SINK THE BELGRANO

MIKE ROSSITER

BANTAM PRESS

LONDON · TORONTO · SYDNEY · AUCKLAND · JOHANNESBURG

TRANSWORLD PUBLISHERS
61–63 Uxbridge Road, London W5 5SA
a division of The Random House Group Ltd
www.booksattransworld.co.uk

First published in Great Britain
in 2007 by Bantam Press
a division of Transworld Publishers

Copyright © Mike Rossiter 2007

Mike Rossiter has asserted his right under the Copyright, Designs
and Patents Act 1988 to be identified as the author of this work.

A CIP catalogue record for this book
is available from the British Library.

ISBN 9780593058428 (cased)
ISBN 9780593058435 (tpb)

Addresses for Random House Group Ltd companies outside the UK
can be found at: www.randomhouse.co.uk
The Random House Group Ltd Reg. No. 954009

The Random House Group Ltd makes every effort to ensure that the papers used in its books
are made from trees that have been legally sourced from well-managed and credibly certified
forests. Our paper procurement policy can be found at: www.randomhouse.co.uk/paper.htm

Typeset in 12/16pt Times New Roman by
Falcon Oast Graphic Art Ltd

Printed and bound in Great Britain by
CPI Mackays, Chatham, ME5 8TD

2 4 6 8 10 9 7 5 3 1

Contents

Picture Acknowledgements

First Section
Conqueror during trials and the *Conqueror* insignia: [2CL/2/C072/ 000] Wirral Museum, Birkenhead.

Sir Rex Hunt: © Julian Calder/Corbis; aerial view of Port Stanley: PA/PA/Empics; Argentine soldiers in Port Stanley and British soldiers surrender: both © Rafael Wollmann /Gamma, Camera Press London; islanders during occupation: FKD 2174 Imperial War Museum/ Ministry of Defence (Royal Marines)/ Crown copyright; Argentine officers in Port Stanley: © Rafael Wollmann /Gamma, Camera Press London; General Galtieri: © Topfoto/AP.

Cartoon and page from the *Conqueror*'s patrol report: courtesy Tim McClement; crew below decks; computer dials; Conqueror on the surface: all courtesy David Hall; Sir John Fieldhouse and staff: PA/PA/Empics; Commander Wreford-Brown and PO Graham Libby: PA/PA/Empics; Rear Admiral Sir John (Sandy) Woodward: Nils Jorgensen/Rex Features.

25 de Mayo: © FR / ROW, Camera Press, London; Argentine pilots: © Alain Nogues/Corbis Sygma; HMS Splendid leaving Rosyth:

Author's Note

In the years following the war with Argentina in 1982, over sovereignty of the Falkland Islands, I interviewed John Nott, the Secretary of State for Defence (commonly known as the Minister of Defence) at the time, Sir Henry Leach, the First Sea Lord, Admiral Sandy Woodward, the commander of the carrier task force, and several others who served on the ships or were part of the land forces. I also read many of the books, both biographical and reportage, that had been written about the war with Argentina. Only fairly recently, however, did I fully appreciate the importance of HMS *Conqueror* and the other nuclear submarines that took part in the conflict. I also came to believe that the sinking of the Argentine cruiser *General Belgrano* was a pivotal event in the war, and that this incident had never been given the attention that it merited.

This realization occurred during a discussion I had in an almost deserted building in Whitehall on a dark winter's day shortly after Christmas a few years ago. I was planning to produce a television series about the history of the Royal Navy called *War at Sea*, and I was talking to Rear Admiral Tim McClement about the possibility of a camera crew spending time on board various warships during a series of exercises called 'The Thursday War'. As our meeting progressed we started discussing the war in the Falklands, and Rear Admiral

McClement told me about his experience as the first officer on HMS *Conqueror*, the submarine that sank the *Belgrano*. I quickly forgot the purpose of my visit as I listened to a wholly new and personal perspective on the navy's war in the South Atlantic.

Our discussions didn't stop at the Falklands, however. For several hours I learned about the activities of British nuclear submarines before and after the war with Argentina. Throughout the years of the Cold War, up until 1989 when hostilities came to an end, the *Conqueror* and other nuclear submarines were engaged in a long-running conflict with the submarine forces of the Soviet Union, carrying out missions that were often so sensitive and dangerous that they had to be authorized personally by the Prime Minister of the day. After that meeting I remained intrigued by what I had been told about HMS *Conqueror* in the South Atlantic, the capabilities of nuclear submarines and the demands placed on the officers and crew of submarines on a patrol. I was determined to try to tell at least some of the stories that I had heard that day, although I realized that the majority of them were and would remain secret.

The opportunity to do this occurred extremely unexpectedly when I talked to my editor at Transworld, Simon Thorogood, about the scope of naval history and how much the modern navy has been influenced by it. I casually mentioned the story of *Conqueror* and he responded enthusiastically. We both knew that the twenty-fifth anniversary of the Falklands War was, in publishing terms, practically upon us, but if a book could be written in time it would be the right moment to publish it. Within days Simon and Transworld had confirmed their interest and I had written to Rear Admiral McClement, explaining what I wanted to do and asking for his help. The rest, dear reader, is history.

The book was not easy to research. None of the documents concerning the Falklands War is yet lodged in the National Archives. Access to them has been granted to the official historian of the Falklands War, Professor Sir Lawrence Freedman, and his findings and interpretation have been published in the two volumes of his history. I found these an invaluable source, naturally, but Sir Lawrence Freedman's focus was not necessarily the same as mine.

My main sources had to be interviews with former crewmembers of the *Conqueror*, though this presented several difficulties. Some are still angry that their actions were criticized in the way that they were, which led to so many conspiracy theories about when and why the order to sink the *Belgrano* was given. Some have seen their views and opinions distorted by the media in the past and now refuse to give any more interviews. In order to deal with this, I insisted that all the interviews were tape-recorded, and that every interviewee had a transcript of the tapes.

But there were other difficulties as well. The events are now twenty-five years old, and the circumstances of an extremely long patrol in a submarine, where people alternate watches every six hours, inevitably mean that events are conflated and memory is very hazy. I was given access to some personal notes and papers, but not until extremely late in the day did a Freedom of Information Act Request produce the submarine's patrol report. Only then could I unravel what seemed to be several very confusing contradictions in the personal descriptions of events.

A final obstacle, it turned out, was the traditions of the submarine service itself, coupled with old habits of secrecy from the covert nature of submarine operations during the Cold War. There are some aspects of these that people are just unwilling to talk about, and no amount of persuasion would change that.

In the end, however, people did volunteer what they could remember and what they thought it was safe to reveal. I would like to thank Tim McClement, in particular, for his help, as well as Dave Hall, Jonty Powis, Graham Libby, Bill Budding, Charlie Foy, Colin Way and Jeff Tall at the Submarine Museum. I would also like to thank Lieutenant Commander Nigel Firth and Lieutenant Commander Mark Thompson for arranging my visit to Devonport and access to HMS *Trenchant*, a modern Trafalgar-class submarine. I should also like to acknowledge the assistance of the Imperial War Museum Archive.

A few years after the war in the Falklands, Martin Middlebrook went to Argentina to write his book *The Fight for the Malvinas*. This was a very useful source, but I also wanted to form my own judgements about the behaviour of the *General Belgrano* and her crew. Argentina was, of course, a military dictatorship during the Falklands War, and the Argentine navy played an important role in the country's internal oppression. I am not sure what archives of the period will be made available, or when.

However, the captain of the *Belgrano*, Captain Héctor Bonzo, and the Asociación Amigos del Crucero *General Belgrano* (Association of the Survivors of the *Belgrano*) are now completely open about their orders and their mission. Everywhere I went I was met with courtesy, and my questions were answered quite candidly. Again, all the interviews were taped and contemporaneous notes were taken. I have to thank the Argentine Naval Attaché in London, Captain Carlos Castro Madero, and Captain Ulloa in Argentina for their help, and also the great assistance of Rear Admiral Carlos Barros. Captain Héctor Bonzo and Commander Pedro Luis Galazi of the *Belgrano* were also very helpful and reflective. I would also like to thank Norberto Bernasconi, Dr Alberto Levene, Oscar Fornes, Juan Heinze, Ruben Otero, Santiago Bellozo, Fernando Millan and Lucas Ocampo.

Thanks are also due to Pablo Touzon and Luz Maria Algranti for their sterling work, both in translating and in organizing an extremely busy schedule.

I must also thank Simon Thorogood at Transworld and my agent, Luigi Bonomi. On a personal note, I would also like to thank my wife, Anne Koch, and my two sons, Max and Alex, for their forbearance while I tried to write this book.

The attack by the *Conqueror* on the *Belgrano* was fundamental to the outcome of the war over the Falklands, but this, and what led up to it, has never been given the attention that other events in the war have received. I hope that this book goes some way to redressing that. Needless to say, any errors in the text are solely my responsibility.

Mike Rossiter
February 2007

Prologue

A LITTLE LOCAL DIFFICULTY

Early in the morning of 29 March 1982, the British Prime Minister Margaret Thatcher was at Northolt Aerodrome, an old wartime RAF base now used for government and VIP flights, located a few miles north of London. With Lord Carrington, the Foreign Secretary, she was on her way to a meeting in Brussels. Before boarding the RAF VC10, she had time to talk to the Foreign Secretary about some troubling events taking place thousands of miles away in the South Atlantic. A group of Argentine workmen – it was unclear exactly who they were – had landed on the island of South Georgia, which was a British possession administered from the Falkland Islands a further seven hundred miles to the west. The workmen, it appeared, had flouted the authority of the British representative on the island and had raised the Argentine flag over their encampment. It looked likely that efforts to remove them would antagonize the

Argentine junta – the military government that had seized power in 1976 – and there were worries that the incident might escalate into a serious international dispute. Margaret Thatcher wanted to beef up Britain's military presence in the area, and asked her office in Downing Street to contact the Secretary of State for Defence, John Nott, about sending a nuclear submarine to the region. That decision taken, she then boarded the aircraft for Brussels. She had no idea that in three days' time what was happening in the South Atlantic would present her with the biggest crisis of her life.

Once ensconced in her seat, the Prime Minister thought only of the meeting to come and the escalating costs of the Common Agricultural Policy. She was in the middle of a series of bitter negotiations with the leaders of France and Germany about the future structure of the European Community, and specifically about the enormous sums of money that were being paid by Britain to support inefficient European agriculture. This was just one of the many problems vital to British interests that had beset her government since its election in 1979. Everywhere members of her Cabinet looked, they faced serious, seemingly intractable difficulties.

As far as the economy was concerned, the prospect for 1982 was dismal. Elected to power in 1979 on the slogan 'Labour Isn't Working', Thatcher's government had done little to curb the sense of decline. The number of people unemployed had reached three million; interest rates were hovering around 16 per cent; in the previous year there had been a prolonged strike in the nationalized steel industry and now there was the threat of one by the country's coalminers.

In 1981 serious rioting had erupted in the streets of cities throughout Britain, the biggest and most prolonged having been

2

in the Toxteth area of Liverpool and in Southall and Brixton in London; most commentators were forecasting another violent summer to come in inner-city Britain. The conflict in Northern Ireland had assumed a horrifying new dimension, with ten detained IRA members dying while on hunger strike, to further their claim for prisoner of war status.

Looking abroad, the landscape appeared equally threatening. War had started between Iraq and Iran, disrupting oil supplies and causing increasing instability in the Middle East. In the Cold War – the global conflict between the United States, its European allies and the Soviet Union – the West had suffered a series of significant reverses during Margaret Thatcher's short period in office. The most obvious and dramatic had been the Soviet invasion of Afghanistan in 1979, when a whole army had marched in and taken over the country. The Soviet Union had also succeeded in establishing port facilities in Angola and Mozambique, and Russian aircraft were conducting long-range reconnaissance flights over the Atlantic and the Indian Ocean.

There was very little that Britain could do about the war in the Gulf, but the creeping Soviet expansion throughout the world, accompanied by a Soviet navy that was getting bigger and rapidly modernizing, was of deep concern. Britain had a nuclear deterrent of Polaris missiles carried on nuclear submarines that needed to be modernized. The preferred solution was to replace them with new, larger submarines carrying Trident missiles purchased from the United States. John Nott, the Defence Secretary, was in the middle of negotiations with other European governments about the acceptability of this, as well as desperately trying to find the money in the defence budget to pay for the new submarines, missiles and warheads. With all these concerns, both domestic and international, hinging on Britain's role as a major economy, a nuclear power, a member of NATO and Europe, and the United States' closest ally, it was understandable that events on a far-off, wind-blasted island seemed a mere irritating distraction.

On that chilly Monday morning John Nott had seen the same information as Margaret Thatcher, and also thought that nuclear submarines should be sent south, purely as a precaution. At that time Britain had only seven nuclear-powered fleet or hunter-killer submarines in service. They were heavily worked. Not only did they protect the missile-carrying Polaris submarines, but they also worked in collaboration with the United States navy conducting intelligence missions and trailing any Soviet submarine that attempted to enter the eastern Atlantic. In 1982 the US and British submarine patrols were facing a crisis. The Russians had recently launched a new class of nuclear sub-marines, which seemed to be much quieter and harder to detect than their predecessors. The West was losing its advantage in anti-submarine warfare. Increased intelligence patrols and new tactics were now being called for.

In order to comply with the Prime Minister's request, the navy decided that a British nuclear submarine currently at sea working with the surface fleet on exercises off Gibraltar might be spared to go to the South Atlantic. HMS *Spartan* was duly instructed to break off from the exercises and head south, but the Ministry of Defence (MoD) felt that perhaps others should also be prepared to go.

There was no love lost between John Nott and senior officers of the Royal Navy, who thought that if money needed to be found to modernize the nuclear deterrent it should come from the Exchequer, not out of the navy's budget; they were only too aware of how stretched their resources were in trying to meet not only the requirements of their own political masters but also the demands of their US allies.

Vice Admiral Peter Herbert, who was in charge of all Britain's nuclear submarines, can be forgiven for feeling that these new orders were unreasonable. 'With twelve scrap-iron merchants creating a stir in South Georgia it is difficult to believe that it is necessary to disrupt *Spartan*'s exercises and send her to the South Atlantic,' he wrote.

Sending *Spartan* was bad enough, in his eyes, but where were the others to come from? HMS *Splendid* had been sent on an urgent mission to find a Soviet submarine; once she had discovered it perhaps that contact and the responsibility for it could be passed over to a US submarine, and *Splendid* might then become part of the effort to deter any aggression from Argentina. As for any others, what choice was there? HMS *Conqueror* was tied up at the wall in Faslane, not currently tasked for anything. Yes, that looked like a solution: *Conqueror* – she could go.

1

'STORE FOR WAR'

The first hint that HMS *Conqueror* was to gain worldwide notoriety was met with absolute disbelief.

On the rainy, cold evening of 30 March 1982, *Conqueror* was tied up at the quayside in Faslane, on the eastern side of the Gare Loch in Scotland, home to the 3rd Submarine Squadron, part of Britain's fleet of nuclear submarines. She had just returned from exercises with the US navy at the Atlantic Undersea Test and Evaluation Center off Andros Island in the Bahamas, and most of the crew had already gone on leave for the Easter holiday. Commander David Hall, the chief engineer, was the senior officer remaining on the submarine. *Conqueror* was scheduled for her five-week-long Assisted Maintenance Period, when the submarine's engineers would work with the shore-based engineering staff to carry out a far-reaching programme of repairs and inspections. Uppermost on David Hall's mind were the problems of mobilizing the equipment and spares necessary for the required work on the submarine's nuclear reactor, turbines, pumps and gearboxes. It was these times in port when the submariners of the 'Silent Service' were reminded most forcefully that they were merely the sharp end of a large and inflexible bureaucracy, of far more importance than a mere warship.

When David picked up the telephone and heard the Faslane duty officer tell him that HMS *Conqueror* was ordered to carry out an exercise known as 'Store for War', his immediate reply was to tell him 'to go and do something very painful. I had a large amount of nuclear maintenance to get through, and had no time for stupid and pointless exercises. And I made it very plain they could go and find another boat.'

The duty officer on the other end of the line persisted, however, and thirty minutes later came on board *Conqueror* to make sure that Commander Hall had got the message. The orders were not an exercise; they came from Admiral Sir John Fieldhouse, Commander-in-Chief Fleet, the most senior seagoing admiral in the navy. *Conqueror* was being scrambled for an operational emergency. David's immediate thought was that there was a crisis in the North Atlantic, that a Russian nuclear submarine had penetrated NATO's defences and that *Conqueror* was being sent to hunt it down.

HMS *Conqueror* was a nuclear submarine, termed an SSN, which stands for Ship Submersible Nuclear. She was not armed with missiles carrying nuclear warheads, like the SSBNs or 'Bombers' that hid quietly in the depths, ready to launch nuclear retaliation against the Soviet Union. The only nuclear element of *Conqueror* was the nuclear reactor that produced heat, which in turn generated steam to drive her turbines and propeller.

Conqueror's job was to locate and trail warships and submarines, and in the event of war to sink them, hence the description 'hunter-killer'.

At rest on the surface, tied up at the quayside, or 'against the wall' as it is known, *Conqueror*'s matt black conning tower rose 30 feet above her curved deck but, like an iceberg, the vast bulk of her hull, 265 feet long and 30 feet in diameter, still lay hidden below the waterline. Almost level with the forward deck, really a narrow walkway about 6 feet in width, and about a quarter of her length back from the bow were two hydroplanes that projected outwards like short, stubby wings on either side. Further aft, all that could be seen of her stern was another black fin sticking free of the water, which was the visible part of the cruciform tail, with, below the waterline, its vertical rudder, and another two horizontal hydroplanes, and one large propeller that drove her through the water at speeds of nearly 30 miles an hour. *Conqueror* had no sharp bow to cut through the waves like a destroyer, or even like an older submarine such as a Second World War U-boat. Her bow slid down in a curve and disappeared into the sea, concealing the sonar receivers mounted on the bow and sides, and her six forward-pointing torpedo tubes. Even resting on the surface, about 85 per cent of the bulk of a nuclear submarine remains hidden below the sea. Once launched, submarines make only a grudging acknowledgement of life above the waves.

HMS *Conqueror* was the most modern expression of a type of warship that had existed throughout the twentieth century and had always carried with it an air of illegitimacy. Submariners were seen as a nasty, piratical bunch, the very nature of the craft they sailed in being unseen and underhand, preying on honest, defenceless merchant shipping. They had proved to be a very effective weapon in the First World War, as the U-boats of the German navy wreaked havoc on Britain's seaborne trade, their reputation confirmed by their success in sinking unsuspecting passenger and merchant ships. When a U-boat torpedoed the liner *Lusitania* it was seen as a callous and unnecessary act, and damaged Germany's relations with the then neutral United States. Germany's submarine fleet was more than just a successful commerce raider, however. The threat the submarines posed to surface warships weighed heavily on the British Admiralty and their lurking presence in the North Sea kept the Royal Navy's home fleet in port in the first two years of the war. Admiral 'Jackie' Fisher, the great modernizer of the Royal Navy and creator of the huge, heavily gunned and armoured dreadnoughts, prophesied that submarines would revolutionize war at sea, and the fear that U-boats instilled in British admirals seemed to bear him out.

Gradually, naval engineers started to work out ways to counter the threat that submarines posed and the balance of advantage shifted to surface warships again. Battleships were built with armour plating along their sides and large bulges on the waterline that would lessen the damage caused by exploding torpedo warheads. The science of sound detection developed, and Asdic, as the British called it, or sonar as it was known elsewhere, proved to be capable of locating submerged submarines. Once detected, they were not fast enough to outrun a warship such as a destroyer or frigate, which could carpet an area of sea with high-explosive depth-charges.

Submarines also had another, fatal weakness. They had constantly to come to the surface, either to replenish the air supply for the crew or to travel on the surface under diesel power to recharge the huge banks of batteries that powered them under water, and consequently both sonar detection and airborne radar greatly reduced their threat. During the Second World War the German navy developed the snorkel mast, which sucked in air and vented the exhaust gases so that submarines could run their diesel engines while submerged at periscope depth. However, airborne radar was quickly improved to detect the snorkel sticking up above the waves. By 1945, when the war came to an end, almost half the German submarines sunk by the Allies had been detected by aircraft when they were running on the surface or submerged at periscope depth; the other half had been sunk by warships at very close range using depth-charges.

In the last years of the Second World War the German navy carried out a lot of work in an attempt to remedy the growing vulnerability of their U-boats. It was clear that they needed to be able to achieve greater underwater speeds and to be less dependent on oxygen from the atmosphere. A system utilizing hydrogen peroxide as a fuel had been developed in the 1930s. Hydrogen peroxide broke down to provide oxygen and heat, and prototypes were developed that were designed to achieve speeds of 25 knots when submerged – enough to outrun a surface vessel in rough seas. These U-boats were still in the construction stage by the end of the war in Europe, and never saw service. There were a lot of problems with hydrogen peroxide as a fuel, despite the seeming advantages it might offer. It was a difficult chemical to store and transport, and it was extremely volatile and explosive when it came into contact with seawater. The Royal Navy took a lot of interest in this captured German technology after the war, and built a submarine called HMS *Explorer* that was powered by hydrogen peroxide. It was nicknamed HMS *Exploder*.

The Second World War had seen another development,

however: nuclear energy, a product of atomic physics. Its devastating nature as a weapon was revealed in the bombs dropped on the Japanese cities of Hiroshima and Nagasaki, but it had a more promising aspect when it was utilized in a reactor, where the energy from disintegrating atoms was more controlled.

It was quickly apparent that here was a source of energy that needed no air for combustion, and was almost unlimited. Its potential was seized upon by US Admiral Hyman G. Rickover, who quickly organized a massive development project to produce a reactor that could be put into warships and submarines. The efforts resulted in the first nuclear-powered submarine being launched in 1955 – *Nautilus*, named after the mysteriously powered submarine in Jules Verne's science-fiction novel *Twenty Thousand Leagues Under the Sea*. The modern *Nautilus* quickly demonstrated its unique capabilities, as impressive as anything that Verne imagined. Voyaging right around the world without coming to the surface, making dangerous journeys under the Arctic ice cap to the North Pole, the nuclear-powered submarine was as revolutionary a warship as Admiral Fisher's *Dreadnought* had been forty-nine years previously.

Putting nuclear reactors in submarines had turned the battle between surface warships and submarines completely on its head once more. The enormous power available from a nuclear plant transformed the diesel-powered submarines of the Second World War, rendering obsolete the destroyers, frigates and corvettes that had been the stars of convoy protection and which had featured in classic war films like *The Cruel Sea*. Submarines now had the power easily to outrun not only most surface warships but also the newly developed anti-submarine torpedoes. Nuclear power also meant that the submarine need never again surface while on a patrol. There was more than enough energy available to provide refrigeration for large stocks of food, desalination plants for fresh water, power to heat it for showers and cooking, and power to electrolyse water to provide oxygen and clean air for the crew. The only effective way of locating the presence of a submarine was by detecting the sound that it made as it travelled deep beneath the surface of the ocean. Nuclear submarines like *Nautilus* could cruise for months on end, the weakest link now being the crew and the limits of their endurance.

The Royal Navy had also started to investigate the use of nuclear reactors for ships and submarines, but was hampered by the type of reactors that Britain's Atomic Energy Authority was designing for civilian electricity generation. These were heavy, cumbersome gas-cooled reactors and it proved impossible to make them small enough for marine use. By 1953 the navy had started to look at simpler designs, like the pressurized water-cooled reactors being built in the USA; but the launch of *Nautilus* showed how far in advance of the British were the achievements of the United States navy.

Help was at hand, however. In 1957 the United States offered to share its technology, and supplied a complete marine reactor and power plant to the British government.

Britain's first nuclear submarine, then, HMS Dreadnought, named in honour of Admiral Fisher's revolutionary battleship of 1906, was commissioned some years after *Nautilus*, in April 1963. The front part of the boat had been designed and built in the Vickers shipyard in Barrow-in-Furness, but the nuclear reactor and most of the machinery surrounding it was supplied by the United States. *Dreadnought* quickly demonstrated what she was capable of, travelling from Rosyth to Singapore and back, a distance of 26,545 miles, submerged.

The next nuclear submarine to be built in Britain, *Valiant*, was again a product of Vickers shipyards, and this time the nuclear reactor was built and supplied by Rolls-Royce. *Valiant* was never completely successful, but the designs that followed, of which *Conqueror* was the fourth in the series, saw increasing improvements in the machinery, hull shape and other technologies. The British designs were aimed at reducing the transmitted noise of the pumps for coolant water and heat exchangers that were a feature of nuclear reactors. The reactor, the steam-generating plant, turbines and gearbox were all placed on a metal raft, which was insulated from the main hull by rubber and hydraulic mountings. The reactors were now wholly designed and built by British companies, and the torpedo tubes were modified to take a modern wire-guided torpedo called Tigerfish.

The next improvement on the design of *Conqueror* was a new class of submarines, the Swiftsure class, which were faster, could dive deeper, and were equipped with a water-pump propulsion system, which was a multi-bladed propeller inside a casing, rotating between two static sets of blades, like a turbine. This made the rear end of the submarine much quieter. By 1982, five of these submarines had entered service.

The nuclear submarines were used to making rapid responses for extremely hazardous operations. A typical incident, albeit in British waters, involved the *Conqueror*. She was moored in Faslane on New Year's Eve 1972 when she was scrambled. Her orders were to trail a ship that was suspected of smuggling guns to the IRA in Northern Ireland and on her return from this task a few weeks later, according to her navigating officer of the time, Roger Lane-Nott, 'We were in the forefront of the emerging situation with the Russians in the north-east Atlantic.' A Russian submarine had been detected entering the

Atlantic, and was suspected of being in the inner Clyde area.

> It was vital to protect the Polaris boat security and we were sent
> to identify it and chase it off. At the time there was no real system
> of command and control, and our rules of engagement were just
> 'make it go away'. It was left pretty much up to us.

Conqueror found the Russian submarine and confirmed that it
was a Victor class. It was harder to know how to persuade the
Russian sub to leave: 'We made close passes, of less than 1,000
yards, using active sonar so he knew we had located him, at speeds
of 28 knots.' The combined speed of the approaching submarines
was around 60 miles an hour, and in confined and shallow water,
with only sonar to guide them, it is easy to see how an incident
like this could result in a deadly collision. The fact that it didn't
was a testament to the ability of the commanding officer and the
crewmembers. Nobody was given command of a submarine
without passing through a special Submarine Commanding
Officer's Qualifying Course, known as 'Perisher' because during
the course so many submariners' hopes of command perished.
But it produced submarine commanders who had been exposed
to extremely stressful situations, and who were supremely
confident of their abilities. They also knew what their submarine
and its equipment was capable of doing. *Conqueror* eventually
persuaded the Soviet submarine captain to leave, but this
incident exposed the lack of a proper command and control
system. In the year following this encounter, the control of
both Polaris and hunter-killer submarines was centralized
in the NATO headquarters in Northwood, a suburb of north
London.

In the light of *Conqueror*'s previous missions, then, an urgent telephone call to the duty officer of a submarine tied up in harbour was not out of the ordinary, but the order that came on 30 March 1982 to 'store for war' certainly was. Commander David Hall was extremely concerned. *Conqueror* had completed a lengthy patrol in the Barents Sea before crossing the Atlantic to the undersea exercise area in the Bahamas. The submarine was now in its tenth year of service and badly needed a period in port for maintenance. Commander Hall's team had already started work on the reactor control equipment and the main propulsion machinery, some of which was already in pieces. Petty Officer Charlie Foy, who was living on the boat, remembers that a lot of the equipment had already been removed to the shore to be stripped down and cleaned. They now had to reverse this process, and quickly.

The first task was to get the remaining officers and crew back from leave and then work out the best way to shorten a planned five-week maintenance programme. The navigating officer, Lieutenant Jonathan (Jonty) Powis, was living in Faslane with his wife, who was expecting a baby in May. He quickly returned to the boat and started to prepare a list of crewmembers and their contact details. Some of the officers had already been telephoned by the Faslane duty operations officer. Lieutenant Commander Tim McClement, *Conqueror*'s second in command, had left Faslane the day before.

I got into the car with my wife and my six-month-old baby and we drove all the way down to Bath to meet my parents, who we were going to spend Easter with. We arrived, of course, and the first thing my father said was, 'Your officer of the day has been on the phone – you've got to go back.' And I said, 'Well, I'm too tired – I've just driven all the way down.' So I went to bed for four hours, then left my wife and my son, borrowed my mother's car and drove myself all the way back. I assumed we were being deployed as the northerly boat. And I just left my wife and young baby.

It wasn't so easy to find other members of the crew. Some of them didn't get phone calls with orders to return to Faslane until 1 April, and these messages were often treated as an April Fool's joke. Graham Libby, one of *Conqueror*'s divers and the senior sonar operator, who had served on the submarine since 1979, was at home in Portsmouth, having been one of the first to go on leave.

I had only been there for a few days when there was a knock on the door and there was this policeman stood there saying, 'You've been recalled. Make your way back to the boat.' It was the morning of April the first he knocked on the door, and I thought this is a wind-up, April fool, so I phoned the boat up in Faslane, and they said, 'Yeah, it's true – you're recalled.' When I got there it was just a hive of activity. There were stores on the jetty, there was a complete new weapons load, everybody was running around, and I thought this is not a wind-up, this is not an exercise, something's going on here.

By the time that Graham Libby arrived at Faslane, all the officers and most of the crew were desperately struggling to store for war, and to find out what their mission was and how they were expected to carry it out. Storing for war meant taking twice the amount of provisions on board than was necessary for a normal patrol. The process involved double-decking, where tins of food were placed on the decks and then hardboard was laid over the tins as a temporary floor. As Graham Libby explained:

> You're limited in headroom anyway; you're now limited by a fifteen-inch layer of tinned food. So you eat your way through the floor once all the fresh food has gone or perished. Even just looking at all this extra food, you knew you were going for a long time.

Faslane, in fact, was extremely busy. HMS *Splendid* had been recalled from her mission to locate a Soviet submarine in the Atlantic, and was tied up at the quay loading a full complement of torpedoes. Her captain, Commander Roger Lane-Nott, had orders to make the best possible speed to the Falkland Islands:

> I received a signal from the First Sea Lord detailing events in the South Atlantic. We had to pull off the Russian sub, head back to Faslane, and put on stores. I arrived at about nine or ten at night, we loaded up and eighteen hours later we sailed under some secrecy.

By now it was clear to most of the crew of *Conqueror* that there was a problem of some sort developing in the Falklands with the Argentinians, and that was where they were going. In the week before the telephone call to David Hall there had been stories in the news that some Argentine soldiers, or workmen – it was unclear what they were precisely – had landed on a remote island in the middle of the South Atlantic called South Georgia, which was British territory, and had raised the Argentine flag. Now there were unconfirmed rumours that Argentine warships were heading towards the Falkland Islands – another British possession, with a population of two thousand British citizens – with the intention of invading them. There seemed to be no logic to these events, and it was hard to see how *Conqueror* could make any difference to what was happening 8,000 miles away. It took some time for a lot of people actually to work out where the Falklands were. One crewmember recalled thinking, 'What are the Argentinians doing off the coast of Scotland?'

The commanding officer of *Conqueror*, Commander Christopher Wreford-Brown, was new to the boat and had thought that he might have time to get to know the crew, many of whom, like Graham Libby or Petty Officer Writer Colin 'The Bear' Way, had served on the boat for several years. As someone remarked, 'He hardly knew the names of the members of the wardroom, let alone anyone in the junior ratings mess.' But now he was ensconced in meetings on shore trying to get as many details of his mission as he could, and under intense pressure to put to sea as quickly as possible. His conversations with David Hall were fraught as the engineer fought against his extremely truncated maintenance period of ten days being shortened any further, but David was astounded at the complete shift in the attitude of the naval bureaucracy. To get essential spare parts, it was no longer a question of endless form-filling and requisitions, to be met with the answer that they would take ten weeks to arrive. Instead, whatever he wanted was offered to him immediately, with some hard-to-get pieces of equipment sent by helicopter if necessary. He could have rebuilt the whole boat if he had time, but that was the one thing that wasn't available to him. Under continual pressure, his original five-week maintenance period was squeezed to five days. Charlie Foy remembers the process as one mad rush, where as much equipment as possible was taken on board for any foreseeable emergency, and work replacing machinery went on twenty-four hours a day.

It was customary that both the commander and the second officer on a nuclear submarine should be command-qualified, and Lieutenant Commander McClement had also just recently passed his Commander's Course. As a colleague remarked, 'He was nails dug in, dead keen to prove himself.' He was, however, only an acting lieutenant commander, whereas the chief engineer was a full commander, very much senior in rank. When McClement had first joined *Conqueror* Commander Hall had taken him aside and said, 'You're second in command and I'll back you in the wardroom, if you will do me the favour of listening to me if I think I can give you some advice.' They had got on well ever since. Both were curious to find out what their new commanding officer was like.

Lieutenant Commander McClement had other worries as well. Petty Officer Charlie Foy was returning to the submarine one night when he saw a bus parked next to the boat with the words Royal Marine Free Fall Parachute Team painted on the side. *Conqueror* was embarking a group of the SBS, the Special Boat Service.

The Special Boat Service was a small group of Special Forces drawn solely from the Royal Marines. As a unit, they were not as famous as the other group of Special Forces, the Special Air Service, or SAS. The SAS had become well known because of their operations in Northern Ireland, and most recently for their role in the 1980 Iranian Embassy hostage crisis in London. A group of Iranian students, opposed to the rule of Iran's leader, the Ayatollah Khomeini, had taken nineteen hostages in the embassy in Kensington. Members of the SAS had abseiled down the front and back of the building, smashing through windows, throwing stun grenades and firing machine pistols. The whole event, broadcast live on television, had been as thrilling as anything Hollywood could produce.

Compared with this, the SBS had a non-existent public profile, but they considered themselves just as highly trained and had been in action in Suez, Aden, Malaysia and Indonesia. They had been formed after the Second World War from some rather esoteric groups. One of them was the Special Boat Section, which was part of an army commando unit. Then there was a small group of marines called the Combined Operations Pilotage Parties, formed in 1942, who were responsible for the clandestine surveillance and charting of possible landing beaches for the Allied invasions of Sicily and France. A third group, whose exploits were the best known, was the Royal Marines Boom Patrol Detachment. This last group, despite its prosaic name, was formed to mount attacks on enemy ships in port. Their most famous operation was an incursion by canoe into Bordeaux harbour with limpet mines, damaging six merchant vessels. Only two men survived, Blondie Hasler and Ned Sparks; a memorial to the ten who died was erected at the SBS headquarters in Poole, Dorset, and a feature film about the mission, *The Cockleshell Heroes*, was made after the war.

The different activities of these various groups give a good indication of the talents of 6SBS, who had turned up on the quay-side by HMS *Conqueror*. Led by their commanding officer David Heaver, 6SBS also comprised a warrant officer and three troops of four men, making fourteen extra berths to be found by Tim McClement. To add to his problems, McClement had received another signal saying that he was to expect a further thirty-six men by parachute once he was under way. He had to sit down in the wardroom with the weapons and engineering officers and work out how small a boat crew they could put to sea with in order to accommodate the extra men.

This troop of the SBS had been on winter and mountain exercises in Norway and had been ordered to make their way straight to Faslane, leaving most of their equipment and weapons to follow. The SBS can carry out a wide variety of activities, from sabotage to reconnaissance and surveillance, and Whitehall had mobilized all the Special Forces, including the SAS, on the principle that it was imperative to get them to the Falklands as soon as possible; they could worry about their specific mission later. Consequently 6SBS had a consignment of equipment that not only replaced what they had left behind in Norway, but which would enable them to undertake whatever task they might be asked to perform. There were new personal handguns and silenced machine pistols, which they had never even test-fired. There were limpet mines, demolition charges, hand grenades, rocket launchers, general-purpose machine guns and ammunition of every calibre. There was re-breathing diving equipment, allowing the user to stay under water for extended periods of time, inflatable dinghies and outboard motors, even winter camouflage suits and skis. Everything was loaded into the torpedo room of *Conqueror* via the weapons-loading hatch on the forward casing. It was the skis that gave the game away as far as Charlie Foy was concerned: 'I thought, what does a freefall parachute team want with skis?'

Altogether 9 tons of equipment were brought on board by the SBS. Tim McClement was approached by a chief petty officer who pointed out that all the explosives and ammunition could not be loaded on to the boat, because under regulations each type of weapon had to be stored in its own type of locker.

> The first war decision that I took [recalls McClement] was to take
> the regulations, put them on top of the nine tons of equipment and
> tell him we could say that the explosives were covered by the
> rules. And that was how it was going to go. A lot of the rules were
> going to be broken and ignored.

The equipment posed other problems for Lieutenant Commander
McClement. As first lieutenant, he was responsible for the submarine's trim – that is, its total weight and attitude in the water.
This is far more critical in a submarine than on a surface ship.
According to McClement, it's an automatic, almost instinctive,
action for a submariner to check the draught marks on the hull of
a submarine every time he walks up the gangway: 'I've never
known anyone on a surface ship to bother.' A submarine needs to
have neutral buoyancy, so that if for any reason the reactor shuts
down the submarine will remain at its set depth; it is highly undesirable to have it sink, and also to have it float to the surface.
The weight of everything that comes on board or leaves the submarine is carefully monitored by the first lieutenant, and that
includes the crewmembers. *Conqueror* had already taken on a
large amount of food and other essential supplies – including
1,000 toilet rolls, 35 lb of laundry soap, 49,000 sheets of photo-
copier paper and 22 rolls of tracing paper for the plotting table in
the control room. In addition to the crew's spare equipment, they
now had the extra 9 tons of equipment for the SBS. The boat was
20 tons overweight – not a large amount, but on a submarine
there is almost no margin for error.

HMS *Conqueror* was ready to put to sea on Sunday 4 April.
Slowly, she eased away from the quayside and headed for the
deep waters of the Isle of Arran to do a test dive. Commander
Wreford-Brown ordered the submarine to dive to 75 feet, then

rise to 60 feet – a manoeuvre known as rocking the bubble – to clear any air in the ballast tanks. Then, with all hatches and compartments reporting clear of leaks, the *Conqueror* surfaced once more. They were going to steam down the Irish Sea on the surface to make the quickest time possible. Also, because the SBS had a completely new set of weapons, they were going to be test-fired from the top of the conning tower, or fin. This was completely in breach of safety rules, but Tim McClement knew this wouldn't be the last peacetime regulation that they ignored. He had only one observation to make: 'Don't shoot at Ireland, boys – make sure you're firing at Wales.' So *Conqueror* steamed on her way, with the bow wave breaking cleanly high up the forward casing and with SBS marines taking it in turns to pour pistol and machine-gun fire into the sea. They were heading south – where, and to do what, they still didn't know.

For years *Conqueror* and her crew had sped as quickly as possible northwards, to intercept a Soviet submarine, to trail it, record the slightest sound it made; then sometimes, to remind the Russian commander who was boss, they would reveal their presence before slipping away. Or they would make a careful passage into Soviet territorial waters, inching ever closer to a military base, or to a port on the Barents Sea, knowing if they were detected there would be a dangerous chase with a Russian sub or surface warship. They had trained day in and day out for the time when the Cold War with the Soviet Union became a hot one. But now they were heading into the unknown. As Commander Roger Lane-Nott said about his voyage south in HMS *Splendid* three days earlier, it was the wrong war, against the wrong enemy.

2

THE PLOT

The reason why HMS *Conqueror* was steaming south down the Irish Sea, the bullets from various small arms ricocheting off the water, was that a long-running diplomatic dispute between Great Britain and Argentina about a group of small islands 8,000 miles away from London had led to bloodshed.

The Falkland Islands, or las Islas Malvinas as the Argentinians call them, consist of two main islands separated by a channel that runs roughly south-west to north-east. These islands, East Falkland and West Falkland, are surrounded by innumerable smaller islands and outcrops of rock, and their coasts are indented with many coves and inlets. They lie on the latitude of 51 degrees south, are 59 degrees to the west of Greenwich and 300 miles east of the southern tip of Argentina. Most of the roughly two thousand inhabitants, who are mainly descended from British settlers, live on East Falkland, and the biggest centre of population here is Stanley, a town on the easternmost tip of the island. What the crew of the *Conqueror* were going to do in the South Atlantic, although they did not yet know it, was influenced not only by the Argentine invasion of these two islands, but also the way in which that invasion had unfolded.

Everything about the Falklands is open to dispute. Samuel Johnson wrote that they were 'a bleak and gloomy solitude, an island thrown aside from human use, stormy in winter and barren in summer . . . where a garrison must be kept in a state that contemplates with envy the exiles of Siberia.' Others have said that the climate, although cold in winter, is relatively balmy, and the islands do have an average temperature higher than the UK's.

There are even different versions of the sixteenth-century discovery of the Falklands. Some accounts claim that they were first seen by Amerigo Vespucci in 1502; others say that a ship from one of Magellan's expeditions first encountered them. Alternatively, their first discovery was by a British ship in 1592, or perhaps by Sir Richard Hawkins two years later. There is a rare consensus, however, that they were first named the 'Sebaldes' by a Dutch mariner, Sebald van der Weent, in the year 1600.

The first actual landing on their treeless terrain was by Captain John Strong of the Royal Navy in 1690, and it was he who named the channel between the two major islands after Anthony Cary, 5th Viscount Falkland, who was later to become First Sea Lord. It took another seventy years before any further interest was shown in the Falklands, and this time it was by the French, who were the first to settle on them – on East Falkland in 1764 – christening them Les Malouines, because many of these French settlers came from the port of St Malo in Brittany. This attempt to occupy the islands drew the wrath of the Spanish government, who considered that the previously ignored archipelago was so close to their vast empire in South America that it fell legitimately within their sphere of interest, and they objected strongly to the French presence. The French gave way, and in 1766 formally transferred the settlement to Spain. The Spanish then placed the islands under the jurisdiction of the province of Buenos Aires, and a Spaniard, Don Felipe Ruiz Puente, became governor of the islands, with Malouines becoming the Spanish Malvinas. This was the first recorded instance of an attempt to establish some legitimate sovereignty over the islands.

The story might have ended there had not Commodore John Byron arrived on the island of West Falkland roughly at the same time as the French were settling on East Falkland, and claimed it for Britain. A year later a British settlement was established in Port Egmont on Saunders Island in West Falkland, in apparent ignorance of the French attempt at colonization in what is now Stanley and in the face of Spanish objections.

The British outpost survived for four years, during which Britain and Spain exchanged diplomatic letters about the legitimacy of the settlement, until in 1770 the Spanish made a determined effort to close the question of the islands' governance once and for all. They sent a force of 1,400 soldiers, backed by five warships, to eject the British and eradicate Port Egmont. However, this expedition was not as decisive as the Spanish authorities on the mainland had hoped. The British settlers left, but the British government threatened war, and the Spanish government allowed the settlers back the following year, while declaring that in doing so Spain was not modifying its claim of sovereignty. Three years later the British colony was closed down voluntarily because supporting it had become too great a drain on British resources at a time when every effort was being made to hang on to the colonies in North America.

Once again the Falklands were forgotten as the European empires fought each other for advantage in other parts of the world, and Spain itself became a battleground in the global conflict between Britain and France. When Spain was occupied by Napoleon's forces, the Spanish colonies in South America took the opportunity to seize their freedom. In 1810 the United Provinces of the Rio de la Plate declared their independence from Spain and eventually in 1816 constituted themselves as the country of Argentina, claiming all those lands and territories that had once come under the jurisdiction of the Spanish authorities in Buenos Aires, as the Falklands, or Malvinas, had. It is on this that the subsequent claim of Argentine sovereignty is based.

But it is one thing to claim sovereignty; it is another thing altogether to exercise it. All attempts by Argentina to impose their authority over the islands resulted in a conflict with a more powerful state, and ended in frustration. In 1829 the new Argentinian government in Buenos Aires gave Louis Vernet, as military governor of the islands, the right to establish a colony and to make money out of trading in hides, meat, wool and seal-skins. Britain sent a diplomatic note of protest, but did nothing else. However, Vernet ordered several United States fishing vessels to be seized, arguing that they were fishing in Argentine waters without the appropriate licences from the Argentine government. This brought retribution from the United States in the form of the USS *Lexington*, a warship that sailed to the Falklands in 1831, arrested the inhabitants and laid waste to the settlement, leaving all the buildings destroyed.

Sensing an opportunity, the Admiralty in London then

dispatched two British warships to the islands, which arrived in December 1832. At the same time, the Argentine government sent its own gunboat and a new military governor, but the forces under him mutinied and he was unable to resist the Royal Navy or prevent British forces landing and claiming the Falklands for Britain.

In a brutally succinct explanation of its actions, the British government wrote:

> The British government at one time thought it inexpedient to maintain any garrison in those islands: it has now altered its views and has deemed it proper to establish a post there. His Majesty is not accountable to any foreign power for the reasons which may guide him with respect to territories belonging to the British Crown.

The Falklands became one more red dot on the global map of Empire, and few countries at that time, certainly not Argentina, were prepared to force war upon Britain. Diplomatically, however, with the exchange of notes and letters, the Argentine government protested, and continued to do so.

With the end of the Second World War, a huge anti-colonial movement forced the dismantling of most of the empires of the European states. Not only was there a large and powerful demand for independence and self-determination, but the old imperial powers, particularly Britain, found the costs of hanging on to empire too great to bear. In Argentina, a military coup in 1943 had brought a young colonel, Juan Perón, into the government. In 1946 he was elected President on a policy of national regeneration, and he started to raise the question of the Falklands in the newly created United Nations. Argentinian politics grew extremely violent during the 1950s, with the armed forces, particularly the navy, attempting to overthrow Perón's government. In June 1955 navy aircraft bombed a Peronist rally in the main square, Plaza de Mayo, in Buenos Aires, killing 364 civilians in a failed military coup; another one in September of that year succeeded in ousting Perón from power.

Whatever happened to the Argentine government, however, the claim for the Malvinas was pursued in the United Nations, and in 1965 Argentina successfuly won a Resolution of the General Assembly calling on Britain and Argentina to negotiate a peaceful solution to the problem of the Falklands. The British government's position was that they could not ignore this Resolution, nor would they really want to, but neither could they immediately accede to Argentine demands. They took the view that what were paramount were the wishes and the right to self-determination of the indigenous population. This was an important negotiating tactic, because it helped to defend British interests in other disputes over possessions like Gibraltar, Belize and Northern Ireland. The population of the Falklands was small, but was almost wholly composed of people who could trace their ancestry over several generations to settlers who had been of British origin. That these settlers were determined to remain British was something that the British government was only slowly to become aware of.

Negotiations started between representatives of Britain and Argentina, but they soon hit the reef of the problem of the Falklanders' interests. The Argentine government wanted nothing less than a full transfer of sovereignty, but the effect of any caveat imposed by the British which was designed to protect or preserve the rights enjoyed by the islanders under the existing arrangements would necessarily reduce Argentina's control. The negotiations could not be kept secret from the islanders either, and the more alarmed they became about the talks between the British government and Argentina, the more the issue became a domestic political question in the UK. The Falkland islanders were able, via the Falkland Islands Company, which owned over half the farms on the island, to lobby a number of backbench MPs and encourage them to start asking awkward questions of various Cabinet ministers. The problem for the British government was that it was unable to offer the Argentine government full and unfettered sovereignty, yet at the same time it was unable categorically to refuse to discuss the issue, because it was unwilling to accept the military and financial logic of a total commitment to the Falkland islanders and their defence.

So for several years negotiations were kept alive by discussions about improving transport links between the islands and the mainland, and various visits to the islands by British government ministers on a mission to encourage the islanders to see their future as part of Argentina. These tactics failed, because they never delivered anything that would satisfy the Argentine government, and at the same time they served to alarm the islanders and so caused problems in Westminster. Their one advantage was that they resulted in endless postponement of a resolution to the problem, but this came at the cost of increasing disbelief in the minds of Argentine negotiators about the possibility of ever solving the dispute.

Successive British governments made efforts to break the deadlock. In 1976, the Labour government under James Callaghan appointed a senior Labour peer, Lord Shackleton, to visit the Falklands and produce a report that would examine the islands' long-term economic future. The hope directly expressed to Shackleton was that such a report would help persuade the islanders that there was no future as a community tied to Great Britain, 8,000 miles away. The choice of Lord Shackleton was an odd one. He was the son of the famous Polar explorer Ernest Shackleton, who was buried on the small island of South Georgia 700 miles to the east of the Falklands. HMS *Endurance*, an armed ice patrol ship that regularly visited the Falklands and patrolled the area, generally providing a visible symbol of Britain's interests, was named after Ernest Shackleton's own ship, which had been trapped in the ice of the Weddell Sea off Antarctica and sank in 1915. The name Shackleton may have been reassuring to the Falkland islanders, but it was certainly not designed to impress the Argentine government, who associated it with everything that they found objectionable about Britain's presence in the region.

Lord Shackleton's visit to the Falklands was also affected by political chaos in Argentina. Perón, who had come to power again in 1973, was dead, and the military were preparing for a possible coup. The Argentine government told Britain that they would not offer Lord Shackleton and his team any facilities or help in travelling to the Falklands; they viewed his visit as a provocation and they would be withdrawing their ambassador to London. The report that Shackleton produced was not good news for the Callaghan government either. He argued that, with enough money from Britain, the Falklands might have a promising economic future. He recommended that the airport runway at Stanley should be lengthened, and that fishing should be developed as an alternative industry to farming. The costs would be high – far too high for a population of just two thousand people – but the government also realized that the report had blown back in their faces: it would strengthen the resolve of the islanders to remain British, as well as confirming the Argentine government's view that negotiations were nothing more than a British delaying tactic.

There had been an indication of the way the wind was blowing in Buenos Aires during Shackleton's visit to the Falklands. A Royal Research Ship – perhaps inevitably named *Shackleton* – was carrying out a scientific survey in Antarctic waters. Six hours from Port Stanley, she was intercepted by an Argentine destroyer, *Almirante Storni*, and ordered to halt. This order was ignored, only to be followed by another instruction to alter course and make for Ushuaia, the southerly Argentine port on the Beagle Channel. When this was also ignored, two shots were fired, with a warning that the third would hit the *Shackleton*. With its captain ignoring everything, the RRS *Shackleton* reached the safety of the harbour at Stanley. There was some concern about how she would escape, but there was no further antagonism and she sailed north, escorted by the *Endurance*.

This incident, however, was something that the British government could not ignore. It was evidence that there had been a fundamental change in Argentine policies towards the Falklands, brought about by a military coup in March 1976. Admiral Eduardo Massera, the naval representative on the military junta, was the most aggressive and nationalistic of the military leaders who had taken power. The navy quickly became a key player in the machinery of internal repression, and at the same time adopted a more aggressive policy in pursuit of Argentine territorial ambitions. Argentina had unilaterally imposed a 200-mile maritime economic interest zone, and the Argentine navy came into conflict with Russian and Bulgarian trawlers that were found fishing inside this limit, exchanging shots and receiving casualties. It was Massera who had now engineered the conflict with the *Shackleton* and took a very hard line about the recovery of the Falklands, believing that military action might be necessary.

The change in Argentine negotiating tactics focused the British government's mind on what their options might be if there was any overt action against the Falklands, which it was thought would take the form of cutting communication links with the islands. The Ministry of Defence believed it would be possible to supply the islands with food and fuel using commercial vessels or Royal Fleet Auxiliary ships. The presence of the *Endurance*, and the detachment of thirty-seven marines on the islands, would, it was hoped, deter any military adventures. It had better, because Britain's ability to reinforce the islands was almost non-existent, short of detaching the aircraft carrier *Ark Royal* and its squadrons of Phantom jet fighters. A new round of discussions was coming up, and the Foreign Secretary David Owen took the question of Argentine military action quite seriously. He pursued the matter in Cabinet, and persuaded the Secretary of State for Defence to authorize the dispatch of a nuclear submarine to the area. HMS *Dreadnought* would be accompanied by two frigates and two fleet auxiliaries, ready to be on station close to the Falklands in December 1977 when talks with Argentine foreign ministry representatives were due to take place in New York. There have been several claims since then that the presence of a nuclear submarine was discreetly brought to the notice of the Argentine junta by Sir Maurice Oldfield, head of the Secret Intelligence Service, and that this helped to deflect a plan by the Argentine navy to mount an invasion. Accounts by the Prime Minster at the time, Sir James Callaghan, and the Foreign Secretary David Owen disagree about whether the junta was informed or not, but it is clear that in Argentina some plans for military intervention were being developed, although there was no evidence at the time that they had got to the stage of mobilizing forces. In any event, the talks in New York concluded fairly amicably, and another set of meetings was scheduled to be held in Lima early in 1978. The British government, however, was now viewing any talks with Argentina in the light of the possibility that the junta might resort to some show of force.

David Owen knew that HMS *Endurance* might shortly be paid off and not replaced, because the Ministry of Defence thought it too costly. It was his opinion that 'I see no prospect for some time to come of our being able to dispense with her . . . I view *Endurance*, together with the Royal Marine contingent on the Falklands, as a vital and visible military presence.'

A new British government was elected in May 1979, under Prime Minister Margaret Thatcher. This was one of the most ideologically motivated administrations to be elected since the Labour government of Clement Attlee in 1945. Margaret Thatcher was determined to cut government spending, reduce taxes and limit the power of the trades unions. She had had to fight the old guard of the Conservative Party to become leader, and once elected she wanted to transform the political landscape of Britain. Economically, Britain was stagnating, with high unemployment and inflation. Internationally, the Cold War was not going well. Russia had increased its presence in Africa, with military bases in Angola, and was intervening with economic and military assistance to Afghanistan, which would eventually lead to the Soviet invasion in December of that year. There were some areas, however, where a new government could clear the decks: the long-running problems with the settler rebellion in Rhodesia and the difficulties over the Falklands might be solved by decisive action. The new Foreign Secretary, Lord Carrington, quickly set about dealing with the problem of Rhodesia, and a constitutional conference in London soon resulted in a settlement and the independence of the country under the name Zimbabwe. This led to the election as President, to Lord Carrington's chagrin and Conservative backbench MPs' fury, of Robert Mugabe, the Chinese-backed leader of the Zimbabwe African National Union (ZANU).

Nicholas Ridley, Lord Carrington's Minister of State and his representative in the House of Commons, was now tasked with dealing with the question of negotiations with the Argentine junta. This was approached with less dash than the issue of Rhodesia, but even so, Ridley was soon visiting Buenos Aires and the Falklands, and a new proposal was beginning to take shape in the corridors of the Foreign Office, based on ideas that had been gradually developing during the slow round of negotiations that had taken place under the last Labour government. This was a formula called 'lease-back' and Ridley now believed it was the only possible way out of the impasse. Under this form of agreement, sovereignty of the islands would be formally handed to Argentina, but the British government would hold a lease for a period of ninety-nine years, or more, to guarantee the security of the islanders and their way of life. Both countries' flags would be flown on the islands, and the Argentine government would have an official representation on the Falklands and on their governing body. The proposal was informally presented to Argentina, in the hope that the parties would be able to agree on some variation of this principle – in particular the term of years – and that the junta would accept a limit to the exercise of sovereignty during the period of the lease.

What would have been the outcome of these negotiations

remains one of the great mysteries of history, however, because when Nicholas Ridley visited the Falklands to seek the approval of the islanders he was met with outright antagonism; they made it plain that they would campaign to 'Keep the Falkland Islands British'. The problem for Ridley was that he could not divulge detailed proposals to the islanders, in case they felt that they were being presented with a fait accompli, the product of secret negotiations with Argentina. On the other hand, the lack of detail exacerbated the islanders' fears, and these were further aggravated by a new nationality bill going through parliament that seemed to be taking any rights to British nationality away from them.

The most powerful opposition to lease-back, however, lay not in Stanley, but in London. As a result of the deal over Rhodesia, backbench opinion in the Conservative Party had hardened against Lord Carrington and the Foreign Office, and no one was prepared to see what they viewed as a second shameful abandonment of kith and kin in the Falklands. The new Conservative government had not, in their view, been elected to sell British interests down the river. Ridley was the target not only of hostile questioning from Conservative MPs in the House of Commons when he returned from the Falklands, but also of accusations from the Labour opposition of reneging on previous commitments to the Falklanders. Lease-back was a dead letter as far as the growing Falklands lobby in the Houses of Parliament were concerned. Continuing talks with Argentine representatives were abandoned or delayed while Ridley waited to see if the mood would change in the islands themselves, but it was useless. When the islanders elected a new Falkland Islands Council in October 1981, it was solidly opposed to any form of lease-back.

Argentina proposed another round of talks to start in 1982 in

New York and continue on a monthly schedule. It wasn't clear that the British would have anything to say.

The Argentine junta had already shown that it was prepared to exert some military pressure on Britain, even if, like the attempt to arrest the research ship *Shackleton*, it never amounted to more than harassment that could be disowned by Argentina if it seemed to be getting out of hand. There had been a lot of these incidents over the years since the junta came to power, taking the form, for example, of unauthorized and unannounced landings on isolated islands that were part of the Falkland Islands dependencies, or unofficial over-flights of the Falklands by Argentine air force jets. It was obvious that these were part of a dual strategy to put pressure on both the British government and the Falkland islanders to take the negotiations seriously. By the end of 1981, the British had exhausted their diplomatic options, lease-back was a non-starter because of opposition in the Falklands and in parliament, and there was no other plan on the horizon.

The military leadership in Buenos Aires, however, was beginning to think that it was time to start raising the stakes over the question of the Malvinas. On 9 December 1981, at the height of the southern summer when the pavements of the Plaza de Mayo and the broad Avenida 9 de Julio were swathed in the purple blossoms of the jacaranda trees, two senior military figures, General Leopoldo Galtieri and Admiral Jorge Anaya, met at lunch to discuss various difficulties that they had with the political situation in Argentina and its current president, General Roberto Viola. The two men were very different. Galtieri was a large figure, slightly overweight, expansive, with grand gestures and the face of the rough, bluff man of action that he professed to be. Anaya was small and lean, a precise figure with a fine ascetic face and dark hair that was slicked back, smoothly, close to his skull. Both were exceptionally powerful and ruthless people.

Argentina had been a military dictatorship since the overthrow of Isabel Perón – Juan Perón's widow – in 1976, and the regime had descended into utter barbarity in its so-called war against subversion. Counter-insurgency operations were mounted in the countryside against revolutionary organizations of agricultural workers and peasants, and detentions, torture and murder were used against opponents of the regime in the cities. The numbers of people murdered by the regime rose into the tens of thousands. The army played the most visible role in the creation of this dictatorship, and its head, General Jorge Videla, became President, but the head of the navy, Admiral Eduardo Massera, played a key ideological role in the formation of the junta and its efforts to kill any opposition. The navy ran its own death squads and turned one of its buildings in Buenos Aires, the Navy Mechanics School, into a centre for the torture and imprisonment of many of the regime's detainees. Naval officers assumed a key role in the special units that carried out the kidnapping of suspects and made helicopter flights which disposed of detainees by dropping them into the sea.

Admiral Massera had argued that the junta should reassert Argentina's historical territorial claims over parts of the Beagle Channel in Cape Horn that were disputed with neighbouring Chile, and over the Falkland Islands or Malvinas. His proposal that the Falklands should be recovered by military means had been met with circumspection by President Videla, who thought that it was a subterfuge to enable the navy, and Admiral Massera himself, to amass greater political influence; it was this distrust amongst the members of the junta that had given the British government some extra breathing space. None the less, Admiral Massera was given permission to draw up contingency plans for an invasion of the Malvinas and it was Admiral Anaya, Fleet Commander of the Argentine navy, who was given the task of producing them.

By the time that General Galtieri and Admiral Anaya were sitting down to lunch in 1981, politics had moved on. Videla had been replaced in March 1981 by General Viola. Thousands had been murdered, and the war against subversion could not be continued indefinitely. The junta was split over what policies it should follow in order to retain military power. President Viola was in favour of some form of political liberalization, and had established contacts with remnants of the Peronistas and the Radical Party. A civilian, Costa Méndez, had been allowed into the government as Foreign Minister. But General Galtieri and other senior military figures were concerned, not only about the threat of some relaxation in the repressive policies of the junta, but also about the developing economic crisis that had brought galloping inflation and stagnant output.

The discussions of these military men centred on the possibility of removing Viola from power. Admiral Anaya, now head of the navy, pledged his and the navy's support to Galtieri, but had one specific proviso: that the navy be allowed to expand its plans to recapture the Malvinas, and to work towards their implementation by the end of 1982. The deal was agreed, the meal concluded and events took their course.

Viola, already somewhat ill, was retired, and General Galtieri assumed his position as President and head of the junta a few days later.

True to his word, in January 1982 Galtieri authorized Anaya to start planning for the military takeover of the Malvinas in earnest. The headquarters of the Argentine navy, on Avenida Comodoro Py, is a huge stone building, approached by an enormous set of monumental steps. Like any large headquarters, it is a hotbed of gossip, and for secrecy the Malvinas planning group was set up in the Navy Club, an old building on the corner of Florida and Avenida Corrientes in the centre of Buenos Aires. The Navy Club is modelled on the exclusive old gentlemen's clubs of St James's in London. Approached via an old-fashioned semicircular, metal-grilled lift, its discreetly quiet and elegant rooms were the perfect place to organize a military conspiracy.

The planning group was headed by the Argentine fleet commander, Rear Admiral Juan José Lombardo, and its strategy was based on the plans that had already been worked up by Admiral Anaya in 1977. These assumed that a small amphibious force of three thousand men could land close to Stanley, immobilize the small detachment of marines stationed there and then effectively continue to hold the islands with a force of just five hundred troops. The view of the admirals was that this fait accompli would leave the British government impotent to effect any change in the situation. This was more than a purely military assessment. Rear Admiral Jorge Allara, who was to become head of the invasion force, had recently returned from a two-year stint in London as the Argentine naval attaché. He firmly believed that Britain was indifferent to the fate of the Falklands and would seek a settlement. As the plans progressed and started to take more concrete form, they were given the name Operation Azul, and the working group moved to the large naval base at Puerto Belgrano. The invasion was provisionally scheduled for the end of the year, December 1982.

There was, however, another operation being worked on in the Argentine navy – a secret within a secret, which had been created by Admiral Anaya and was running parallel to Operation Azul, and which the planning group knew nothing about.

To the south-east of the Falklands lies the island of South Georgia, which was also a British possession, having been discovered by James Cook in 1775. It had for many years housed a group of settlements that were supported by the whaling industry. It was here in May 1916 that Shackleton, in his small boat the *James Caird*, had landed after crossing miles of stormy ocean to seek rescue for his crew stranded on Elephant Island 800 miles away. Despite Cook's landing on the island, it had remained unoccupied until 1909, when a Norwegian whaler, Captain Carl Larsen, founded the Compania Argentina de Pesca and established the first whaling station here. He did so without any reference to the Falkland Islands government, which was, in British eyes at least, responsible for the administration of South Georgia. Eventually Larsen, under pressure from a British warship moored in Grytviken harbour, applied formally to the Falklands governor in Port Stanley for a lease, which was granted. In 1909, in response to the growth of Larsen's whaling interests, a civilian station was established at King Edward cove, along the coast from Grytviken, and a stipendiary magistrate appointed, whose function was to act as the British representative

The whaling industry flourished and, as well as Grytviken, whaling stations were established at several points on the sheltered north-east coast, at Leith Harbour, Stromness, Husvik and Ocean Harbour, Prins Olav Harbour and Godthul. Some of these stations were set up, as their names imply, by the Norwegian companies involved in whaling in the South Atlantic, but a Scottish firm, Christian Salveson, was expanding and beginning to dominate the whaling industry. They made their own base in Leith Harbour, later expanding to Stromness and Prins Olav. Salveson brought modern industrial techniques to the industry: they tried to make profits from the entire whale, not just its oil, so machinery and processing plant was installed to produce fertilizer and animal feed from the bones and flesh of the whale's carcass.

The demand for whale products started to decline after the Second World War, and by 1963 Salveson had withdrawn from the whaling business. The thriving communities on South Georgia died, leaving behind their houses, churches and the extensive factories for producing whale oil and other products. Now just scrap, the machinery sat there rusting and decaying, and the population of South Georgia was reduced to the occasional scientific expedition and the handful of volunteers from the British Antarctic Survey who were stationed there.

In 1979 Christian Salveson were approached by an Argentinian who wanted to salvage the scrap metal contained in the abandoned equipment and plant of the former whaling stations. A contract was signed, and for the sum of £160,000 Constantino Davidoff acquired the rights to salvage the remains of Christian Salveson's whaling business. The total amount of scrap metal could be worth several millions of pounds, but there were a lot of costs that Davidoff would have to meet, one of the largest being the transport of men and equipment across the 1,400 miles of stormy seas that separate South Georgia from ports in Argentina. He approached the Argentine navy for help and was met with interest. Navy supply ships travelled up and down the eastern coast of Argentina, and they were available for hire.

Davidoff's first task was actually to travel to South Georgia to make a preliminary investigation of the various sites to which he had purchased the rights and to work out a schedule for the dismantling of the whaling factories. The navy were pleased to help him, and on 16 December 1981 he left Buenos Aires on board the Argentine ice-breaker *Almirante Irízar*, commanded by Captain Cesar Trombetta. Davidoff had become unwittingly involved in the Argentine navy's plotting, for Trombetta was operating under the orders of Admiral Edgardo Otero, former head of the torture and murder centre in Buenos Aires, the Navy Mechanics School. Otero was close to the head of naval intelligence and also to Admiral Anaya. For several months they had been working on a plan to capture South Georgia, a plan code-named Operation Alpha.

Davidoff had sent notification of his visit to South Georgia to the British Embassy in Buenos Aires on the same day that the *Almirante Irízar* had left Argentina. Presumably to avoid any unwelcome enquiries or last-minute objections from the British Ambassador, Captain Trombetta maintained radio silence throughout the four days it took his ship to travel the 1,650 miles from Buenos Aires to South Georgia.

The correct protocol was for Captain Trombetta to stop first at Grytviken to obtain entry clearance from the British representative on South Georgia, the commander of the British Antarctic Survey, but instead he steamed straight on and dropped anchor at Leith Harbour in Stromness Bay. Davidoff and a small group of employees went ashore to make an inventory and take photos of the abandoned whaling station. Someone chalked on the side of a building '*Las Malvinas son Argentinas*'. After four days the ice-breaker left and returned to the mainland.

On 4 January 1982, the British Ambassador in Buenos Aires issued a stiff reprimand to the Argentine Foreign Office about the flouting of entry formalities by the captain of the *Almirante*

Irízar and warned of undesirable consequences if there was any repeat of this behaviour. Despite this, Davidoff made a cordial visit to the British Embassy in February and told officials that he was planning another trip to South Georgia to start the salvage operation in earnest; he assured Embassy staff that he would take personal responsibility for the conduct of his ship, its crew and its passengers. This time an Argentine naval supply ship, the *Bahía Buen Suceso*, a ship of about 5,000 tons, would take forty-one workers to carry out the dismantling of the scrap machinery, with enough supplies for them to stay there until the job was finished.

Regardless of Davidoff's previous reassurances, the *Buen Suceso* left Buenos Aires on 11 March without a landing permit, and this ship too ignored the formalities of calling at the British Antarctic Survey base, instead sailing directly towards Stromness Bay. On 16 March they anchored overnight because of fog, then early in the morning they went slowly into anchor at Leith. Their first task was to repair the jetty. Once this had been done the equipment and stores were unloaded, the Argentine flag was raised and work started on dismantling the derelict machinery.

Two days later, on Friday 19 March, four members of the British Antarctic Survey left their base in King Edward Cove at Grytviken and went by boat to Carlita Bay, from where they were going to trek across the headland to Leith Harbour. They were in the middle of a planned project to prepare emergency rations and shelter for the coming winter. As they crested the hill overlooking the bay, they saw the *Bahía Buen Suceso* berthed in the jetty at Leith with heavy equipment being unloaded and a mobile crane moving crates from the jetty to one of the warehouses. They also saw what they believed were men in some type of military uniform.

The scientists walked down the hill to the harbour, where they saw workmen engaged in demolition work using oxyacetylene cutting tools, dismantling various sections of boilers, tanks and pipework in the old whaling station. But they also found that Davidoff's workers had broken into the two houses that were being used by the British Antarctic Survey and that furniture and emergency food containers had been smashed and pillaged. Once again, the Argentine flag was flying from a building.

Two of the four went down to the jetty, where they were invited on board the *Buen Suceso* and met Captain Briatore. They explained to him that he should go to King Edward Cove to get a landing permit, and that his men should respect British Antarctic Survey property. The captain assured them that he had received permission to land by radio, and offered them overnight accommodation on the ship.

The members of the Survey team declined, returning instead to their building to join their colleagues. There they set up their radio and contacted the commander of the BAS in Grytviken to report the presence of the Argentine ship and the damage to BAS property. The commander, Steve Martin, eventually managed to pass on this information to Rex Hunt, Governor of the Falklands, who in turn transmitted a long message to the Foreign Office in London.

Hunt signalled back to the BAS team a message for Captain Briatore:

You have landed illegally at Leith without obtaining proper clearance. You and your party must go back on board the *Bahía Buen Suceso* immediately and report to the Base commander Grytviken for further instructions. You must remove the Argentine flag from Leith. You must not interfere with the British

Antarctic Survey depot at Leith. You must not alter or deface the notices at Leith. No military personnel are allowed to land on South Georgia. No firearms are to be taken ashore. Ends.

In London the decision was taken to inform the Argentine government, via the British Embassy in Buenos Aires and the Argentine Ambassador in London, that Her Majesty's Government regarded the incident as serious and that if the *Bahía Buen Suceso* was not withdrawn immediately the British government would take whatever action seemed necessary.

These were brave words, but British options were limited. The nearest warships were in Gibraltar, 5,000 miles away. The Antarctic Survey vessel *Endurance* was, however, in Port Stanley and her continued presence was designed precisely to prevent these niggling incursions by Argentina. The Ministry of Defence ordered *Endurance* to put to sea urgently, which she did early on the morning of Sunday 21 March. Before leaving, the Royal Marine detachment on *Endurance* had been brought up to troop strength from the garrison at Stanley in case there was any resistance from the Argentinians at Leith. While the *Endurance* was en route to South Georgia, on the evening of 21 March the *Bahía Buen Suces*o sailed slowly out of Leith Harbour into Stromness Bay and headed back to the Argentine mainland, leaving the salvage workers behind. The Argentine government was told that *Endurance* was on her way to evict the demolition workers, but then there was a change of plan in London and Nick Barker, captain of *Endurance*, was ordered to anchor at Grytviken and not, as he had previously planned, to go straight to Leith Harbour to land the marines.

Endurance remained at anchor 20 miles from the Argentine presence on South Georgia. The Foreign Office and the Ministry of Defence hoped that a slight pause in the effort to remove the demolition workers would allow a breathing space in which diplomatic relations between the British and Argentine governments could cool down. In reality, the pause gave just enough time for the man who was the driving force behind the invasion plan, Admiral Anaya, to step up the momentum. The premature exposure of the covert plan to land Argentine forces on South Georgia had always threatened to undermine a successful operation to capture the Falklands. Now it appeared that Davidoff's demolition operation might do exactly that. Anaya was faced with some hard choices and very little time to make them, as the possibility grew, in Argentine eyes at least, that Britain would send reinforcements to the Falklands. There were three options open to Admiral Anaya and his fellow officers in the junta. The main invasion timetable of Operation Azul could be adhered to, in the hope that in a few months' time any reinforcements on the Falklands would have been withdrawn. But the junta would have to back down over South Georgia now, which was unpalatable, and there were no guarantees about the future. The plan could be abandoned and resuscitated at a later, unspecified date, but this represented a personal defeat for Anaya, and he might never be in a position to impose his will on Galtieri again. Or the project could be rapidly advanced, and the invasion plans put into motion before Britain had time to send significant forces to the island. It was this course that Anaya chose.

On 24 March he ordered Rear Admiral Allara, commander designate of the invasion force, to bring the preparations forward and report the earliest date on which the navy could sail. Allara, together with Admiral Juan Lombardo and Rear Admiral Carlos Busser, met with General Sigfrido Garcia and the air force's Brigadier Mayor Plessel to issue emergency orders to bring forward the mobilization of the ships and men needed for the invasion.

A day later, on 25 March, the 9,600-ton *Bahía Paraiso*, with a detachment of special forces commanded by Lieutenant Commander Alfredo Astiz, and its Alouette helicopter docked in Leith Harbour. If the British marines embarked on *Endurance* were going to attempt to remove the demolition workers, their job had now become far more difficult, and their landing might be opposed. At the same time, Admiral Anaya ordered two corvettes – ships that would be better known as frigates in the Royal Navy – *Drummond* and *Granville*, both armed with anti-ship missiles, to take up a position between South Georgia and the Falkland Islands. Once stationed there they might be able to intercept *Endurance* returning to Port Stanley.

On 26 March the members of the junta held a crisis meeting. Admiral Anaya went to it fortified with the information given to him on the previous day by Admiral Lombardo: the task force would be able to sail by 1 April. The junta wasted little time in debate. General Galtieri in particular was keen to go ahead. His role as President depended on Admiral Anaya's support, but there were other pressing issues that faced all of them that day. The economic situation was worsening, and despite the years of the 'Dirty War' with its murder and torture of left-wingers and unionists, the powerful Peronist trades unions had called a general strike for the end of the month. The junta's grip on power was weakening. The population's loyalties might instead be mobilized once again behind the junta if it sought to recapture the nation's birthright of the Malvinas. Even the one civilian presence in the government, the Foreign Minister Costa Mendez, who had up until now been negotiating with the British Foreign Office, supported the invasion.

The die was cast. On 28 March 1982, the first of the thousand troops that were going to spearhead the Argentine invasion force were marching aboard their transport ship in Puerto Belgrano.

3

'THE MALVINAS ARE OURS!'

The plans to invade the Malvinas had been drawn up over a fairly lengthy period, and despite the fact that the group of officers working on them had been small and extremely secretive, the plans were sufficiently developed that being asked to bring them forward by two months, and to prepare for embarkation in only five days, presented little obstacle. But the immediacy of the decision meant that the organizational tasks required a very concentrated effort. Rear Admiral of Marines Carlos Busser, who was in charge of the amphibious operation, was asked on the evening of 23 March how quickly he could bring the plan together. The naval and military bases that would supply the main forces were close together: the naval headquarters were at Puerto Belgrano, while the military barracks and staff headquarters were in Bahia Blanco, just 23 miles away. Working through the night and the next two days, Vice Admiral

Juan Lombardo, in overall command, was able to drive to Buenos Aires on the 25th and report to Admiral Anaya and the other members of the junta that the invasion would be possible on 1 April, just one week away. In order to achieve this timetable, everything – ships, men and equipment – would need to be fully operational and mobilized in Puerto Belgrano as early as 28 March.

The overall plan envisaged a large naval presence of fifteen vessels to accompany the landing forces, but there was one ship that would not be included in the invasion fleet. It was ironic that the most famous ship in the Argentine navy would not take part in the recovery of the Malvinas. The cruiser *General Belgrano* had not been considered for the invasion plans because she was moored in Puerto Belgrano undergoing a regular period of mechanical maintenance. The *General Belgrano* had served in the Argentine navy for thirty years, but even before then she had seen an enormous amount of combat. Launched in 1938 in Camden in the state of New York, the *Belgrano* had formerly been the USS *Phoenix* and had survived the surprise attack on Pearl Harbor by Japanese bombers in December 1941. While battleships exploded in giant balls of fire, and enormous thick columns of black-brown smoke climbed into the Pacific air, the crew of the *Phoenix* bravely put to sea, defying the bombs and torpedoes of the Japanese navy.

In April 1951 the *Phoenix* was bought by the Argentine navy and renamed the *17 de Octubre*, an important date in the political career of the Argentine President Juan Perón. When he was overthrown in 1956, the cruiser's name was changed again to ARA (Armada Republica de Argentina) *General Belgrano*, after General Manuel Belgrano who had fought with great success in the war of independence in 1816.

The *Belgrano* was a heavily armed cruiser, with fifteen guns firing 6-inch shells mounted on five turrets. She also had eight guns that fired slightly smaller shells, of 5-inch calibre, that were intended for use mainly against aircraft, and several smaller, quick-firing anti-aircraft cannon. The *Belgrano* was elderly, but she had been modernized over the years and fitted with modern radar sets that could provide accurate target information for the main armament, as well as searching the air and sea for hostile ships or aircraft. A hangar in the rear of the hull below the main deck carried two helicopters, and recently the *Belgrano* had been fitted with two British-manufactured Sea Cat anti-aircraft missile launchers.

The *Belgrano* became the flagship of the Argentine navy, and remained so until the arrival of the aircraft carrier *Veinticinco de Mayo*. Even then the *Belgrano* remained a vital symbol of Argentina and its naval power. The *Belgrano* was considered a happy ship, one of those vessels where a combination of good officers and experienced older hands created a bond of solidarity amongst the crew. Every year 1,200 conscripts were selected randomly for military service in the navy and they would arrive at Puerto Belgrano, the main naval headquarters. The ones who learned that they were destined to serve on the *Belgrano* and receive instruction in gunnery, seamanship and damage control were thought to be very lucky. The *Belgrano* was considered to be a plum posting, and her status as an icon of the Argentine navy was enhanced by the number of conscripts and junior officers who had served on her for their initial training period. Perhaps not surprising for a ship whose main armament was fifteen 6-inch guns, and which had been built in the era when gunnery was king, the crew of the *Belgrano* always succeeded in gunnery competitions. Their accuracy and precision was remarkable. The recoil from firing a salvo of all fifteen main guns at once was enough to move the ship back in the water by more than 6 feet, but even so, fifteen 6-inch shells could be fired a distance of 12½ miles, all landing inside a target 100 yards long.

The *General Belgrano*'s maintenance period had to take place after every thousand hours of steaming and was expected to last for two months. The work included inspection and repairs to the main guns and turrets, and checks on their alignment. The main turbines were dismantled and inspected, as were the eight boilers and their steam tubes. The work that was carried out in the engine room was very important because, although the ship had been extremely well built in the American shipyard, there were problems in the reduction gearing that took power from the turbines to the propeller shafts, and in the saturated steam boilers, which had lost some of their efficiency over the years. They were now limited to 70 per cent of their maximum output, unless in an emergency, and this imposed a maximum speed on the cruiser of 18.5 knots.

In addition to this essential work on the propulsion system, the opportunity was taken to fix problems with the electrical circuits of the Sea Cat anti-aircraft missiles and carry out other general maintenance, such as painting the decks and superstructure, replacing aerials and rectifying the general wear and tear of a previous training voyage that had seen the *Belgrano* journey south to Tierra del Fuego and beyond.

During the maintenance period, while the ship was moored at the quayside, the rest of the crew were given instruction in classes on board and in the base, and continued a lot of their training in fire control, damage control and other exercises.

*

In the second week of March, Rear Admiral Allara came to Puerto Belgrano and addressed the main operational leaders of the navy: all the captains in command of seagoing ships like the aircraft carrier; the heads of the frigate division and the two destroyer divisions; and the captain of the *Belgrano*, Captain Héctor Bonzo were included. The meeting was secret, but according to Captain Bonzo the Admiral indicated that soon the navy and the marines would begin preparations to go on a combat mission to assert Argentinian control of the Malvinas. After this meeting, and presumably as part of the build-up to the operation, the activity in Puerto Belgrano started to increase. In particular, the marines started to carry out exercises and manoeuvres involving embarkation and landings from the *Cabo San Antonio*, the large tank-landing craft that had been delivered to the navy four years earlier.

The second in command of the *Belgrano*, Commander Pedro Luis Galazi, had formerly been commanding officer of *Cabo San Antonio*, but had left the ship to go to the *Belgrano* in February 1982. When he learned of the invasion plans on 24 March, and realized that his former ship was going to take part and that he was going to stay in port, he was furious: 'I almost cried when I realized that I was not going to the Malvinas. But otherwise I was very happy about it.'

The first troop movements were the mobilization of the Special Forces, the '*Bustos Tacticos*', and marines who were to make the initial assault and disarm the detachment of British Royal Marines stationed in Port Stanley. It was an important part of the calculation that the small garrison should be overwhelmed, avoiding any bloodshed. The junta was adamant in its belief that Britain would negotiate in the face of a fait accompli, and so it was vital that no damage to British property, or deaths or injuries to British citizens, should become an obstacle to talks. Consequently a comparatively large number of Special Forces and marines would land on the island of East Falkland.

The invasion forces would be made up of groups of soldiers from the HQ and Communications Unit, 387 men from the 2nd battalion Marine Infantry, ninety-two men from an amphibious commando company, and twelve men of the *Bustos Tacticos*, for beach reconnaissance. There were forty-one men from the Marine Field Artillery Battalion who would travel with six 105-mm-calibre howitzers, large, long-range guns that were capable of laying down a heavy fire over long distances; and a reserve force of sixty-five men from the 1st Battalion of Marine Infantry. The troops were to be landed and to be mobile on the islands with twenty Amtracs – amphibious armoured-tracked troop carriers – and there would be a transport unit of heavy lorries, the drivers and crews of which totalled 101 men. A further platoon of thirty-nine men was drawn from the army's 25th Regiment. All in all there was, including some administrative staff, a total of 904 men to be transported to and disembarked on the islands. The 2nd Battalion of the marines were a highly trained unit, who had been involved in an exercise with US marines at the end of 1981; they were probably the best troops available. With their armoured troop carriers they were a mobile and impressive force, quite capable of overwhelming just forty-nine British Royal marines, who had no armour or artillery.

One other addition to the force was destined not for the Falklands, but to reinforce the Argentine Special Forces that had landed with Davidoff's demolition workers at Leith in South Georgia and to complete the takeover of the island. The ship that would take them there was the frigate *Guerrico*. This too was in dry dock for repairs, but the work was quickly completed so that she could set off with the rest of the invasion force on her 1,400-mile journey. All the troops were located close to the port of embarkation except the soldiers from the 25th Regiment, who had to be flown over 1,000 miles from their bases in the south at Colonia Sarmineto. Most of the troops would be loaded into the *Cabo San Antonio*, along with the Amtrac amphibious troop carriers.

The days of 26 and 27 March were important for planning all the aspects of the operation. Everything had to be done, and orders had to be given so that the men in the units concerned were still in the dark about what was really happening. Secrecy was paramount. It all had to look like an exercise, just routine training. About twenty officers were now part of the planning staff, and they had to prepare a communications plan, a schedule for embarkation and a detailed timetable for loading stores and equipment. Activity in Puerto Belgrano reached very high levels, and became very noticeable. Lieutenant Commander Norberto Bernasconi, who was in charge of maintenance work on the *Belgrano*, started to see a lot of activity with landing craft and personnel carriers. He wondered whether another coup was being prepared.

On Sunday 28 March at 08.00 the marines started loading on to the ships at Puerto Belgrano. The cover story for the press, and also for relatives, was that there were to be joint anti-submarine exercises with the Uruguayan navy. This was clearly not appropriate for the members of the 25th Regiment, and their officers were briefed sooner than the rest of the task force and given a different cover story. Juan José Centurion was a lieutenant in the 25th Regiment and, along with the other junior officers, was briefed by their commanding officer one morning and sworn to secrecy.

Right then he gave us the full details of operations. That same night my company was to leave by plane for the Espora base on Puerto Belgrano and we were to embark on the *Santísima Trinidad* and the *Almirante Irízar* the next day. We were given a scenario for deceiving our families that we were going on an exercise in Rio Gallego. We left that same evening. We left with drums and cymbals and with the secret circling around us. We viewed the Malvinas as a lost treasure with a sentimental longing that everyone in Argentina shared.

Many of the other troops had an inkling of their destination, and there was an air of anticipation and excitement aboard the ships. It was a sunny day with little wind. It seemed auspicious.

The ships sailed at midday, and over lunch the rest of the officers were told of their destination and given their first briefing about the overall operation and the details of the landing.

The invasion fleet was divided up into two task forces, code-named Task Force 20 and Task Force 40. Task Force 20 was essentially the Argentine navy's largest ship, the aircraft carrier *Veinticinco de Mayo*, the flagship of the group, carrying the flag of Vice Admiral Juan Lombardo, with an escort of four destroyers, *Comodoro Py*, *Hipólito Bouchard*, *Piedra Buena* and *Segui*, all of them ex-US warships. The role of this group of ships was to provide aerial reconnaissance and long-range cover for Task Force 40, which was the amphibious group, responsible for the landings under the command of Rear Admiral Busser. These ships, the tank-landing craft *Cabo San Antonio*, the transport *Isla de los Estados* and icebreaker *Almirante Irízar* were escorted by four ships and a reconnaissance submarine, the *Santa Fe*. In command of this unit was Rear Admiral Allara on his flagship *Santísima Trinidad*, one of the two destroyers that were modelled on the British Type 42. The *Santísima Trinidad* had been built in Argentina; the other Type 42, the *Hércules*, had been purchased from Vickers shipbuilders. There were also two small frigates, Type 69s, purchased from France, the *Drummond* and the *Granville*.

There was no real reason for this show of strength. Such a large number of ships setting out from Puerto Belgrano could easily have destroyed the so far successful efforts at secrecy. It was the troop numbers that were going to be the decisive element in the seizure of the islands, not the overwhelming force of the Argentine fleet at sea. But there was a very important element of pageant and symbolism to the affair. For the first time a decisive move was being made to heal the wound that the Malvinas represented in the body of the nation. It was a turning point in history: a glorious victory was about to be delivered, almost as significant as the creation of the nation itself, and of course what was being demonstrated was that it was the navy that was the source of this salvation and renewal.

The route planned for the invasion forces was a first leg down, parallel to the coast of Argentina in a southerly direction, then at the latitude of Santa Cruz to head east and pass to the south of the Malvinas, then on the final leg to head north again so that the approach to Stanley would be from the south-east. However, the weather in the South Atlantic now showed its hand, and on the morning of Monday 29 March the winds rapidly increased and a powerful storm developed. All the ships had to reduce their speed, and the *Cabo San Antonio*, somewhat over-loaded with 880 men, started to roll ominously. Conditions were not much better in the Type 42 destroyers, which had a very poor reputation for sea keeping. Cramped between decks, the air vile with the smell of fear and vomit, jolted relentlessly by huge waves that crashed against the shuddering hull, it was a dreadful and debilitating two days for the soldiers and marines of the task force. The seas were so violent that one of the Puma helicopters on the *Almirante Irízar* broke loose and was so badly damaged it was no longer usable.

The plans obviously needed to be changed. The landing planned for 1 April was postponed by twenty-four hours and the task force changed course, heading for Stanley by the shortest route, passing the Malvinas to the north.

Rear Admiral Busser's overall strategy had been to capture Government House and the Royal Marine barracks at Moody Brook almost simultaneously with an overwhelming force advancing from many directions, to emphasize to the marines, and anyone else who might think of putting up resistance, that the invading force had a crushing superiority. Amphibious troops would be landed on a beach 2 miles from Stanley, while the main landing force would drive ashore in their amphibious armoured personnel carriers from a landing point to the north of the airstrip. The plan also called for a helicopter to land troops from the *Almirante Irízar* to occupy Goose Green and Darwin, other smaller settlements on East Falkland, but the damage to the Puma in the storm meant this was no longer possible.

To complicate the situation for Rear Admiral Busser further, the departure of the invasion fleet had been detected by the British government and a warning had been sent to the Falklands Governor, Rex Hunt. The islanders were now expecting some type of landing, and this information had been transmitted to Buenos Aires by Argentinians in the airline office in Stanley. Now it seemed likely that the original landing beach would be defended and intelligence reached Rear Admiral Busser that the airstrip would also be blocked. Busser took a helicopter from *Cabo San Antonio* to the *Santísima Trinidad* to work out the best way forward. Jointly, Rear Admiral Busser and Admiral Allara decided on a rapid readjustment of their forces, and selected some alternative landing sites.

The landing beach was changed to one in Yorke Bay, to the west of Stanley, and a Hercules flight bringing more troops of the 25th Regiment from Comodoro Rivadavia was abandoned. The main platoon of armoured amphibious troops, which had originally been intended to take Government House, was directed to capture the airstrip, and a small force of marines, who were going to land in boats, were ordered to march north and take Government House as well as the Royal Marine barracks at Moody Brook.

Early on the morning of 2 April the *Santísima Trinidad* launched twenty-one rubber inflatable dinghies powered by outboard motors, and a detachment of ninety-one marines scrambled aboard them, heading for the shore near Seal Point. They had trouble with some of the outboard motors, which started to run erratically, and some of the inflatables became trapped in thick beds of seaweed, but eventually they made it ashore. There they split up, the main party under Lieutenant Commander Sabarots heading for the Royal Marine barracks, while a smaller group under the command of Lieutenant Commander Giachino went to capture Government House.

At the same time, to the north of Stanley, the submarine *Santa Fe* launched a small group of Special Forces swimmers who were to reconnoitre the landing beach for the body of the marines in their Amtracs on the *Cabo San Antonio*, which was now gently holding its position to the east of the submarine.

At this time, the operation had passed the point of no return and the troops on board the *Cabo San Antonio*, now recovering from their extreme discomfort during the storm, were told of their mission aims. Rear Admiral Busser announced over the tannoy, 'We have been drawn by destiny to carry out one of the dearest ambitions of the Argentine people: to recover the Malvinas islands.'

The troops exploded in cheers, waving their hands in the air and grinning at each other – it was like a goal being scored in the World Cup. At 06.00 the marines climbed inside the Amtracs and started the engines, filling the decks with a deafening noise and fume-laden exhausts. The bow doors were opened, a green traffic light at the front of the deck flashed on and the first vehicle entered the water. Every thirty seconds another drove on to the ramp until they were all afloat, their propellers driving them through the mercifully calm sea. The vanguard of the assault force was guided to its landing point by signals from the Special Forces, who had swum ashore from the *Santa Fe* and landed two and a half hours earlier, at 04.00. At 06.30 the first Amtrac hit the beach, its tracks biting into the fine white sand.

The first four Amtracs advanced, their commanders expecting to come into contact with the Royal Marines close to the landing beach. But they had got as far as the outskirts of Stanley before they were met with gunfire from a group of marines who had set up a position in three white houses by the side of the road. The first rifle fire was very accurate, and the Amtrac on the right was hit. Then a rocket launcher was fired at the group of personnel carriers; it went wide, but it was enough for the crews of the Amtracs – the Argentines drove off the road and took cover. An anti-tank rifle was fired at one of the houses, but the Royal Marines still returned fire. A mortar carried by one of the troops in the Amtracs was brought forward and a total of three mortar bombs were fired, with one getting a direct hit on the roof of one of the houses. After this there was no more fire from the house, and the Royal Marine detachment retreated and sought to avoid capture.

Meanwhile Lieutenant Giachino's detachment had walked for some miles across the rough, hummocky land towards Government House. It was dark and it had taken them far longer than they expected to cross the rough terrain. Because they had no clear idea of the layout of the house, they first stormed some empty servants' quarters next to the residence itself. As they regrouped and moved towards the main house, the Royal Marines, who had decided to turn Government House into a defensive strong point, opened fire; Giachino, hit in the leg, went down. So too did one of his companions, Lieutenant Quiroga. Badly wounded, Giachino was left where he lay, clutching a grenade. It was stalemate.

In Stanley the Amtracs had by now driven noisily through the town and taken up positions around it. Rear Admiral Busser was directing the six 105mm howitzers to be deployed near Yorke Bay, where they could shell both the airstrip, if necessary, and Port Stanley. By 08.00 Stanley was occupied.

Rear Admiral Busser and the main party of amphibious commandos who had travelled from Moody Brook went to Government House. There Governor Hunt had decided to surrender, much to the displeasure of the marines. Busser approached the house, unarmed and with a white flag, and was allowed into the residence. After a few almost ritual exchanges concerning the illegality of the Argentine actions, the British garrison and the Governor surrendered. The Malvinas was now firmly in the hands of the government of Argentina.

At a stroke, the Argentine navy and marines had produced a

stunning, historic victory. Argentina was filled with a delirious euphoria. Hundreds of thousands of people filled the squares and streets of Buenos Aires, holding aloft wave after wave of Argentine flags, like a blue-and-white cornfield rippling in the breeze. Just a week before the city had been paralysed by a general strike, its streets filled with the sound of chanting strikers, the clatter of police batons against their riot shields, the explosions of tear-gas cartridges and the screams of injured demonstrators; now they were filled with rapturous shouts of 'Viva Argentina! Viva las Malvinas!' As General Galtieri appeared on the balcony of the presidential palace, it seemed as though the junta had achieved the geographical unity of Argentina and the spiritual unity of the Argentinians. 'The legitimate rights of the Argentine people,' he announced, 'postponed prudently and patiently for a hundred and fifty years, become a reality.'

On South Georgia, Captain Trombetta, commander of the Bahía Paraiso, which had landed the group of Special Forces at Leith a few days ago, radioed to the marines at the British Antarctic Survey base to tell them that the Governor of the Falklands had surrendered unconditionally and suggested that they do the same. Trombetta then ordered all personnel to assemble on the beach. The frigate Guerrico had completed its 1,400-mile journey from Puerto Belgrano and had launched its helicopter, which circled over the British base at Grytviken. It had just landed a small party of troops near to the jetty there when the Royal Marines opened fire, hitting the helicopter several times and causing it to crash. The ensuing battle lasted for two more hours. The Guerrico steamed closer to the shore to assist the Argentine troops, but she too was hit several times with anti-tank rockets, causing her captain to withdraw to safety.

The *Guerrico* could, however, use her main gun to bombard the marines' position, and another helicopter was still landing more troops. The Royal Marines could not win, but had killed three Argentine soldiers, destroyed a helicopter and inflicted heavy damage to the frigate. In their view they had put up as much resistance as they could without pointless losses, and now they surrendered.

In Puerto Belgrano the news was announced to the sailors on the *Belgrano*, which had of course remained in port. Some of the crew were drawn up on the dockside with other sailors and told the news. Fernando Millan had been conscripted into the navy in 1981 and had trained as a radio telephonist. He had only one month left to complete his national service, after which he expected to pack his bags and go home. As he stood on the dock and heard the news, he felt very proud: 'It was great. When you are nineteen years old the world is at your feet. So we were very happy.' On board the ship, those working on the machinery and carrying out other repairs were mustered on the forward deck and told that the Malvinas had been recovered. Ruben Otero, another conscript in the engine room, also felt good about it and didn't believe that the British would do anything: 'They [the islands] were so far away, and so insignificant for Britain.' Others felt slightly differently. A gunner, Santiago Bellozo, had studied history: 'I did not think that the British would just sit on their hands.' Lucas Ocampo also worked in the engine room as a volunteer. He had been on the *Belgrano* for over two years and, being two or three years older than the conscripts, was looked up to. 'Slapping the Brits in the face made us feel strong,' he said. 'But I knew it would not end there. I thought, Britain will do something.'

In the wardroom, opinion among the officers was similar.

Hardly anybody in Argentina thought anything other than that the Malvinas rightly belonged to them. They were part of Argentina, as much as Buenos Aires was. There was also great pride in the successful conclusion of the military operation; it had gone without a hitch and had been conducted in an extremely humane way. Lieutenant Commander Bernasconi, who was living on the *Belgrano*, spending much of his time in the engine room, remembered: 'I was very surprised. I was told on the first of April, tomorrow they are landing on the Malvinas. In the wardroom most officers were extremely cheerful – it was very good news. Two, I think, had a serious face and were not affected by the mood. I said to some people that I have my reservations about this.'

4

A DIVERSION

HMS *Conqueror* headed steadily south through the Irish Sea, the bow wave creeping back over the forward casing as if the sea was eager to welcome the submarine and its crew back to its dark interior. On Tuesday 6 April, two days after departing Faslane, she left the crowded and relatively shallow waters of the Irish Sea, and Commander Chris Wreford-Brown signalled his intention to dive and make the maximum speed that he could. The watchkeepers on the fin went below, the order was given to shut and clip the upper lid, the main vents were opened and the submarine dived to 425 feet, with her speed set at 24 knots. Apart from coming to periscope depth for signals every twelve hours, *Conqueror* maintained this depth and speed for the long transit south.

Just a few days into the patrol, however, a problem started to develop that brought Commander Wreford-Brown to a fury and

threatened to compromise the mission. It was not a great introduction to his first command. The central, most overwhelming
asset of a nuclear submarine is the availability of unlimited
power from its nuclear reactor. This supplies abundant electricity
to provide fresh water, hot showers, refrigerated food and a constantly replenished clean, fresh atmosphere. Electricity powers
machines to scrub the atmosphere in the submarine, removing
dirt and carbon dioxide. It is also used to produce oxygen by the
electrolysis of seawater. The machine that did this, a very
complex piece of equipment, was situated on the main deck in
the engineering compartment to the rear of the reactor. The
process needs high-voltage electric current to be passed through
water maintained at high pressure, producing oxygen and
hydrogen, the two component chemicals of water. These two
gases in combination can be highly explosive and the electrolysis
machine was always treated with respect. The engineers in the
rear of the submarine used to say, 'If it has a green light showing
you walk past it; if it has a red light showing you run past.' In
order to remove dangerous concentrations of hydrogen and
oxygen, the system was periodically flushed out with the inert
gas nitrogen, which was stored in high-pressure containers outside the main hull of the submarine, under the casing. After a few
days it became obvious on board *Conqueror* that nitrogen was
being lost and that this was caused by a leak outside the submarine. There were several immediate worries. Was the leak
going to make too much noise when they reached their operational area? Was the gas going to leak into the ballast tanks and
affect the trim of the submarine?

Crucially, without the oxygen-making machine, the
Conqueror would be forced periodically to vent the submarine
by using the snorkel – the Second World War invention that

enabled German U-boats to run their diesel engines while submerged. But this would mean that *Conqueror* had to come to periscope depth, reduce her speed and potentially reveal her presence on the surface. At the end of the snorkel mast is a very big head, called the 'snort', so it is easily detectable by radar and is also a visual target. In addition, a large fan is turned on to help pump in air, and it can be a problem choosing when to run a big, noisy pump once a day for forty minutes. This all negates the main benefits of nuclear power that made nuclear submarines so potent – their speed, endurance and secrecy. The carbon-dioxide scrubbers and the air-conditioning system would help to some extent, and there was a back-up system that used large 'candles' made of sodium hydroxide to produce oxygen; these were placed in metal containers at either end of the boat and then ignited. The decision was made to continue the patrol, but Wreford-Brown was very unhappy about starting a possibly long and completely unknown mission with a potential fault like this.

On board HMS *Splendid*, the first nuclear submarine to have left Faslane, three days earlier than *Conqueror* and travelling on a different course, they discovered that they had the opposite problem: their electrolysis machine was working perfectly but their snorkel was defective, which would make things difficult if they ever needed to resort to their emergency diesel engines.

Conqueror, *Splendid* and *Spartan* had slipped out of port in secret. Their journey was not a public show to put pressure on the Argentine junta; instead it was a real threat, a weapon that could be used as soon as they were in a position to go into action. All three submarines were heading south at the best speed they could make, but only *Conqueror* had a detachment of the Special Boat Service on board. When the orders to prepare for Operation

Corporate – as the campaign to defend the Falklands was code-named – were first issued, it was thought to be extremely urgent to mobilize as many of the Special Forces as possible and to get them on to the Falklands, carrying out reconnaissance and gathering information about the state of Argentine forces and their deployment. So SAS contingents went to Ascension Island, which was going to be used as the British supply base in the Atlantic, while the SBS arrived in Faslane. The extra thirty-four SBS marines that Tim McClement expected to be parachuted into the sea next to *Conqueror* for embarkation never did materialize, but a few days out, on 10 April, among the masses of signals that were being sent covering rules of engagement, the latest intelligence briefings and political updates, *Conqueror* received a signal instructing Commander Wreford-Brown to change course. Unlike *Splendid* and *Spartan*, they were not going to be heading for the exclusion zone around the Falklands after all. *Conqueror* was going to take its special cargo of SBS troops to the desolate island of South Georgia, carry out reconnaissance and assist in support of SBS operations.

The members of the SBS were extremely physically fit, experts in demolition and underwater reconnaissance, who trained regularly in Arctic conditions in Norway. 'The Booties', as they were known on board *Conqueror*, were a novel addition to the crew. It wasn't usual for them to spend anything longer than forty-eight hours on a submarine for a special mission, but now they were in for a long trip. What exactly 6SBS were going to do when they arrived in South Georgia had still not been worked out. On the way down it occurred to their commanding officer, David Heaver, that if the SBS were going to be landed by boat, it might be a good idea if the *Conqueror* could lay down some covering fire against enemy positions if it was needed.

Nuclear submarines don't normally carry machine guns, but a solution was quickly worked out:

> We said, is there any way we can mount this [machine gun] on the top? We didn't want all the shell cases to go inside the casing of the fin because they might damage the masts going up and down, so one of our chief petty officers worked out and built a general-purpose machine-gun mount with a semicircular swivel, just by looking at the machine gun, looking at the top of the fin, working out the weight, welding some pipes together and adding a sheet-metal box for the shell cases. We named it after him – the Barlow Mount.

The SBS detachment created some problems on board the boat. It's a mistake to think that nuclear submarines are spacious. They are much bigger than conventional submarines and the facilities for the crew are better, but most civilians would find them extremely cramped. The walkways are narrower than on a surface warship and there are not enough bunks for the crew. The most junior ratings 'hot bunk' – in other words, share bunk space with junior ratings on the opposite watch – or sleep in the weapons-stowage compartment next to the torpedoes. Many prefer this, because the bunks provide not much more personal space than could be found in an expensive coffin. The torpedo room, on the other hand, is one of the few compartments in the boat where there is a feeling of space, stretching as it does across the whole 33-foot width of the hull. It is only the fact that a third of the crew is asleep in their bunks at any one time that allows the other crewmembers to move around the boat with any ease.

The fourteen men of 6SBS exacerbated this problem, because Lieutenant Commander McClement and Commander

Wreford-Brown had decided that the Booties should have their own bunks so that they could stick to their own routine throughout the journey south. They needed an area for physical training, and they were given space to do it in the weapons-stowage compartment. They wanted their own areas where they could continue to do weapons training and drill, and where they could plan their operation when the time came, so they were given access to both the ratings' messes. So that they weren't seen as inconvenient passengers, Tim McClement told them that they would have to make sure that they integrated into the crew, doing their share of watchkeeping, or at least turning up regularly in the same space. So the SBS actually took their turn on the throttles for the engines and on the steering positions in the control room. They each wanted to keep their personal weapon, usually a 9mm pistol, with them all the time, and they were allowed to do so as long as it wasn't loaded. They very quickly integrated themselves, though like most Special Forces they took advice from people they did not consider equals with a pinch of salt. Because of the failure of the electrolysis machinery, there were occasional peaks in the carbon-dioxide content of the boat's atmosphere. The medical officer gave the SBS a briefing about this, warning them that physical exercise would not do them much good and, moreover, would give them a splitting headache and lay them out for twelve hours. Their response was that they were in the SBS, were highly trained and had to maintain their physical condition, so they continued to do their exercises in the torpedo room. The medical officer was proved correct.

The SBS men fascinated the members of the crew, who learned from them the secrets of unarmed combat, silent killing, demolition and covert surveillance. Sprawled over high explosives in the weapons compartment, their guns and knives hanging from pipes on the deck head, they gave a piratical air to the forward part of the ship. Occasionally, however, they demonstrated that they hadn't quite understood the routine of the boat or the special nature of life underwater.

Petty Officer Graham Libby, or 'Horse' as he was known, was the leading sonar operator on board *Conqueror*. He had wanted to join the fire brigade as a young boy, but was too young, so he joined the navy instead and was promoted to acting leading seaman, but demoted after a 'bit of trouble' on shore. Unwillingly drafted into the submarine service, he was ready to leave the navy, but then he experienced the adrenalin of the 100-foot-deep escape training tower and realized that he might after all enjoy submarines. HMS *Conqueror* was his first posting, and he joined her at Faslane in 1979, so by now he had served continuously on board for three years. As well as operating the sonar, Horse was the ship's 'scratcher' – the crewmember responsible for the outer casing of the submarine, making sure that everything was properly maintained and that the capstans, winches and cables were all properly secured so that no noise was made when the boat was under way. He was also the most senior diver on *Conqueror*. Graham Libby thought the SBS were brilliant, but they gave him an alarming moment at the beginning of the cruise.

We were heading down, making good speed, doing a noise check, when suddenly we heard this massive thumping noise. It sounded like part of the boat was rattling and we thought, 'What the hell is that?' You don't like it because it means you haven't done your job properly, or we have to surface and fix something. And we have guys on the boat that can go round with a little portable device to isolate where the sound is coming from. Because we have to fix it, you can't make those sorts of noises when you're operational, you have to be quiet. And we listened and we couldn't pin down what it was. Eventually the noise monitors came back. The banging was the SBS guys doing their exercises in the fore part where the torpedoes were stowed. They were banging against the metal grating and it was being transmitted out to the ocean. It was a hell of a racket. So we had to put rubber mats down whenever they wanted to work out. But to have an SBS unit on board was unusual, and you thought, 'What the hell's going on?' We knew we were going south but we didn't know why we had these chaps on board.

The SBS tried to train hard, as much as they could in the cramped space of a fully loaded torpedo room, but it was inevitably less than they would have liked. For the rest of the crew on the submarine, however, the tempo of training increased far beyond what was normal.

Even on a regular operation against a Soviet target in the North Atlantic there would be at least one exercise every day, training for an emergency like a fire or a spillage somewhere on the boat, but on the voyage down south the exercises were more complicated, with a fire at one end of the boat quickly followed by an emergency somewhere else. There were constant weapons and fire-control exercises as well.

Commanding officer Chris Wreford-Brown, and the executive officer, Tim McClement, were having to do the same research that all the other ships in the task force were starting to do. They were trying to assess the state of the Argentine forces and what sort of enemy they could expect to meet. Beyond the standard reference manuals they had little to go on. *Conqueror* had really had only one mission since she was launched, and that was to counter the threat from the Russian submarine fleet in the north-east Atlantic and the Barents Sea. Now they were heading into the South Atlantic – literally heading into the unknown. Neither officer had much idea about how the situation would develop, but Tim McClement's rule of thumb was simple. Respect your enemy and believe that his equipment is as good as yours:

We didn't say oh well, they're Argentinians and it's Second World War equipment, therefore we don't have to worry. Our war mentality was to think of them as threatening, as though they were our own forces, our own people with the same level of training, because that's the only way we would win.

So I worked the ship's company hard because that's my job, trained them whether it was anti-ship, anti-submarine, landing SBS, surveillance. I didn't know what we were going to be called upon to do, so we worked everyone up so we could ensure that we were ready. People talked about Suez, but they forgot that we had landed and started fighting before the US intervened. Funnily enough, we had to change the Cold War mindset: against the Russians it was either peace or the end of the world, but here we were now going to a local war without the Americans. It was my view, and I made this clear to everyone, that Galtieri would not change his mind; neither would Mrs Thatcher. I thought we could expect bloodshed. We trained eighteen hours a day. It was a fine balance, really, just to arrive in good shape but not knackered.

There was so much training, in fact, that one officer complained to Tim McClement that he was creating a blood lust in the crew. Such is the atmosphere on board a submarine, where it is literally true that everyone will sink or swim together, that McClement thought that the officer was perfectly entitled to raise these objections. But he didn't have to agree.

> I said that's my job, and he said but they're going to get so frenetic and gung-ho that when we don't fight – because we won't – you'll have to unwind them. I said OK, well if I have to unwind them I'll unwind them, but in case we do have to fight we'll be ready. And we were.

On *Splendid*, a few days ahead of *Conqueror*, a similar regime of training had been introduced. *Splendid* was heading directly for the exclusion zone, so the training was immediately orientated towards attacking Argentine shipping and submarines. The journey took days, travelling down parallel to the coast of South America – 'Brazil seemed to go on for ages.' On *Splendid* there was a marked difference in the crew between what its commanding officer Commander Roger Lane-Nott referred to as Hawks and Doves. The younger crew members were eager for action, wanting to get stuck in. The more senior ratings were more cautious. They had served for longer and were looking forward to a shore posting. They tended to have wives and a family.

Roger Lane-Nott decided that the only way to run the boat was to keep people informed as much as possible about what was happening in the outside world. This was not easy on a submarine. There was a domestic shortwave radio on board that would receive the BBC World Service when the submarine was at periscope depth. It was kept at the bottom of the companionway on three deck, and the crew would cluster round to listen to it. It became an important lifeline as the journey went on, and crewmembers would often go down just to look at the radio, as if seeking some reassurance that a normal world existed.

On *Conqueror* there was slightly less communication. The crew never knew exactly where they were going or what they were going to do, and there was a lot of speculation. They had less access to the outside world and felt more in the dark. Graham Libby believed that he 'was only told things that the senior officers thought we should be told', as they received updates of the state of negotiations and the imposition of the exclusion zone. 'We'd get told that Mrs Thatcher's doing this and this has happened, and rules of engagement are changing. Although we were never told specifics, you know. You were kept in the picture but you were kept in a little tiny picture in the corner of a big picture.'

Life on a submarine is remarkably confined. One hundred and twenty people are enclosed in a submerged bubble of air that is speeding through a lightless ocean for days on end. Consciousness itself takes on the limits of the steel hull that defines this isolated world. The rest of the crew's life was remote: 'You didn't forget your family; its very strange, you have your family but they're over there in England in a box, and you very quickly come down to the only thing that matters is the submarine and the job it's doing and your mates.'

Conqueror crossed the equator on 12 April. There was little time for any traditional Crossing the Line ceremony. Certificates were printed out on the boat's duplicators, with a drawing of a bearded Father Neptune, signed by Christopher Wreford-Brown, and on the reverse a drawing of six heavily booted SBS marines with snorkels and paddles astride a snarling submarine. Apart from these certificates, there were hand-outs, leaflets and the daily bulletin. There was also the boat's newspaper, the *Black Tin Fish,*

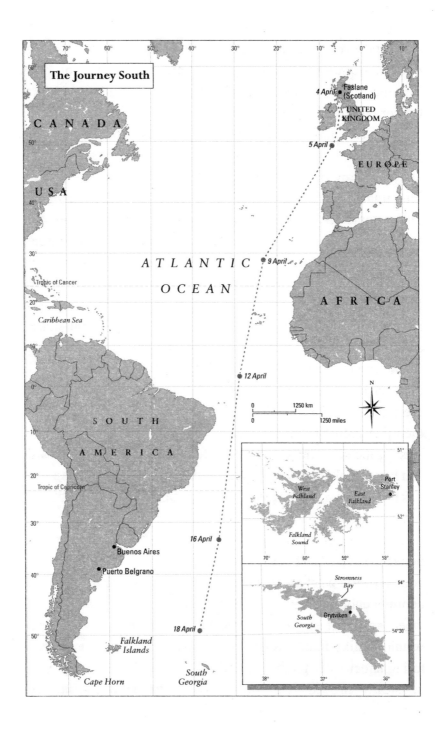

produced every few days, which contained a lot of 'dits' (or ditties), stories, jokes and cartoons that help to keep the crew informed and to boost morale. This was another job for the first officer, Tim McClement.

Conqueror had been making maximum speed south for nine days, the crew fully occupied with their normal watchkeeping and their programme of exercises, but it was an extraordinarily long transit with little other action. The strain was beginning to tell on some people. One of the more senior hands was the chief stoker, who, normally friendly and talkative, grew quiet and withdrawn the further south they went. McClement became concerned, but a few days later the man cheered up. He told McClement that he was no longer depressed, but had settled in his own mind that he would never see his wife and children again, and was now content.

The crew were established in two watches, with each watch on duty on a rota of six hours on, six hours off, starting at one o'clock in the morning. It was almost possible not to see some of the other crew on the alternate watch. Petty Officer Colin Way was on the seven to one watch. He would wake at 06.15, wash and have breakfast, then go on watch in the control room at seven.

The control room was located on the first deck, underneath the fin. The two periscopes, one for an attack, the other for observation, were raised and used from here, and to the right of the periscope wells was the plotting table, where the submarine's course would be charted and the track of various ships would be continuously marked. This is the navigator's responsibility or, when he is off watch, the responsibility of the officer of the watch. Unlike the American navy, where the plot is kept by a rating under supervision, the officer of the watch keeps the plot, physically marking the position of every contact, sonar and visual, on what is called the constant evaluation plot. Tracing paper on a large roll travels over an illuminated table, with a point of light shining from underneath to represent the submarine's position. The bearing of every contact in relation to the submarine is marked on the paper and plotted over time as the paper slowly rolls across the table. In the first instance this is for safety, to ensure that a contact is not on a collision course. When the contact is a potential enemy, the plot becomes an essential aid in trailing the target.

At the front of the control room were the desks and chairs where the sonar operators sat listening to the variety of sonar sensors that were mounted in the bows of the submarine and arrayed down the side of the hull. There was also another sonar listening device that was trailed behind the submarine. Called a towed array, it was a permanent fixture, clipped on to the rear hydroplane before leaving port. It allowed noises to be heard from a position away from the background noise of the boat, its machinery and propellor, and in certain low frequencies it was extremely sensitive.

Forward of the control room were the officers' wardroom and cabins on the same deck, with the captain's cabin immediately to the rear. After days at sea the commander and the senior officers would be so attuned to the condition of the boat that any change, any unfamiliar noise, would be almost instinctively sensed, and they would be just a few steps away from the control room.

The submarine's course and running depth was controlled by a rudder at the rear, two sets of horizontal planes, or stabilizers, one set at the rear forming a cross shape with the rudders, and two at the bows, level with the number one deck. These control surfaces were operated from a console placed at the right of the control room.

Two operators sat side by side: Colin Way, who was the after plane operator, on the left, and the forward plane operator, who also controlled the rudders, to his right. The rudder and planes were moved by a control column, similar to that of an aircraft. In front of the two operators were various dials showing the course, depth and speed of the submarine. The rear plane operator also had an instrument like a spirit level to show the attitude of the boat in the water, and dials that showed the angle of the planes. The dive angle of the boat is controlled by the after planes, and because of the great forward speed of the submarine, operating the after planes requires concentration. On *Conqueror*, Colin Way normally only ever served two hours at a time on the planes during his six-hour watch. It doesn't take long for a submarine to reach a depth where its hull might fracture, especially if it is diving at a speed of 25 knots. There are other dangers involved in fast dives, too, and Colin had an incident on *Conqueror* when the submarine was at periscope depth.

The officer on the periscope saw a light coming towards the submarine, which you know is an emergency – go deep! I will always remember this day because I put down ten degrees manual and we went shooting down and I sensed everybody behind me because we didn't have much water underneath – that's why they were all standing behind me ready to grab me if I made a cock-up. So you do have to be aware all the time.

On a long voyage to a patrol area, the submarine will be operating on autopilot, but there are always dangers in this. Weapons Electrical Artificer (WEA) Charlie Foy, whose watchkeeping position was on the after planes, was on watch in the South Atlantic, keeping maximum speed and running deep, making for

South Georgia. The submarine had just dived to 750 feet to check the difference in sound velocity at various depths, and had come back up to 425 feet again. The Weapons Engineering Officer had just come on watch; he decided to switch on the active sonar to check that everything was working before entering the exclusion zone that the Argentinians had declared around South Georgia. He abruptly ordered 'All in hand' – the command to the planesmen to go into manual control – reduced speed and made a 5-degree up angle on the planes. The manoeuvre was so severe that Bill Budding thought the back half of the submarine would be torn off. The *Conqueror* had been speeding towards an uncharted seamount and had narrowly avoided colliding with it.

All three submarines in the South Atlantic were under the control of the Flag Officer Submarines in Northwood and had two ways of communicating with them. One was by a very low-frequency (VLF) radio signal transmitted from the purpose-built radio station at Anthorn in Cumbria and other sites, which was received on the submarine by a long, trailing aerial that was deployed from the rear of the fin, and once deployed was left trailing. The aerial was made of buoyant cable and floated just below the surface when the submarine was at periscope depth. It was important not to allow the aerial to float on the surface. Photos had been taken of a line of sea birds perching on the floating aerial of a Russian submarine, giving the game away!

Signals were sent out from Northwood to all submarines every four hours. Compressed and coded, the signals would consist of general news, background information and intelligence updates that were of use to every submarine. Then would follow signals directed at individual submarines. Each submarine in the Falklands task force was on a twenty-four-hour watch during their transit to their operational area; in other words, they were expected to take their signals once every twenty-four hours. Signals for individual submarines, which often specified what course the submarine should follow, would be called 'vitals', and numbered sequentially.

VLF transmissions can penetrate water to a depth of around 30 feet, so submarine VLF broadcasts are the safest way to impart information, because the submarine can remain below the surface. The amount of information is limited, because low-frequency signals cannot transmit as much information as higher frequency, but with a submarine listening to at least one broadcast every twenty-four hours there would be a high level of assurance that the signal had been received.

The second method of communication was a very high-frequency (VHF) transmission via a satellite, which was broadcast every fifteen minutes. This package was called the 'all call', which lasted for two minutes, and then for a minute after that there were the individual submarine messages, identified by the individual submarine call sign. Receiving satellite communications requires the submarine to go to periscope depth and raise an aerial out of the water, increasing the risk of detection. The navy's new satellite system, which had become operational on 31 March, was called Gapfiller. It was designed for submarines that were part of the NATO forces aimed at the Soviet threat, so the signals become more and more unreliable as the submarines proceeded further south past the equator. If signals hadn't been picked up, then the submarine was expected to signal to Northwood saying that the vitals had been missed.

Wreford-Brown tried to coordinate the times when he came to periscope depth to pick up signals and replenish the boat's air at night, to avoid being seen, although both the aerial and the snorkel were also good radar targets. The lighting in the control room and the wardroom next to it was switched to red for half an hour before coming up to periscope depth. Black lighting is switched on – or, rather, red lighting is switched off – at periscope depth so that the commander on the periscope has perfect night vision and even the faintest light of an approaching aircraft or a surface vessel can be picked up. Black lighting is just very faint, with just enough light on the dials for people to see. As *Conqueror* reached its patrol area, and was coming to periscope depth more frequently, the light in the control room and the wardroom and captain's cabin was kept permanently at red. Cards are played endlessly, to pass the time, but in red light it's impossible to see the red suits, Diamonds and Hearts. Tim McClement persuaded the medical officer, who had a lot of time on his hands, to outline in black ink all the Hearts and Diamonds in the packs of cards in the wardroom: 'He was pleased to have something to do.'

One incident, however, caused concern throughout the boat. The reactor was operating at full power almost constantly to keep the required speed to South Georgia; orders from Northwood were to maintain 'a mean rate of advance of 23.5 knots', an average hourly speed that takes into account not only the maximum speed achievable, but the delays for taking routine signals and any other incidents. The reactor, along with the steam turbines and generators that provide thrust to the propeller and electricity to the boat, are located naturally enough in the rear part of the boat. The reactor itself is located amidships, and the reactor compartment is separated from the rest of the submarine by two bulkheads. Access to the reactor compartment is gained via an airlock in the side of a passageway that joins these two bulkheads and gives access from the front part of the boat to the main machinery space. Entry to this passageway from either end is also controlled by airlocks. The deck of the passageway has a

HMS Conqueror, *during her sea trials. Like a giant whale on the ocean's surface, the tall fin dwarfs the crewmen on watch. Launched in 1969 at Cammell Laird's yard in Birkenhead, she was the fourth wholly British nuclear-attack submarine to be built.*

Sir Rex Hunt (right), Governor of the Falklands, in full imperial splendour, ostrich feathers blowing in the wind. His warnings about Argentine intentions were not taken seriously, and the Argentine troops, posing happily before the Governor's residence (below), were easily able to overpower the small garrison of British soldiers on the islands.

(Right) Photos of Royal Marines forced to lie on the ground after surrendering to the Argentinians inflamed public opinion in Britian.

(Right) Argentine amphibious armoured-troop carriers lined the main street of Stanley, while the islanders wondered what would happen next. General Galtieri, leader of the Argentine junta (below right), thought it was all over, and accepted the cheers of the crowd from his balcony on the presidential palace.

However, the Argentine military leaders now on the Falklands wondered whether they would be able to defend the Islands in the long term (below).

This Royal Marine form NO 3201A is ___
___tify that T.McClement_ was allowed to cross
__ Equator whilst in our transport HMS CONQUEROR
__ 12 April 1982. Signed: David Weaver   Chief Bootie
                                          Captain

(Above) *In addition to its own crew, HMS* Conqueror *embarked a unit of the Special Boat Service for the voyage south. With time on their hands, their artistic talents flourished, as this crossing-the-line certificate shows.* (Below) *The course and speed of* Conqueror's *torpedoes were calculated on this mechanical computer, still set to the solution for the Belgrano attack.*

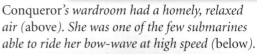

Conqueror's *wardroom had a homely, relaxed air* (above). *She was one of the few submarines able to ride her bow-wave at high speed* (below).

Conqueror's *Captain, Commander Christopher Wreford-Brown, and Petty Officer Graham Libby are seen here with* Conqueror *in the background. Libby's recall from leave turned out to be anything but an April Fool's joke.*

In Northwood, Sir John Fieldhouse (third from left) was in charge of the most difficult operation since the Second World War. His staff included Flag Officer Submarines Vice Admiral Peter Herbert (far left).

This page from Conqueror's patrol report shows her journey south. It was a very fast passage, keeping an average speed of almost 22 knots.

Rear Admiral 'Sandy' Woodward, in charge of the task group, had to fight the Chiefs of Staff at Northwood for control of Conqueror *and the other submarines. He was highly critical of the rules of engagement imposed upon him.*

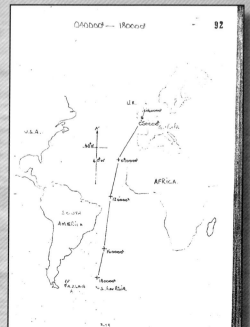

(Above left and right)
The biggest threat to the task force was the Argentine aircraft carrier Veinticinco de Mayo *and its Skyhawk bombers, which could strike from hundreds of miles away. HMS* Splendid *(below left) was ordered to find it.*

A sideshow on South Georgia threatened to become another calamity. The remote glacier-covered island was Conqueror's first port of call, and there they carried out a covert reconnaissance of Grytviken.

The initial SAS landing was a disaster. This photo (right) shows troopers on the ice shortly after their helicopter crashed. The SBS on Conqueror *could only watch and wonder.*

The Argentine submarine Santa Fe *was eventually attacked by navy helicopters and put out of action. This dramatic reversal of fortune demoralized the Argentine forces, and enabled South Georgia to be taken. The victory buoyed up the politicians at home.*

The invasion of the Falklands caused consternation in Westminster, but First Sea Lord Sir Henry Leach (right), argued that action was necessary, and possible. John Nott, Francis Pym and Margaret Thatcher (below) had no other option but to listen.

As it became clear that Britain was not going to let the Argentine junta off the hook, reaction in Argentina became uncertain. Their press branded Margaret Thatcher a pirate (top), and public demonstrations became belligerent, particularly during visits by Alexander Haig, the US Secretary of State, seeking a peace plan (left). Meanwhile, mothers of conscripts started knitting warm clothes for their sons on the Falklands, who often lacked basic comforts (above).

hatch covering a window into the reactor compartment, where stainless-steel pipes and aluminium-covered shielding gleams in the fluorescent lights. The pressurized water reactor is a stainless-steel cylinder that contains enriched uranium, surrounded by water which is kept at high pressure. The water is for cooling, and it also acts partly as a radiation shield. The reactor produces heat because the uranium gives off atomic particles that collide with other atoms of uranium, causing those atoms to split, producing heat and more nuclear particles to continue the process called a chain reaction. When the reactor is running, and producing energy, it is said to be 'critical'. Of course a lot of radiation is produced, and the reactor and its cooling water are kept inside a hexagonal silver container of lead and polystyrene bricks. The heat from the reactor is taken from the cooling water by a separate system of pipes that goes to a heat exchanger where water is heated to produce steam. This steam then drives turbines, which are connected by gearing to the propeller and which drive dynamos to produce electricity. If the nuclear reaction in the reactor starts to speed up, then there is only one way to avert disaster: graphite control rods slam down into the uranium pile, absorbing nuclear particles and stopping the reaction. If this happens, the reactor has been prevented from becoming a bomb but the submarine is now without power, which is a potential emergency. Two back-up systems are installed on board: diesel engines, which require the submarine to surface to periscope depth and use its snorkel, and finally a set of batteries, which are only able to power the submarine for a short time.

Much of the monitoring of the reactor systems is done automatically, and if a problem is detected it will trigger an automatic shutdown. This is exactly what happened on *Conqueror*'s voyage south. The control rods lowered and the reactor went into a partial shutdown.

Chief engineer David Hall and his crew urgently started to investigate the problem. At the back of their minds was the question whether something had been overlooked in the desperate rush to finish essential maintenance and get the boat to sea. Would people have to suit up and enter the reactor vessel – an extreme step? When the reactor stops it is impossible to forget that submarines exist in an extremely hostile environment. It is necessary to maintain some forward motion so that the planes can keep the boat at the right depth, but this drains the batteries, and their power may be needed to restart the reactor. The only real option is to surface to periscope depth and run the auxiliary diesel engines, but this can be very difficult if the sea is rough. But there was no other indication of a developing fault in the reactor. What had triggered the shutdown?

Then at last David thought he had found the solution. All the reactor controls and instruments are replicated and the automatic safety equipment operates on a voting system. If two instruments detect a fault in the system, they will override another one saying that the system is safe, and will automatically trigger an emergency procedure. This is what had happened: two sensors had failed simultaneously and it became a simple matter to replace them and start up again. Within twenty-five minutes the reactor was running again. There are no more comforting words on a nuclear submarine in that situation than the two sentences 'Reactor is critical. Full electrical power is restored.'

It's a tense situation when the only source of power is switched off, but everyone on the boat is aware of what is going on. The crew of a submarine is trained to know enough about every area of the boat, wherever their main duties are:

... and that includes operating major parts of machinery [remembers Libby], which valves to open in the event of flooding in the engine compartment. I would know that, same as the guys that worked back half would know which valves to open or close if they were in the front of the boat and something happened, like major hydraulic lines, water supplies, coolants ... you'd know where all the electrical breakers were, so that if something did happen and you're in an unfamiliar area you're still aware of what to do to save the boat, basically, and you're trained so hard you know what to do even in the dark. So there was never a them and us – fore and aft part of ship – rivalry, because it's a small ship and we all got on, we all ate together. By the end of the patrol we knew each other's dreams.

5

THE VOYAGE OF THE *BELGRANO*

On 6 April the Argentine ships that had taken part in the recovery of the Malvinas arrived back in Puerto Belgrano. The huge aircraft carrier moved slowly through the canal that connected the harbour to the open sea and moored at her normal place on the wall along from the *General Belgrano*, still in the middle of her mechanical maintenance. There was enormous excitement and activity as the crews disembarked from the carrier and the escort destroyers that followed her into port.

In the few days that had elapsed since the Argentine marines had landed on the islands, the work on maintenance of the *Belgrano* had rapidly speeded up. Lieutenant Commander Bernasconi, one of the senior engineers, was working round the clock and so were his men. 'We had a very short period in which to complete everything,' he remembers. 'And suddenly there were a lot of other things that we had to do.' The plan to invade the Malvinas had been put together on the basis that Britain would not take any action to recover the islands. However, by 5 April a British task force had sailed from Portsmouth and Britain had declared the imposition of a maritime exclusion zone around the Falkland Islands starting on 12 April. There was now a real threat that the British fleet would have the capacity actually to go on the offensive to recover the islands. If there was a war, the *Belgrano* would be required and her crew would need time to be worked up and trained.

For Bernasconi it was exhausting:

There then started a very intensive period which never seemed to end. Many days we spent loading munitions, until two in the morning. We put munitions everywhere, even under the beds; we loaded stocks, enormous stocks, of food, enough for a long extended war cruise, and maintenance work started on everything – the main armament, the radars, everything to prepare for war.

The admiral's quarters at the rear of the ship were used to assemble all the operational intelligence that Captain Bonzo and his senior officers could locate: 'Charts, manoeuvring diagrams, lists of different warships and their armaments and characteristics and any other data that we could find. A leading lieutenant, Gerardo Canepa, took over the organizing of our intelligence data.'

As part of the change to a war footing, the number of personnel was increased, with the addition of extra lieutenants and lieutenant commanders. In all, the crew complement was 629 permanent crew members, with 408 conscripts, plus 56 officers. Most of the conscripts had already been serving on the *Belgrano* during its summer cruise. Some, like Fernando Millan, had their return to civilian life blocked as a result of the recovery of the Malvinas. In Millan's view it took very little time before the conscripts saw the *Belgrano* as their home – 'We felt we owned it.' There was in general a lot of enthusiasm and excitement on the part of the crew, despite the hard work. But the more thoughtful were aware that the situation had changed radically and that no one knew what might happen.

The ship's surgeon, Lieutenant Alberto Levene, was in Buenos Aires during the operation to recover the Malvinas. He had witnessed the ecstatic scenes in the Plaza de Mayo when hundreds of thousands of Argentinians had thronged the city, waving their blue-and-white flags. He and his wife had been privately dismayed by the news. He had arrived on board the boat at Puerto Belgrano on the 12th, and spent the next few days inspecting the medical supplies, the first-aid equipment stored in the action station casualty centres, and the equipment in the operating theatre. In his cabin he wrote a letter to his wife, and enclosed his wedding ring before sealing the envelope. He believed that the British fleet was not coming to negotiate and that the *Belgrano* could be in a battle. The cruiser was vulnerable, and he had read enough stories about the Second World War to know that there were always very few survivors. 'It was going to be a risky business, and I knew something was going to happen. But as a doctor, with over one thousand crewmembers, at least my task was clear.'

Conscript Ruben Otero managed to slip away from Puerto Belgrano and take the ten-hour bus journey to see his mother in Buenos Aires before the *Belgrano* sailed. His family were very worried about him. Ruben believed that nothing would happen, and assured his mother that if he went into battle he would put on his life jacket and get into a life raft. He believed he led a charmed life. Then he returned to the ship to continue his work in the engine room, checking water levels and steam pressure in the boilers.

There were two members of the crew who could easily have left the ship. They were civilians, brothers, Heriberto and Leopoldo Avila, who ran the refreshment bar in the recreation area on the second deck, commonly known as the 'Soda Fountain'. But they had been on the *Belgrano* longer than any crewmember, since 1969, and they told Captain Bonzo that they had no intention of leaving the ship.

In the final stages of the maintenance period, Captain Bonzo and his senior officers were involved in lengthy discussions and planning meetings in the port. The navy knew that their military doctrines and training would not be enough for the coming war. Their operational plans were based on the possibility of a conflict with neighbouring Chile and other medium powers in the region. It could never be admitted openly, but they were at a severe disadvantage because of the political role that the navy had played for some years as part of the military dictatorship and in the 'Dirty War'. This was not the best training for confronting a professional navy that exercised continually with NATO and had serving officers with war-fighting experience, not only from the Second World War but also from Korea and Suez.

The officers looked at various options for the deployment of their fleet. They were confronting a situation that was changing quite rapidly. Their assumptions were that there would be no units of the British fleet in the vicinity of the Malvinas until 26 April, but on 10 April the frigate *Granville* was travelling from Stanley to Puerto Belgrano when it detected radar signals that it took to be from an enemy ship. The electronic warfare officers assumed that the transmissions were from a nuclear submarine, because it was far too early for any surface warship to be in the vicinity. It was clear to Admiral Lombardo, the commander-in-chief in Puerto Belgrano, that the arrival of British nuclear submarines was evidence that the Royal Navy's task force was not just for show, and that its deployments were very serious. It also showed, in the words of Captain Bonzo, 'that if the negotiations made little progress there would be a continuation of politics by other means'.

The presence of British nuclear submarines seriously affected the balance of naval forces in the region. They were much more powerful than Argentine surface forces, and the Argentine navy knew that its own conventional submarines were really inadequate for dealing with a nuclear sub. It was impossible to ignore their presence; any operations in the conflict would now be a calculated risk.

During the meeting in Puerto Belgrano, several options for deploying the *Belgrano* were discussed. One view was that she should be stationed in the Malvinas, in the port in Stanley. Her main armament would be effective against surface ships up to $12^1/_2$ miles away, and she could be used as artillery to bombard troops during a landing. But the ship would be vulnerable to air attack, and positioning her in the harbour in the Falklands would limit her use and the value of her mobility would be lost. There were also doubts about the ability of the *Belgrano* to get through the exclusion zone in one piece. The junta was unclear about what tactics the British would use, and were afraid of leaving the Argentine mainland undefended. It was Captain Bonzo's view that:

a lot of the information we received on a daily basis from newspapers and magazines about the actions of the British fleet added to our confusion. It was hard to understand what was true and what was probably part of the enemy's attempts at mis-information. Much information was designed to give the impression that there was an inexorable escalation of the conflict.

The British War Cabinet was well aware that any attempt to attack the Argentine mainland would rapidly bring to an end the diplomatic and military support that they were receiving from the United States, Chile and European countries. But it was thought useful to raise the possibility of such an attack in the minds of the junta, so that they would have to take military precautions to guard against it. So Admiral Sandy Woodward, in command of the task force, maintained a course for the battle group that appeared to head initially for Buenos Aires. At the same time in London, several backbench MPs dropped off-the-record hints to newspapers that Vulcan bombers were being prepared for raids on various mainland airbases and ports, and that a raid on the Argentine capital had been contemplated.

The plans that were put together in the days before the *Belgrano* sailed were the best that the command in Puerto Belgrano could come up with. Despite the meticulous plans that had been prepared for the recovery of the Malvinas, little thought had been given to preparations for a British response, and the unexpected size of the fleet that was advancing on the Argentine forces in the Malvinas, together with a profound uncertainty about where this fleet was heading, meant that Argentina's plans had to remain very flexible. As Bonzo described it, 'We had to increase our capacity to act by putting the best groups of ships together that we could. We had to develop tactics that would use our best strengths, and the missions had to be built around the distinctive capabilities of the ships and their armaments.' The fact that this might divide the available forces and reduce their ability to defend each other was something that could not be avoided. 'We also had to look at the way to work when we had to have radio and signals silence, and also reduce radar emissions to a minimum. In this war we knew that the electronic signals would give us away very quickly.'

The defence of the Malvinas would be the responsibility of Naval Task Force 79, under the command of Admiral Lombardo in Puerto Belgrano. The task force would be made of three groups. The first, 79.1, under the command of Captain José Sarcona, would be the aircraft carrier *Veinticinco de Mayo* with its embarked aircraft Skyhawk A-4Q fighter bombers, and a group of escort vessels – three corvettes, the *Guerrico*, *Drummond* and *Granville*, and the destroyer *Santísima Trinidad*, with the fleet tanker *Campo Durán*. The second group, 79.2, would be under the command of Captain Juan Calmon, and would be a flotilla of five destroyers, the *Piedra Buena*, the *Hipólito Bouchard*, the *Segui* and the *Comodoro Py*, with the flagship of this group, the destroyer *Hércules*. Finally, the third group would be a single ship, the cruiser *General Belgrano*.

Captain Bonzo's orders were to sail with the *Belgrano* and take up station in the area of the Isla de los Estados, the small island to the east of Tierra del Fuego, and once there to maintain a patrol controlling access to the zone of operations around the Falklands, to intercept enemy units and prevent them from transiting through the Horn to reinforce the British fleet. This was considered to be important because there had already been reports of HMS *Exeter*, a Type 42 destroyer, passing through the Panama Canal with an oiler, which it was suspected might be on its way to rejoin the fleet.

*

The maintenance work on the *Belgrano* was finished by 14 April and Captain Bonzo reported to Admiral Lombardo that she was ready to put to sea. An Alouette helicopter had recently been embarked and was in place in the hangar under the main deck at the stern.

The day before the *Belgrano*'s departure was another long day for the engineer Lieutenant Commander Bernasconi. It takes a lot of time to get the steam plant working; temperatures have to be raised slowly and pressure has to be increased bit by bit. The ratings in the after compartments didn't go home the night before. But according to Bernasconi the crew were in very good heart: 'Their spirit was good, people didn't seek to go on leave, they wanted to stay with the ship.'

Before the *Belgrano* went to war, the officers knew that the crew had worked hard and were tired. When Captain Bonzo walked the 300 yards between the Navy Command and the gang-plank of the cruiser, he knew that the human factor was going to be crucial. There was the utmost need for training for both conscripts and regular crew alike. Could they, he wondered, maintain their *esprit de corps* and their emotional balance as the conflict developed? How would they fare under the stress of battle?

On 16 April, the *General Belgrano* put to sea. There were no waving crowds, no television cameras or escorting ships to celebrate the departure of this symbolic ship. Only military personnel from the base saw the *Belgrano* gently leave the jetty. Conscript Fernando Millan recollects that it was a perfect day, calm and sunny, and from his place on the bridge the ship looked clean and smart from her days in harbour.

The *Belgrano* slipped her cables and was slowly towed out of the narrow entrance to the harbour, before the captain ordered slow ahead, and she headed down-river to the sea. The ship was gleaming, freshly painted in a coat of battleship grey, canvas tarpaulins shining white; everything was working well, as it usually did on this ship, the pride of the Argentine navy. She had a war crew of 1,093, a third of whom were conscripts. There was an air of anticipation. Nobody had wanted to remain behind. The atmosphere was good: Argentina had recaptured the Malvinas and everyone on board had supped, however thoughtfully, at the cup of victory. Now they and the *Belgrano* were off to war. But there was a lot to be done. There were very many raw crewmembers, inexperienced and unsure of themselves and their capabilities. The senior officers knew there was plenty of training to get through before the crew would be ready for combat – but just how much time they would get they didn't know.

Captain Bonzo was going to take the *Belgrano* to her allotted patrol area in the south, near the Isla de los Estados, but he was going to stay close to the mainland, inside the 12-mile limit and in shallow water. He wanted to avoid any possible contact with submarines, and also had orders to avoid contact with any merchant ships. He knew that the crew needed a period of very serious training, and this started as soon as they were clear of the harbour.

Conscript Santiago Bellozo was part of the gun crew in Turret One, the 6-inch gun turret closest to the bows. There were three guns in each turret and, with the gun crews and ammunition loaders, there were sixty sailors in each. It was hot, hard work, and his chief petty officer called them together to say, 'Gentlemen, we are not going to a ball, we are going to war.' It was important that everyone in the turret continued to perform their task: 'We had very specific instructions, if we got into combat, that we as a group don't stop shooting to save the injured.'

Alarms were meant to be responded to immediately – the crew had to be taken out of their routines to do so. There were exercises not only for surface action, but also anti-aircraft training, damage control, training for casualty parties and also in abandoning ship. They also had to start training to keep a darkened ship; no smoking on the upper decks was allowed and portholes were kept shut. The boilers were cleaned properly and burners changed regularly so that there would be no smudge of smoke to give away the location of the ship.

While the exercises were taking place, the senior officers had this one opportunity to organize the crew most effectively. The first officer, Commander Galazi, explained:

> We had conscripts and a new set of crew, so that we had to keep a watch on those that were not naturally happy or had difficulties with the task that they might have to do in action. Every task should be allotted to people who were most capable of doing it, so over the next days we looked at the way that people performed and slowly looked for those personalities that had some natural leadership and initiative.

All day and night the alarms and calls to action stations went on, until on 19 April the *Belgrano* arrived on station off Isla de los Estados.

The *General Belgrano* was a Second World War vessel and had the thick armour that was standard for that period – up to 8 inches thick in some areas. She would not be seriously damaged by the guns carried by most surface ships, like the Royal Navy's general-purpose 4.5-inch gun. A salvo from the *Belgrano* would be a far greater threat to a surface ship than the guns on the British destroyers and frigates, but Captain Bonzo's orders were to avoid contact with enemy ships that had surface-to-surface missiles, like the French-built Exocet, because these would be able to outrange the *Belgrano*'s main armament.

Now that they were in the remote waters of Tierra del Fuego, Captain Bonzo could organize a live firing practice with the *Belgrano* weapons. Conscript Bellozo found the noise in his gun turret deafening when the 6-inch guns were fired. Ruben Otero's action stations were in the boiler rooms, checking water levels in the feed tanks. Every twenty minutes he had to squeeze between two enormous boilers, which were very noisy and hot, to check the level of water in a glass tell-tale at the back of them. During one exercise, as he was squeezing between the boilers the main armament fired a live salvo and he thought that a disaster had occurred. There was an incredible explosion, and the whole ship leaped and shuddered in the water.

The calls to action stations were not always exercises, and the mood on the ship was becoming increasingly sombre. On 20 April the *Belgrano* was on a course of around 300 degrees passing along the coast of Tierra del Fuego when a radar signal was detected by the sailors on watch in the operations room. There was no record of a merchant ship in the area, so immediately the officer of the watch ordered a change of course, headed towards the bearing of the signal and called the captain. The siren for action stations sounded and the guns were cleared. Everybody was closed up and there was considerable tension on the bridge and in the control room as they waited for the order to fire. The strange ship was not showing lights, and a star shell was fired from one of the anti-aircraft guns to illuminate the target. The intercepted ship was ordered to stop and it did so immediately, and started switching on not only its navigation lights but every light that was on the boat. It was a merchantman that had developed technical problems, whose captain had not bothered to tell the command in the port of Ushuaia that it had been delayed by two days. It was a moment away from being fired upon, and the 6-inch shells of the *Belgrano* would have destroyed it utterly. The incident had a profound effect on Conscript Bellozo and many others in the crew, who felt that the training and the exercises might now very quickly become real action. The cruiser, he realized, was now in a state of war.

On 22 April the *Belgrano* left its station to go to Ushuaia. This small city and naval base is the capital of Tierra del Fuego and claims to be the world's most southerly city. It stands on the Beagle Channel, the sheltered waterway that separates the main island of Tierra del Fuego from the smaller islands of the archipelago and forms a passage between the Atlantic and the Pacific Oceans. Ushuaia is on the northern coast, in a small bay where the channel is at its widest. There was a possibility that the *Belgrano* would be sent to reinforce the Argentine troops on South Georgia, so Captain Bonzo wanted to keep his fuel tanks topped up ready for the coming conflict. In Ushuaia he could also replace some ammunition for the 40mm cannons that the live firing exercises had proved to be defective. Other ammunition was going to be topped up, and live rounds for the Sea Cat anti-aircraft missile launchers were going to be loaded.

Travelling up the channel required precise navigation and they reached Ushuaia at 18.30 hours. When they arrived, the ammunition was already waiting on the jetty and they started to load it. Conscript Juan Heinze was one of the Sea Cat missile operators, and when he saw the boxes of live missiles being loaded he felt a shiver down his back. The situation in the Beagle Channel, and for the base in Ushuaia too, was delicate because there was also a dispute between Chile and Argentina over the two countries' borders in the Beagle Channel itself. An important question was whether Chile would remain neutral in the conflict with Great Britain. So far that appeared to be the case, but even so the *Belgrano* maintained a regime of radio silence and reduced electronic signals and emissions. Captain Bonzo believes now, however, that information about the *Belgrano*'s departure was sent to Britain via the port authorities in Punta Arenas, the Chilean port.

The refuelling and re-arming done, *Belgrano* prepared to leave Ushuaia on 24 April at 08.30 hours. Softly, with gentle power on the propellers, the cruiser eased into the channel and headed east, into the morning light of the polar autumn.

Captain Bonzo reflected on the condition of the enemy approaching. There was a mobilization of warships in the Atlantic that the world had not seen since the Second World War, and there was now a fleet of warships, aircraft and troops heading to the Falklands, with a major resupply base in the Atlantic on Ascension Island, which lies 1,000 miles from the coast of West Africa. The British had effective satellite communications and direct links to their H.Q. in Northwood. They also possessed, thought Bonzo, a considerable amount of intelligence on Argentine forces, with information about all the wavelengths of the radars and communications equipment that they used; they knew all the codes and had access to very good satellite systems, with excellent intelligence about the movement of Argentine warships.

As the *Belgrano* headed out, they received a signal saying that a reconnaissance aircraft had spotted the location of the British task force at 35 degrees south and 28 degrees west, heading at 13 knots on a course to the south. The battle group was about 1,500 miles to the east of Buenos Aires, and was made up of two aircraft carriers and seven destroyers. Significantly, on a direct course, it would take about three days to arrive at the Malvinas.

Several hours after the *Belgrano* left Ushuaia, one of the senior petty officers, Arturo Catena, reported to the sick bay with severe stomach pains. On examination, the nurse realized he had acute appendicitis. He needed an operation immediately. The ship slowed, and Captain Bonzo ordered the helicopter to fly the sick man back to port, but the ship's surgeon, Lieutenant Levene, didn't see why the operation couldn't be carried out on board. 'I said, if we cannot operate on an appendix when we are about to go to war, what are the crew going to think about us?' The petty officer was given the choice, and he elected to stay on board. 'He didn't want to leave his comrades. He was taking two big risks: going into battle and being operated on on board the ship. Personally, I think the battle was the bigger one.' The *Belgrano* slowed to just a few knots and the operation took place in the Beagle Channel.

Late on Saturday 24 April there had been a change of plans for the coordination of Task Force 79. The naval command had placed most of their forces to the north of the Falklands, because they thought that this was where the British task force would concentrate its attack. So the aircraft carrier the *Veinticinco de Mayo*, and the Exocet-armed destroyers and frigates, had all been deployed in the north, in two separate task forces.

The Argentine high command were not sure what Admiral Woodward would do, but believed that he might make a frontal assault on Stanley and attempt to capture it as a prelude to

forcing negotiations on the junta. Although the Argentine landing had succeeded in taking Stanley, they had made their attack
on an undefended island and been able to head straight for the
centre of population. The situation that confronted Britain was
that the islands and the airfield at Stanley were now well
defended, and Woodward wanted to avoid civilian casualties. He
was still unsure of his strengths and wanted to weaken the
Argentine navy and air force before making a landing, but it
suited his plans to make the Argentinians think that a landing was
imminent.

Now as the British task force approached, Admiral Lombardo
in Puerto Belgrano started moving his ships around. Two
destroyers, the *Piedra Buena* and the *Hipólito Bouchard*, were to
be detached from Task Group 79.2 in the north, and along with
the tanker *Puerto Rosales* they would join up with the *Belgrano*
to form a new Task Group 79.3 (TG79.3). In coordination with
the major force to the north, TG79.3 was ordered to remain outside the total exclusion zone, an area of 200 miles' radius around
the Falklands imposed by Britain, and be prepared to intercept
enemy units when ordered.

The two destroyers that were to accompany the *Belgrano* had
both been built in the Second World War for the United States
navy, and were fitted with six 5-inch guns. Bought by the
Argentine navy, they had recently been modernized and fitted
with Exocet ship-to-ship missiles, the appropriate fire-control
radars and a sonar anti-submarine unit. Both ships had a
maximum speed of 22 knots.

On 26 April the Swiss Embassy in Buenos Aires delivered a
diplomatic note on behalf of the British government to the
Argentine junta. It stated that from 30 April Britain would, in
the interests of self-defence, consider that any warships or

aircraft moving towards the position of or appearing to threaten the British fleet would be subject to attack.

In retaliation, the junta issued a decree that any ship or aircraft, military or civilian, in the zone of 200 miles off the coast of Argentina, which included 200 miles off the coasts of the Malvinas, South Georgia and the South Sandwich Islands, which they now claimed as Argentinian territory, would be considered hostile.

The situation was rapidly escalating, with both sides giving public warnings and the British fleet steadily approaching the Malvinas. The threat of war was growing, and the crew were beginning to feel it. As the *Belgrano* reached the open sea and headed for the rendezvous with the two destroyers, there were few on the *Belgrano* who had any illusions left about what they were heading into.

6

THE MOMENT OF TRUTH

The invasion of the Falkland Islands by an Argentine force of amphibious troops sent shock waves through the British government, causing outrage in the press and amongst politicians of all parties. In a move unprecedented since the Second World War, an emergency debate in both Houses of Parliament was called on a Saturday, the day following the invasion.

In 1977, as we have seen, a military threat from Argentina had caused anxious discussion in the Cabinet, and the Prime Minister of the day, James Callaghan, had been instrumental in the dispatch of a nuclear submarine and two supporting frigates to patrol off the Falklands. How was it that within the space of just five years, when another crisis was brewing as the policy of some form of lease-back agreement with Argentina collapsed, the British government could have been so taken by surprise?

Ever since Juan Perón had raised the question of the

sovereignty of the islands in the United Nations, Britain's armed forces had been in decline. The question now on everybody's lips was: had that decline gone so far that the Argentine junta could invade British territory with impunity? Did Britain have the forces for a military campaign halfway round the globe and, just as important, was there the political will to mount one? Or was the cartoonist's image of Britain as a toothless, crippled old lion closer to the truth than anyone wanted to admit?

The tension between the responsibilities that the British government claimed to accept and the money it was prepared to make available to the military came to a head with the election of the Conservative government under Margaret Thatcher in 1979, and more particularly with the appointment of John Nott, former President of the Board of Trade and an arch-monetarist, as Secretary of State for Defence in January 1981.

Defence spending was way over budget, exacerbated by the steep economic downturn that the government had caused by its squeeze on public finances. Many defence contractors suffered a loss of civilian orders and made deliveries to the Ministry of Defence ahead of schedule, stretching the Ministry's budget. The main culprit, however, according to the Defence Secretary, was the cost of the navy's ships and the unrealistic size of the fleet compared to what was required for Britain's real defence needs. John Nott was working on a new defence White Paper that would scrap the last vestiges of the aircraft carriers. *Hermes*, now being refitted to carry Sea Harriers, and *Invincible*, the first of the new purpose-built through-deck carriers with its complement of Sea Harriers, were to be sold to India and Australia respectively. In addition, fifteen of the navy's surface ships were to be scrapped. John Nott argued – plausibly, some thought – that the sole threat to Britain came from Russia and the Warsaw Pact, and that opposing this threat was where the money should be spent. Anti-submarine warfare, confined to the protection of the Polaris nuclear deterrent, was all that was required of the navy. There could be no pretence of a need to protect Atlantic convoys or anything of that nature, because any war in Europe would rapidly escalate into a nuclear confrontation which would by its very nature bring the war to an end. If deterrence failed, so the argument went, conventional forces would be useless. Privately, John Nott was scathing about the Royal Navy and 'its floating gin palaces'. He hadn't a good word to say about the navy or its senior staff, finding their arguments and presentations self-serving and inadequate.

The Defence Secretary, however, found an unexpectedly aggressive antagonist in this fight to reduce the Royal Navy: Admiral of the Fleet Sir Henry Leach. Physically, Sir Henry was a slight figure, but he had a forceful personality. He spoke as though every sentence he uttered had been carefully composed beforehand, and because of this he could appear slightly cold and aloof, but in fact his precise and deliberate persona concealed an anarchic sense of humour.

Leach was Royal Navy through and through, the embodiment of its history and Nelsonian tradition. At the age of fourteen he had entered the naval college at Dartmouth, and as a midshipman on the evening of 10 December 1941 had walked along the quay at Singapore naval base asking for news of his father, Captain John Leach. Commanding officer of the battleship *Prince of Wales*, Sir Henry's father had been killed when the *Prince of Wales* and the *Repulse* were attacked and sunk earlier that day by Japanese torpedo bombers. The decision to send the *Prince of Wales* and her companion battleship to Malaya despite the absence of any protection from air attack had been taken at a very high level. From then on Sir Henry Leach had a healthy suspicion of politicians and armchair strategists.

Later in the war he commanded a gun turret on the battleship *Duke of York* against the German warship *Scharnhorst* at the battle of the North Cape. Despite specializing as a gunnery officer, Leach was not a dyed-in-the-wool traditionalist. He had learned to fly, and was proud of the fact that in his career in the navy he had managed to fly most of the aircraft with which he came into contact. His vision of the navy was that it should be a rounded and flexible force, capable of defending Britain's nuclear deterrent from the Soviet fleet as well as being able to send troops and carrier-borne aircraft to Kuwait or another ally if called upon to do so.

Leach could not accept that the Royal Navy should bear most of the cuts that were being made to Britain's armed forces by John Nott. The navy's share of the defence budget was around 4 per cent greater than that of the RAF, but naval expenditure had been affected heavily by the introduction into service of a fleet of hunter-killer nuclear submarines, like *Conqueror*, that were designed to take on the growing Russian fleet. What was even more unjust in Leach's eyes was that the navy was being asked to bear the cost of modernizing Britain's nuclear deterrent with the purchase of Trident missiles and the submarines to launch them.

Nott attempted to characterize Leach as a man governed by prejudice, whose views were solely motivated by self-interest. Yet Sir Henry felt that dangerous precedents were being set:

What would have been normal was that there would have been a debate between the chiefs of staff about where the cuts would fall. His [Nott's] plans lacked any consultation with people that knew anything, and two weeks before they were to be announced his office sent out the list of main areas to be cut to the defence staff. This was the first time we had seen it. It was the most traumatic defence review for a great many years, greater than 1966, or even 1957, after Suez.

Sir Henry Leach and his minister loathed each other. Nott did not have a very high opinion of Sir Henry's intellectual worth, saying that he was 'not exactly "cerebral man"'. But Leach did not know the meaning of defeat, and continued in a persistent and highly personal lobbying campaign against measures that he believed would destroy the navy and were dangerous for the country. Exercising his constitutional right as chief of the navy he sought a meeting with the Prime Minister, Margaret Thatcher, but was put off. In a letter sent as a substitute for a face-to-face meeting, he summed up his objections:

> The navy was projected to bear 62% of the total reduction in defence spending, amounting to a quarter of its total budget. When implemented in 1983 it would cut the carrier force from three to two, and by 1991 the surface fleet, including fleet auxiliaries, would be halved . . .
>
> War seldom takes the expected form and a strong maritime capability provides flexibility for the unforeseen. If you erode it to the extent envisaged I believe you will undesirably foreclose your future options and prejudice our national security.

In a last desperate effort to persuade the Defence Secretary to reverse his decision to sell the new carrier *Invincible* to Australia, Leach travelled by train down to St Austell in Cornwell to see Nott, who was visiting his constituency in St Ives over the weekend. He offered to find the £175 million – the amount that the Australians were paying the British government for *Invincible* – by pensioning off other warships, so determined was he to maintain an aircraft-carrier element in the navy. He got nowhere.

All Sir Henry's arguments were in vain. But in the fight over the big-ticket items in the budget, both sides had been searching around for cuts of a few million here and there. Desperate to save the price of a frigate, the navy had suggested to Nott that various inessential items of expenditure should be cut. At the top of the list was the Royal Yacht *Britannia*, shortly needing an expensive refit. As Nott said, to expect a Tory government to scrap *Britannia* was absurd, so second on the list was HMS *Endurance*, Britain's flag-bearer in the South Atlantic. Despite last-minute objections from the Foreign Minister Lord Carrington, *Endurance* was due to be disposed of after the financial year 1981–2. As we have seen, opinion in the Ministry of Defence was that *Endurance* was inadequate to deter Argentine aggression, but the final, long-postponed decision to axe the sole naval vessel regularly deployed in the Falklands served as another indication for the Argentine junta, and particularly Admiral Anaya, that Britain would be indifferent to the fate of the islands.

There had been some slight warnings to the British government that the Argentine junta would take an increasingly militant line after the appointment of General Galtieri in December 1981. The newspaper *La Prensa* was particularly vociferous in its calls for military action, and the British Ambassador, Richard Williams, and the Military Attaché, Colonel Steven Love, in Buenos Aires tried to inform London of the shift of emphasis in Argentine attitudes to the issue of the Malvinas that was now apparent.

It was not, however, until late in March 1982, when there was clearly a crisis in relations with Argentina over South Georgia, that Margaret Thatcher and her government really started to pay serious attention to what, if anything, they might do if the junta tried to cut flights to the Falklands, or intervened militarily in the attempt to remove the scrap-metal workers from Leith Harbour. There was no thought, even at this late stage, that there might be a bigger crisis over the Falkland Islands themselves.

On 19 March the Overseas and Defence Subcommittee of the Cabinet had asked the Commander-in-Chief of the Fleet, the most senior operational officer, to investigate what options existed to send some ships to the Falklands, as a show of British resolution and to substitute for the loss of HMS *Endurance*. Nothing immediate was requested; it was thought that any deployment within the next nine months would be adequate. The answers were depressing. Any deployment was considered to be too expensive. A frigate might be diverted from a patrol off Belize, but because of the distances involved it would need to be accompanied by a Royal Fleet Auxiliary Tanker, and the deployment would be disruptive to other equally pressing commitments elsewhere. Generally speaking, assessments of what actions were possible in the event of military activity by Argentina relied on the work that had been carried out during the last crisis in 1977. It was the considered opinion that military options were extremely limited.

The Argentine navy had in its fleet an aircraft carrier and a cruiser, four submarines, nine destroyers – two of which had been bought from the United Kingdom – maritime patrol aircraft and patrol vessels, and five marine battalions. They could mount a substantial naval operation if they so desired.

In addition to this, the navy had its own land- and carrier-based aircraft, while the Argentine air force had over two hundred aircraft. There was the added advantage, of course, that the Falklands were geographically close to the mainland.

As far as Britain was concerned, it was possible to deploy a nuclear-attack submarine, but this would take time and its presence would ideally need to be supplemented with one or two surface ships, Type 42 destroyers or frigates. These ships would need refuelling, so a fleet auxiliary ship carrying fuel oil and provisions would also need to be on station. A permanent re-inforcement of the Falklands would require a serious commitment of men and ships. The MoD concluded, 'Our scope for military action is extremely limited; almost anything we could do would be too late and/or extremely expensive.' As one official commented, 'It would be a practical nonsense, besides which Suez would look sensible, for us to attempt to engage in serious operations against a perfectly competent and well-equipped local opponent off the toe of South America.'

However, the countdown had started. On Friday 26 March in Buenos Aires, at a quarter past seven in the evening, the three members of the Argentine junta decided to set in motion the military recovery of the Malvinas. The next day, the 27th, an intelligence report was received in London and circulated to ministers, saying that there were indications that all the Argentine navy's submarines had left port. John Nott, at home on Sunday the 28th, was going through his ministerial red boxes, the cases that contained the intelligence and political briefings that were sent to him daily in his role as a senior minister. As he read this intelligence about the submarines, it made him think, not that the Falklands were under threat, but that the situation in South Georgia was now much worse than he expected.

Intelligence of Argentine intentions now started to arrive like a remorseless drum beat. On 28 March British Intelligence intercepted a signal to the Argentine submarine *Santa Fe*, a large diesel-electric submarine that had been purchased from the United States in 1971. The signal ordered the submarine to go to a set of coordinates and carry out reconnaissance of the beach in preparation for disembarkation. If the duty officer in the Ministry of Defence had had the time to examine the geographic coordinates that were in the signal, he would have seen that the *Santa Fe* was being sent to a place just east of Port Stanley in the Falklands. But the signal was just one of hundreds he received that day and he routinely forwarded it to the South America desk officer, where it was only closely examined a day later.

By then the Argentine fleet had set sail on its journey to the Falklands. The fourteen surface ships were detected at sea on 30 March when they were some 800 miles from the Falklands, but again the Ministry of Defence officials believed that this was an exercise aimed, if at anything, at influencing the situation in South Georgia.

On the evening of 30 March severe weather in the South Atlantic forced the Argentine fleet to slow, then to change course to avoid the worst of the mountainous seas that were being generated by the storm. On 31 March Rear Admiral Busser, in command of the landing force, radioed to Buenos Aires that because of the bad storm the invasion had been postponed by one day, from Thursday 1 April to Friday the 2nd. This signal was also intercepted by Britain. GCHQ (Government Communications Headquarters: the government signals intelligence agency) decoded it and passed it immediately to the Ministry of Defence, the Foreign Office and the Joint Intelligence Committee, the unit of the Cabinet Office that produces intelligence assessments for the Prime Minister. This was the signal that enabled Rex Hunt, the Falklands Governor, and the marine detachment in Stanley to make some preparations for the Argentine invasion.

In London the news was a body-blow to Margaret Thatcher and her senior Cabinet ministers. When John Nott met Mrs Thatcher in her room in the House of Commons that evening, they had no idea what to do. 'We spent three-quarters of an hour, I think, going round and round in circles, wondering what we could do diplomatically,' recalled John Nott later. It was quite revealing that even then, with the evidence of an Argentine invasion fleet before them, neither the Prime Minister nor her Defence Secretary considered that a military response was possible. In fact, apart from John Nott and his Permanent Secretary there was no other person from the Ministry of Defence nor any representative of the Chief of Defence Staff in the meeting, although senior civil servants from the Foreign Office had also come to the Prime Minister's room. In that small office in the House of Commons, on the evening of 31 March 1982, the leaders of Britain were confronting the sad and humiliating end of Britain's power and influence.

If everything had ended there, the Argentine invasion would have been a complete success, and Admiral Anaya's belief that Britain would no longer fight over a few islands thousands of miles away would have proved to be absolutely correct. However, in the short space of time between the junta's decision to bring forward its invasion plans and the moment that the crisis over the defence of the Falkland Islands exploded in the British government's face, certain measures had been taken by the Royal Navy – what Sir Henry Leach referred to as 'one or two minor preparations', in case there was some escalation of the stand-off in South Georgia.

An annual exercise called Springtrain was being carried out by the Royal Navy off Gibraltar, and some of the ships taking part had already been selected as possible reinforcements for HMS *Endurance* in South Georgia. Admiral Sir John Fieldhouse, Commander-in-Chief Fleet, was in Gibraltar and, after a conversation with Leach, talked on the evening of Tuesday 30 March to Rear Admiral Woodward, in command of Springtrain, about the deteriorating situation in the South Atlantic. HMS *Spartan*, a Swiftsure class SSN, had already been detached from the Springtrain exercise and ordered to load up with her war complement of torpedoes in Gibraltar. HMS *Splendid* was diverted to Faslane and ordered to make ready to sail south, and, of course, the duty officer on HMS *Conqueror* had received a telephone call. As John Nott said, 'The navy picked up the ball and ran with it.'

But these preparations were just that, and in any event, by 31 March, with the Argentine invasion fleet at sea, they looked like the proverbial bolt in the stable door. However, the signals that had brought John Nott to Margaret Thatcher's office had also been placed in Admiral Sir Henry Leach's in-tray on his desk in the Ministry of Defence. That Wednesday Sir Henry had been on a visit to inspect a naval shore establishment in Portsmouth and flew back that evening by helicopter. By 6.30 he was in his office and reading what he described as two completely opposed documents. One brief was from the Naval Staff and one was from Intelligence.

The Intelligence brief really put their head on the block and said: on this occasion we really think the Argies do mean business and that they will invade during the first week of April. The Naval Staff brief said, to my shame, keep your cool, this is the mixture as before, it has all blown over in the past and it will blow over again; we are vastly over committed, do nothing. The two briefs were incompatible and my reaction was – what the hell is the point of having a navy if you don't use it for this sort of thing in these sorts of circumstances?

Sir Henry went to see his minister in his rooms in the ministry building, but was told that Nott was being briefed at this moment in the House of Commons. Afraid that Nott was being instructed on the basis of the Naval Staff brief, he went straight away to the House of Commons, still wearing the full uniform he had worn during his tour of inspection that day. John Nott was not in his office, and while a messenger went to search for him Sir Henry had to kick his heels in the whip's office.

Finally making his way to the meeting in Margaret Thatcher's room, Leach found Nott with Margaret Thatcher and Permanent Secretaries from the Ministry of Defence and Foreign Office. The atmosphere in the meeting was, according to Sir Henry, extremely doom-laden.

The Prime Minister invited him to say what he thought. There had been doubts expressed by the officials in the meeting, not only about what could be done but also, even now, whether anything needed to be done. Leach was absolutely clear, and his calm, deliberate and forceful voice cut through the confusion and doubt.

On the basis of the latest intelligence, I think we must assume that the Falkland Islands will be invaded, and that this will happen in the next few days. If it does there is no way the garrison can put up an effective fight against what we know to be embarked on the Argentine fleet. Nor now is there any effective deterrence that we could apply in time. Therefore the islands will be captured.

But all was not lost. He believed that the islands should be re-captured. 'To do so would require a very considerable naval task force. I believe we should assemble such a task force now with-out further delay.' The task force could be assembled in forty-eight hours, he told the Prime Minister, and he was quite clear about what he was seeking. He wanted permission to assemble a task force ready for orders to sail down to the South Atlantic if necessary, and in his view it was necessary. The Prime Minister said to him, 'Why do you say that?' Sir Henry replied, 'Because if we do not, if we muck around, if we pussyfoot, if we don't move very fast and are not entirely successful, in a very few months' time we shall be living in a different country whose word will count for little.'

Sir Henry got what he wanted. When the meeting finally broke up he left with full authority to assemble the task force on the lines that he had proposed, but not to sail it until further instructions.

John Nott remained behind with Margaret Thatcher. He was highly sceptical of Sir Henry's proposal. He had absolutely no confidence in Leach's judgement, and said so to Margaret Thatcher. He had severe doubts, not least about the logistics of fighting a war 8,000 miles away without air cover from land-based aircraft. It was not until the next day when he was given a full briefing from the Acting Chief of Defence Staff that Nott accepted that a task force was a viable proposal. Much of the briefing, however, would not have been prepared had it not been for Sir Henry Leach's having talked to the Acting Chief, who was Sir Edwin Bramall, Chief of the Army General Staff. He took Leach's word that the task force would be able to defend itself against air attack, which he considered to be the crucial question. There was a Cabinet meeting on the evening of Friday 2 April, the day of the successful invasion, and Margaret Thatcher was given authority by the Cabinet to order the task force to put to sea.

So, when the Prime Minister and her government had to face the fury of the House of Commons in the emergency debate on the morning of Saturday 3 April, she was able to say that a task force was being prepared and made ready to sail. It was the one thing that prevented Thatcher and the majority of her Cabinet from being forced to resign. After eighteen months of conflict, fighting a relentlessly determined struggle against the inflexibility and disdain of his minister, Admiral Leach had thrown his Prime Minister and her government a lifeline. It was due to his obstinacy, his self-assurance and his determination to talk to John Nott on that Wednesday night that they were in a position to grasp it. On his own initiative, Sir Henry Leach had reversed a sixteen-year-old defence policy that had seen the mental horizons of Britain's politicians and defence establishment limited by the borders of NATO. The Royal Navy was now about to embark on a campaign 8,000 miles from Britain.

After the Cabinet meeting on the Friday evening, Michael Heseltine, Secretary of State for the Environment, and Cecil Parkinson, Chairman of the Conservative Party and the Paymaster General, went to their club for dinner. 'He and I sat', said Parkinson, 'as a couple of politicians over dinner, speculating about what it would do to the government if this was a failure. And it would be a disaster.'

7

ENGLAND EXPECTS

As at many other times in Britain's history, everything now rested on the Royal Navy. The Cabinet had given orders to send a task force to the South Atlantic, and the government under Margaret Thatcher had survived a tumultuous and extremely critical emergency debate in the House of Commons on Saturday 3 April. Lord Carrington, the Foreign Secretary, had accepted that his department was at fault in not paying enough attention to Argentine intentions and had resigned. John Nott had offered his resignation to the Prime Minister, but was easily persuaded not to go. Now the really difficult things had to be carried out, and whether or not the participants in that tense and anxious meeting in Margaret Thatcher's room in Westminster realized it, the initiative had passed into the hands of Admiral of the Fleet Sir Henry Leach and such men and ships of the Royal Navy as Britain still had left in 1982.

The fleet of surface warships based in Portsmouth was organized into squadrons, made up of groups of frigates and destroyers, whose numbers varied; sometimes there would be five frigates in a squadron, sometimes a destroyer and four frigates. There were altogether eight squadrons, with another four destroyers and six frigates organized separately. These squadrons and unattached warships were divided into two flotillas, the First and Second Flotilla, each of which was commanded by a rear admiral. The large helicopter assault ships *Fearless* and *Intrepid* and the two aircraft carriers *Hermes* and *Invincible*, which were now earmarked for sale, were part of the Third Flotilla.

The First Flotilla had set out from Portsmouth in the middle of March, sailing to Gibraltar for the Springtrain exercise. This was an annual event involving not only destroyers and frigates, but also nuclear and conventional submarines, fleet auxiliaries and aircraft flying out of Gibraltar. This large group of warships carried out a variety of anti-submarine warfare and anti-aircraft exercises, testing communications procedures and training crews in the complicated tasks of coordinating warships, helicopters and various weapons systems in different types of conflict. Two nuclear submarines from Devonport were taking part in the anti-submarine exercises, and Royal Fleet Auxiliaries – large multipurpose ships carrying stores, provisions and fuel oil – assisted exercises in replenishment at sea, the process of refuelling warships from accompanying tankers while under way. In short, they were the normal manoeuvres and exercises that a surface fleet had performed for decades.

The navy had changed dramatically since the last time a large fleet had put to sea in earnest, to invade Egypt and the Suez Canal in 1956. It was considerably smaller now, of course, but there had been other changes that affected the way the fleet organized itself and the way it fought. The most profound was the development of nuclear submarines and their increasing importance in naval warfare.

One indication of the growing importance of submarines was that, slowly and quietly, officers from the submarine service had started to achieve high rank. Two of these submariners were now to be of fundamental importance in the coming conflict over the Falkland Islands. The Flag Officer of the First Flotilla, or FOF1 for short, was Rear Admiral 'Sandy' Woodward, and he was in overall charge of the current Springtrain exercise. Admiral Woodward had a distinguished career in the navy, serving on the conventional submarine HMS *Tireless*, as well as having commanded HMS *Valiant*, the second of Britain's nuclear submarines, and then commanding HMS *Warspite*, the follow-on nuclear submarine from *Valiant*. He then became an instructor on the Submarine Commanding Officer's Qualifying Course and had been offered the job of Flag Officer Submarines, in command of the whole submarine fleet, before becoming FOF1.

The other key figure was the man who had flown out to Gibraltar to observe the Springtrain exercise, and had brought with him at the last minute Sir Henry Leach's request to make preparations for a possible task force. Admiral Sir John Fieldhouse was the first peacetime submariner to reach the rank of admiral, let alone the position of Commander-in-Chief Fleet. John Fieldhouse had been the commanding officer of Britain's first nuclear-powered submarine, HMS *Dreadnought*, then Flag Officer Submarines (FOSM), in command of all Britain's submarine fleet, before being promoted to his current post as C-in-C Fleet.

These submariners – and there were quite a lot of other former submarine commanders who were commanding some of the surface ships in Woodward's First Flotilla – were a new type of leadership in the navy, who had experienced command at the cutting edge of the Cold War, on covert and dangerous missions against the Soviet Union. They were used to taking risks on these operations, entering harbours, trailing Soviet warships and submarines as closely and silently as they could. They came to trust their own judgement, and that of their crews, operating as they were under very limited control from the Flag Officer Submarines. They came closest to those captains of 180 years earlier, at Trafalgar, who had sailed into battle under Nelson with the injunction 'No captain can do very wrong if he places his ship alongside that of an enemy.'

It was the existence of these officers and their influence in the navy that helped to maintain a level of professionalism in a service that still boasted it was the best navy in the world. It may have been this *esprit de corps* that kept it so during the recent history of decline, cancellations and cuts that in terms of equipment meant the surface fleet was dangerously inadequate. Such deficiencies may have been easy to put to the back of one's mind during an annual exercise, however much it was designed to stretch people's abilities. Admiral Woodward was now about to have those deficiencies placed firmly at the forefront of his concerns when his commanding officer arrived in Gibraltar on 29 March.

It was perfectly normal for Admiral Fieldhouse to fly out to Gibraltar to inspect the ships on Operation Springtrain, but this time the C-in-C Fleet was bringing news of the developing situation in South Georgia and had to report back to Sir Henry Leach on what ships could be quickly mobilized into a task force. On that evening, Fieldhouse and Woodward met in the admiral's cabin on board the big county-class destroyer HMS *Glamorgan* and worked out how a task force might be built up from the ships currently taking part in the Springtrain exercise. These ships were the obvious candidates for the job, because their crews were already worked up and well trained from the exercise; they were used to working together on manoeuvres and they were 1,000 miles closer to the South Atlantic than warships in the UK. The problem was that the ships had sailed to Gibraltar for an exercise, not to fight a war or to go on an extended patrol. The nuclear submarine HMS *Spartan* had been withdrawn from Springtrain already to go south to the Falklands, but first had to dock in Gibraltar and load live torpedoes and extra stores from the conventional submarine HMS *Onyx*. A similar operation would have to be carried out for any surface ships that went south, and it would be difficult to keep that operation secret. In any event, as a preparation Woodward returned to his flagship, *Antrim*, and sent an immediate signal to all the ships taking part in Springtrain – a Short Notice Operational Readiness Check, which requested them to report their current status, their fuel stocks, stores and mechanical condition.

During the two admirals' discussion, Fieldhouse was at the same time making an assessment of Woodward's suitability as leader of any task force. He was not the most senior admiral that Fieldhouse could call on, but, like the ships he was commanding, Woodward was available, was in Gibraltar and had been actively involved in a series of strenuous and demanding exercises over the past three weeks. Woodward knew his ships' capabilities and that of the officers and crews.

There was considerable irony in Woodward's appointment. Earlier in his career, he had served for some time in the Ministry of Defence in Whitehall as Assistant Director (Warfare) in the

Directorate of Naval Plans. While there, in 1974 he had participated in producing the Position Paper on the feasibility of defending the Falklands against an Argentine invasion. It came, of course, to the conclusion that it would be impossible. A great deal had changed in the nine years since the paper was first produced, but one thing that had not improved was the number of ships and the effectiveness of the weapons systems that were available to the Royal Navy. When, very early in the morning of 3 April, Woodward received the signal to form a task force and prepare to head south on Operation Corporate, the accuracy of that previous Position Paper weighed heavily on his mind. It was now going to be his job to prove it wrong.

Over the next few hours those ships selected to head south were supplied with fuel, ammunition and stores of all sorts from those of the flotilla that were to return to the UK. Shells were delivered by helicopter and winched from deck to deck on straining cables. Ships steamed close to each other and heaving lines were fired by Grapnel guns; heavy fuel hoses were hauled across the narrow gap of sea and thousands of gallons of fuel oil and aviation spirit were pumped from ship to ship. It was an urgent frenzy of activity that left eight ships out of twenty-five heading south, not to the Falklands, but to another island dependency in the Atlantic, Ascension Island. Here, Woodward and the ships that were being mobilized in the UK would meet and form up into a proper task force before heading towards the Falklands, and possibly war.

When on the night of 31 March Admiral Leach proposed to Margaret Thatcher and her sceptical Defence Secretary the assembly of a task force, Nott remained behind to voice his doubts and his lack of respect for Leach's judgement. In the days that followed, the Chiefs of Staff of the other two services privately shared their minister's reservations about the plan. Sir Edwin Bramall, head of the army, accepted that there was a political and diplomatic case for sending a task force and believed that the navy probably had made a correct assessment when they said that they could defend their ships in the South Atlantic, but he was doubtful about their chances of gaining sufficient control of the airspace over the Falklands to give safety to the amphibious ships and the troops that would attempt to land on the islands:

> I don't think there was any doubt in any of our minds that it was going to be a highly difficult operation. It was going to be undertaken 8,000 miles away, outside range of any of our airbases. So any air cover was dependent on floating platforms in the South Atlantic. We were right under the lee of the Argentine airbases and well within their range.

The 'floating platforms' to which Bramall referred were the two so-called 'through deck cruisers' HMS *Hermes* and *Invincible*, which John Nott had earmarked for sale to India and Australia respectively. They could carry between them just twenty Sea Harriers, the seaborne version of the vertical take-off and landing 'jump jet' ground-attack aircraft that had been built for the RAF. Fully loaded with weapons and fuel, the Sea Harriers needed a 'ski-lift' – an upward-sloping extension to the flight deck – to help them get airborne. They had barely been introduced into service, and had only just finished a trial period with the first Fleet Air Arm Squadron to evaluate them. These twenty aircraft would have to defend the task force against the supersonic Mirage and Kfir fighters of the Argentine air force, as well as the carrier-borne Skyhawks and Etendard fighter bombers of the Argentine navy. Argentina possessed an overwhelming superiority in aircraft numbers, and if they were prepared to use the runway at Stanley as well as their aircraft carrier, they would enjoy a great deal of tactical flexibility, being able to attack the task force with a large number of aircraft from several directions using radar-guided Exocet anti-ship missiles that could hit ships 25–30 miles away. The Royal Navy's last fleet carrier, HMS *Ark Royal*, along with its squadron of fast Phantom fighters and Buccaneer bombers, and its early-warning search aircraft, had recently been scrapped. *Hermes* and *Invincible* would not carry early-warning aircraft that could search beyond the visual horizon; neither were they equipped with catapults, so could not launch aircraft quickly after recovering them. For this reason as well as the constraints of capacity, the loss of or serious damage to either of Woodward's carriers would be a body-blow that would cause the failure of the operation. So the Sea Harriers of the Fleet Air Arm were going to be vital in the defence of the task force and the success of any attempt to recapture the islands.

If the defensive screen of Sea Harriers was breached by Argentine fighters and bombers, the next line of defence for the carriers would be the missiles carried on the surface warships. These showed the gaps and deficiencies caused by years of decline and lack of funds. Of the eight ships that had left the Springtrain flotilla and were heading south, the two big county-class destroyers, *Antrim* and *Glamorgan*, had been designed around a missile system called Sea Slug, developed to be fired against high-altitude Soviet bombers that might attack the fleet with an atom bomb. It was not quick to load and fire, and the missile's control and guidance system, like that of the other missiles in the fleet, could be overwhelmed if there was more than one possible target. Sea Slug was twenty years old and quite simply obsolete, although the missile itself was so heavy that it might be effective if fired against a warship. There were three Type 42 destroyers, *Sheffield*, *Coventry* and *Glasgow*, in Woodward's eight ships, and these all carried Sea Dart, an anti-aircraft missile that was designed to hit very fast targets – supersonic aircraft flying at altitude – but the Type 965 radar on the Type 42 destroyers could not deal with more than one target at a time; neither could it track low-flying aircraft. If Argentine bombers made low, high-speed attacks, which would be the most intelligent thing for them to do, then the only weapon that might counter them was a system called Sea Wolf, a quick-firing missile system designed to attack low-altitude targets. However, only HMS *Brilliant*, a Type 22 frigate, was fitted with this modern system. Of the remaining two ships, HMS *Plymouth* was an elderly Type 12 frigate which had the Sea Cat anti-aircraft missile, a short-range system carried by several ships in Woodward's group. This too was approaching the end of its usefulness. It was manually guided and slow, totally unsuited to anything but head-on interceptions where the operator had plenty of warning and time to prepare the missile, arm and fire it. HMS *Arrow*, a Type 21 frigate, was similarly equipped.

In the Second World War, when groups of warships adopted a collective defence against air attack, each ship was given the responsibility of using its guns to defend different parts of the air space around a fleet or a convoy. With the missiles and their radar guidance that were mounted on Woodward's destroyers and frigates, this type of coordinated overlapping defence was almost impossible. None of the missiles' radars would lock on and direct its missile to an aircraft that was not heading directly towards it, so collective area defence was very difficult. More warships were on standby in the United Kingdom, ready to join the task force, but none of them had systems that could lessen Woodward's vulnerability to air attack from bombers or sea-skimming anti-ship missiles like the Exocet.

Woodward pondered these and other problems; they would weigh heavily on his mind in the coming days. He had no experience operating aircraft carriers or their aircraft, and hoped that there would be good enough support on board to prevent its becoming a problem. By the time that his ships left the area of the Straits of Gibraltar, the nuclear submarines *Splendid*, *Spartan* and *Conqueror* had already started their journey to the Falklands ready to prevent the islands being reinforced by sea. The submarines were going to be his first line of defence against the Argentine navy, and he hoped against its fleet air arm as well. He knew the submarines' capabilities intimately and was confident that controlling them would be no problem. In any event, things would become clearer when the task force met up in Ascension.

Ascension Island is located about 500 miles south of the equator and 1,000 miles from the coast of Africa, at the same latitude as the northern borders of Angola. It is an extinct volcano, part of the mid-Atlantic ridge system, rising out of the ocean like a giant humpbacked whale. A cap of white clouds permanently floats above the highest point of the island, the Peak. It is extremely remote, barely 50 miles square. Ascension was disregarded for years, but occupied by Britain when Napoleon was imprisoned on the island of St Helena, which is the closest piece of land to Ascension. During the Second World War, the United States built an airstrip here, called Wideawake Airfield, and the USA later took a lease from the British government on the facility. The facilities offered to the British fleet would be a test of the United States government's attitude to the dispute, but even if they were fully cooperative – as indeed they were – the airstrip and port facilities were basic. Ascension housed a listening post for the British signals intelligence organization GCHQ and similar facilities for the United States, as well as a missile-tracking station for the National Aeronautics and Space Administration (NASA) and a US government missile-proving range. Ascension had never been designed as a base from which to mount a major naval battle in the South Atlantic, but within a few days of the task force being ordered south, the airstrip at Ascension Island was going to become extremely busy, with more aircraft movements a day than Chicago International airport.

The biggest and most important ships in Woodward's task force were going to be the two aircraft platforms, HMS *Hermes* (the larger of the two) and HMS *Invincible*. They left Portsmouth on 6 April, the harbour and the wall along the old Martello tower lined with crowds of wellwishers, cheering and waving as the ships slowly headed out into the Channel. The crews and their aircraft were lined up along the flight deck. It could not have been a more public sailing to war, nor a clearer announcement that Britain was prepared to use force.

Hermes had been in the middle of a refit when the invasion of the Falklands occurred, and it had taken enormous efforts to get her in a condition to go to sea, with the dockyard workers labouring round the clock. She was to become Admiral Woodward's flagship when the two carriers linked up with the rest of the task force at Ascension Island, and many of Woodward's staff therefore joined the ship at Portsmouth. With three submarines making maximum speed down the South Atlantic already, Woodward would need officers to manage communications and coordinate their movements.

Lieutenant Commander Jeff Tall had recently spent some time on attachment to the US navy's Pacific Fleet, where he had been closely involved with their efforts to integrate their submarine fleet with their aircraft carrier task groups. Now back at Faslane, he was ordered to catch a plane from Glasgow and be in Portsmouth by 20.00 the same evening, 4 April.

So I went. Bonnie, my wife, had just put the lamb in the oven. I remember her driving me to Glasgow Airport with my hold-all. 'See you in a couple of weeks,' I think I said. You reported to the British Airways desk. I said I was Lieutenant Commander Jeff Tall. 'Hang on. Yeah, you're on the flight. Go!', and at Heathrow there were buses and you jumped on a bus and it took you to Portsmouth. And there was *Hermes*. It was extraordinary. She had everything coming out, you know; there were pipes and valves, and leads and scaffolding being struck down, aircraft landing, and this poor commander who actually was a very good, old-fashioned seaman saying 'Who the fuck are you? Oh, submarine team leader. Right, go to the bar and we'll sort you out later.'

On the voyage down to Ascension Island, Woodward started to exercise his ships for the war that he knew he must expect to fight. Lacking any carriers to provide anti-aircraft exercises, he confined himself to anti-submarine exercises and working out plans for confronting the Argentine navy. He was, however, hampered by the lack of any realistic intelligence about the state of the Argentine armed forces. British Intelligence, along with the rest of Britain's defence establishment, had been focused for many years almost exclusively on Europe and the threat from the Warsaw Pact. One of Woodward's first signals to Fleet

Headquarters in Northwood, on 5 April, had been a request for as much information as could possibly be gleaned from other friendly governments, and also from defence companies that had sold arms to the Argentine government. Woodward desperately needed to know not only the composition and state of readiness of the Argentine navy and air force, but the performance of much of their equipment, particularly the modern weapons that had been supplied by Germany, France and Israel.

The most pressing concern for him was the performance of Argentina's two new Type 209 submarines, *Salta* and *San Luis*, and their anti-ship torpedoes, purchased from Germany. The submarines were diesel-electric, and they were very quiet, with up-to-date sonar equipment. The torpedoes were modern, wire-guided missiles that could be directed by sonar to their target, theoretically making evasion very difficult.

Secondly, Woodward was concerned about the Exocet anti-ship missiles and just how many of them were available to Argentina. He had no accurate information on the number of Argentine ships that had been fitted with them, nor what their effective range was, although according to the published information the Argentinians possessed eleven ships fitted with these missiles. If the warships of the Argentine navy managed to break out into the open sea, Woodward's only counter to them would be his own Exocet missiles, which were carried on some of his frigates and on the county-class destroyers *Antrim* and *Glamorgan*. The Sea Harriers might be used to attack Argentine surface ships with bombs, but this would be a serious diversion from their principle job of providing air defence.

There was also the worrying question of the size and extent of the air forces that Argentina might be able to launch against the task force of Operation Corporate. Argentina had bought modern supersonic French fighters known as Mirages, and an Israeli-manufactured version called the Kfir. The Argentine navy had also started to buy from France an aircraft called the Super Etendard, which could take off from an aircraft carrier and would carry an airborne version of the Exocet missile. It was believed the Super Etendard had a range of about 400 miles, and that it could be refuelled from a tanker aircraft in flight, probably adding another 200 miles to its combat radius from the carrier, which could steam anywhere. The Super Etendard carried the AM.39, an air-launched version of the Exocet, which could be launched when the aircraft were barely in range of the radar carried on Woodward's ships. Their presence in the Argentine armoury was an unsettling prospect for Woodward, who commanded a fleet without any early-warning aircraft.

The greatest advantage that the Argentinian forces possessed, however, was that their ships and aircraft were operating very close to home. The 1,600-mile supply line to Ascension that Woodward had to deal with seemed very long indeed. If the Argentine navy threatened to attack, Woodward proposed to withdraw his carriers very rapidly east and hope that two attack groups of three Type 42 destroyers and the *Glamorgan* in the company of two Type 21 frigates would be able to take them on with their own Exocet missiles.

The Argentine navy and marines had recently taken part in exercises with US forces, and Woodward now asked Admiral Fieldhouse to obtain as much information as possible from the United States about the way that the Argentinians operated their aircraft carrier, *Veinticinco de Mayo*, and the performance of the US-built Skyhawk A-4Q fighter bombers that flew from its decks. The list of unknowns was a long one, and the answers to some of Woodward's questions might prove to be very depressing.

Whatever the answers, it was clear that it would be far better if the nuclear submarines could prevent the Argentine navy coming anywhere near his surface fleet.

Woodward toured the ships in his battle group, attempting to boost morale and confidence by minimizing the dangers posed by Argentina, a process that he referred to as threat reduction.

Hermes and *Invincible* arrived off Ascension Island on 14 April and were met by Admiral Woodward in HMS *Glamorgan*. He proceeded to transfer his command and his staff to the admiral's quarters in *Hermes*. They had sailed with *Fearless*, a ship designed to carry troops. She also carried landing craft, which could be floated out by flooding compartments in the stern. No sooner had the carriers and *Fearless* arrived – bringing the commanders of the amphibious and land forces, Commodore Mike Clapp and Brigadier Julian Thompson, respectively – than Admiral Fieldhouse flew in with his staff to lay down some ground rules for the control of the operation and to brief the commanders on the current thinking in London.

Fieldhouse wanted to impress on people what Woodward had already inwardly digested: the leadership of the Royal Navy, First Sea Lord Admiral Sir Henry Leach and Chief of the Defence Staff Lord Lewin, knew that if the Argentine government did not back down, a war was inevitable, British ships would be sunk and lives would be lost. They were not certain that any of the politicians in the Cabinet, or in the House of Commons, or the population at large had grasped that fact, or really understood what it meant. 'This operation', said Fieldhouse, 'is the most difficult thing we have attempted since the Second World War.' He assured the assembled officers on *Hermes* that the government was committed to recovering the

Falklands, and that if diplomacy failed then there would be absolute political support for the task force. It was hard to square this with the obvious fact that the ultimate aims of the task force had yet to be clarified. Was it just to secure a bridgehead for British troops on the islands? Or would the campaign continue until the Argentine forces on the Falklands had been defeated? All that had been decided, it seems, was that the battle group would proceed to the Falklands and enforce a blockade. They would start the air and sea war, and carry out the essential reconnaissance missions to gain the intelligence needed to plan for a landing.

In overall command of the task force was Admiral Fieldhouse. He reported directly to the Chief of Defence Staff Admiral Lewin, who reported directly to the Prime Minister. Margaret Thatcher had organized a small War Cabinet around her of the Defence Secretary, John Nott; the Foreign Secretary, Francis Pym, now that Carrington had resigned; the Home Secretary, William Whitelaw; and the Chairman of the Conservative Party and Paymaster General, Cecil Parkinson. A lot of things were still left in the air, and there was some confusion in the minds of the senior commanders of the task force about who was in overall charge. Woodward clearly was the senior officer, but did his remit run to the amphibious forces and the troops? One area of command and control was decided, however, and that was the issue of the nuclear submarines, which were going to be constituted as a separate task group designated 324.3 within the overall task force, under the control of Flag Officer Submarines Vice Admiral Herbert in Northwood. He would be under the direct control of Admiral Fieldhouse. This was not to Woodward's or Jeff Tall's liking.

Lieutenant Commander Tall attended some of the meetings

where command of the submarines was discussed: 'I was privy to a couple of discussions, and I went in there with John Fieldhouse who'd arrived with his team, and it was obvious to me there was disagreement. It was clear that he was not going to give away command and control of his submarines.' Some people have suggested that this was purely a matter of inertia – Vice Admiral Herbert didn't see any real reason to change a system that had functioned well up until now – but Jeff Tall thinks there were wider policy issues at stake:

> There's no doubt in my mind that the overriding consideration was do not lose a reactor in the South Atlantic. Because the political ramifications of that, I think, would have been extremely serious. The other issue was the US. We had removed three front-line SSNs from the Cold War battle and I don't think they were happy with that, because the Americans relied on us, in the case of a flare-up, to actually fill the forward billets. We could get there days before they could.

Whether this was the reason for maintaining a NATO command and control structure is not clear. Whatever the reason, the result wasn't welcomed on *Hermes*, Woodward's flagship. Jeff Tall remembers:

> So Sandy did not get what he expected, which was, I think, Submarine Element Core. He did not get the direct support role over the submarines as he expected. The choice was made that I would go as the submarine support man, basically because of my understanding of support operations. And everybody else disappeared. I hung on to one Radio Supervisor, Petty Officer level, who was capable of listening into SSIS – Submarine Support

Indicate Information Exchange System, essentially the submarine satellite link.

Political pressures were also affecting other aspects of the task force operations and were demanding more immediate attention from Woodward. Negotiations taking place in the UN, and concerns about the extent to which public opinion in Britain would remain in support of the use of force for any length of time, meant that two separate missions were imposed on Woodward.

The British delegation in the United Nations had successfully secured a Resolution of the UN Security Council that condemned the use of force by Argentina but committed both parties to seek a solution by diplomatic means. It was this caveat that the British government regarded as a hostage to fortune and it meant that the diplomatic negotiations were continuing, given further impetus by the intervention of Alexander Haig, the United States Secretary of State, who flew back and forth between London, New York and Buenos Aires in an attempt to broker some form of deal.

The United States government was totally split over the policies it should adopt in the conflict between Britain and the Argentine junta. Casper Weinberger, who was the Secretary of Defense in charge of the Pentagon, was determined to support Britain if it came to a war and did everything he could to speed up supplies of modern equipment, particularly the most advanced air-to-air missiles for the Sea Harriers, and to provide other support at Ascension Island. The US State Department, the foreign-policy arm of the US government, however, was dominated by people who believed that support for the military dictatorships in Argentina, Chile and other countries, and US interests in Latin America generally, were of far more overriding importance than support for Britain. The main proponent of this view was Jeane Kirkpatrick, the US Ambassador to the United Nations, who was proving very difficult in the Security Council. With the Argentine Foreign Minister continually casting his government's occupation of the Malvinas in an anti-colonial light, the State Department was also very nervous about alienating many of the countries of the Third World, who were a well-organized bloc in the UN General Assembly. The British government had to maintain the position that it was open to negotiations and anxious to avoid a war, whilst not allowing those negotiations to weaken Britain's position militarily. This diplomatic posture was not maintained solely to avoid condemnation within the United Nations. The government was anxious to overcome the criticism it had endured about its various failures in preventing the invasion of the Falklands, and wanted also to keep up the momentum for decisive action that had been generated by the emergency debate in parliament on 3 April.

This debate had been misleading, however, because the general clamour for action that had been heard from the government backbenches and an opportunistic Labour opposition had not necessarily accurately reflected the mood of the country. The Labour leadership under anti-nuclear campaigner Michael Foot might now be committed to war, but many ordinary members of the party were dubious about its success. Despite the scenes of tearful departures for the warships leaving Portsmouth, and the later stirring emotional farewells to the troops crowded on the deck of the P&O liner *Canberra*, pressed into service as a troop carrier, the country was not totally united behind war. The press by and large reflected this attitude. The *Financial Times* had argued that the best way forward in the crisis was to use economic sanctions against Argentina, and was opposed to the use of force. So too was the *Guardian*. The *Sunday Times* argued that an attempt to repossess the islands would be a shortcut to a bloody disaster, and only the *Daily Telegraph* and *The Times* were unequivocally in favour of a military campaign.

So negotiations continued, and the government had to be seen to be going along with them. As long as the possibility of a settlement existed, it became extremely important to establish a military position as advantageous to Britain as possible. For this reason, Woodward was ordered to send some of his ships – three of the Type 42 destroyers, *Sheffield*, *Coventry* and *Glasgow*, and the frigates *Brilliant* and *Arrow* – ahead of the main task force. They went followed by a tanker, with the plan to proceed as fast as they could until they had exhausted two-thirds of their fuel, and then they should loiter until the tanker caught up with them and they could refuel at sea. They would cover about 1,160 miles and would establish the strongest force possible as far south as possible, just in case the diplomats imposed a freeze on any further military movements pending a negotiated settlement.

In addition to this advance guard, on 7 April the War Cabinet took the decision to recapture the island of South Georgia, where the salvage workers' landing had been the catalyst for this unprecedented lurch to war. The island was of very limited military value, but the Chiefs of Staff had approved the operation. Possession of South Georgia would give Britain a bargaining counter if negotiations over the status of the Falklands started. A successful effort to recapture it would show to the Argentine junta and to the world at large that Britain was not bluffing about the use of force, and might encourage the Argentinians to back down. Finally, there was a view that several weeks would elapse before the task force and the amphibious group would be ready to land on the Falklands themselves, and some form of action before then was desirable to keep up the political appetite for a war. The armed forces also wanted to demonstrate to the government that they were capable of fighting. Two warships, *Antrim* and *Plymouth*, therefore picked up a detachment of Special Forces at Ascension Island and, in the company of another fleet tanker, *Tidespring*, went at full speed onwards to South Georgia.

Also heading for the island at high speed was the nuclear submarine HMS *Conqueror*. In fact, as we have seen, *Conqueror* had received notification of its destination on 10 April, in a group of signals that included rules of engagement for the Falkland Islands, assessment of Argentinian forces and an initial indication that *Conqueror*'s task was to conduct some surveillance operation around the island. As the plans to retake South Georgia developed, *Conqueror*'s role would change. With 6SBS and all their weapons on board, they could play a vital role in any landing.

Also on Wednesday 7 April, the government announced in parliament that a 200-mile maritime exclusion zone was going to be established around the Falklands, with effect from the following Monday, 12 April:

> From the time indicated any Argentine warship and Argentine naval Auxiliaries found within this Zone will be treated as hostile and are liable to be attacked by British forces. This measure is without prejudice to the right of the United Kingdom to take whatever additional measures may be needed in exercise of its right of self-defence, under Article 15 of the United Nations Charter.

It was not an empty threat. The first nuclear submarine to be ordered to the South Atlantic, HMS *Spartan*, which had left Springtrain loaded with war shot torpedoes at Gibraltar and then hurried south, would be in the area when the exclusion zone was due to take effect. What action the submarine would take remained to be seen but, following the announcement of the exclusion zone, on 8 April the War Cabinet endorsed rules of engagement for the nuclear submarines. Once Argentine warships, submarines and naval auxiliaries had been positively identified inside the exclusion zone, they could be attacked. If the SSN were attacked, commanders were authorized to retaliate as necessary for self-defence both inside and outside the exclusion zone.

These rules were subsequently modified in respect of submarines. It was feared that if an SSN waited to identify an Argentine submarine positively before attacking, it carried the risk of being detected and attacked itself. Therefore if a conventional submarine was detected it could be assumed to be Argentinian and attacked on the SSN's own initiative. With HMS *Splendid* also expected to arrive in the vicinity of the Falklands a day after *Spartan*, the war might start sooner than anyone had expected.

There were now a large number of unknowns for Woodward to deal with. Perhaps the most unsettling – far more so than his fears about the Argentine forces – was the realization that, even though he would be fighting in a remote, inhospitable ocean 8,000 miles away from home, the Chiefs of Staff and the War Cabinet would still be trying to exercise control. The success of the operation and the lives of his sailors would depend on them getting it right.

8

THE BATTLE FOR SOUTH GEORGIA

By 18 April HMS *Conqueror* was coming into sight of South Georgia. The submarine had steamed over 7,000 miles since leaving Faslane on the morning of 4 April. Apart from coming to periscope depth every twelve hours to receive signals and fix their position from a satellite, since 6 April they had remained submerged throughout the course of the voyage. The *Conqueror* had travelled past Spain, Gibraltar and the Azores, through the warm, tropical waters off the west coast of Africa, and into the wide expanses of the South Atlantic.

Submarines are extremely dependent on their knowledge of the sea around them. They need to know its temperature, its salinity, the direction and depth of the various currents in the ocean, whether they are made of warm or cold water, the depth of the sea floor and much else – everything that will affect how sound is transmitted through the water. Submariners' knowledge of the North Atlantic can be almost instinctive, but for *Conqueror*'s men the southern ocean was completely uncharted. The further south they travelled, the more they relied on their own measurements and sensors to assess the nature of the water they lived in. Almost every other day the *Conqueror* would descend to 750 feet and launch a small buoy that would be used to measure the changes in the velocity of the sound as it rose to the surface. At various depths there were layers that would be able to transmit sound over great distances, and it was vital for those on duty in the control room to know where those layers were, particularly if they were trying to locate a target or avoid detection.

The main navigational tool on board *Conqueror* was a Ship's Inertial Navigation System, which used gyroscopes and accelerometers to measure changes in the position of the submarine and the speed of those changes. It was built before the age of digital technology and Lieutenant Jonty Powis, the navigator, used to think that it looked as though it had been put together in an afternoon by Blue Peter. It was accurate in measuring changes in latitude, but it needed constant adjustment to work out longitude. This was achieved by receiving a signal from a satellite that *Conqueror* downloaded every twenty-four hours. This too was a fairly basic system, one of the first satellite navigation systems to be fitted to Royal Navy submarines. The operator on board had to listen to the signal from the satellite and manually track it so that the signal remained strong enough for the computer to work out a unique position. It was accurate enough within 100 yards, and the navigator could then feed this position into the Inertial Navigation System to update it. It was a complicated process, and Jonty Powis was pleased with himself when they arrived at South Georgia.

The latitudes of Faslane and South Georgia are the same bar 3 degrees: Faslane is 56 degrees north and South Georgia is 53 degrees south, but their climates are very different. Without a warming Gulf Stream, South Georgia is much colder, flayed by fierce gales and dominated by massive glaciers.

Conqueror slowed to 10 knots and approached the island with care, at a depth of 590 feet, because there was the possibility, even after the southern summer, that there might be some icebergs in the water. It was getting dark, so the final approach to the island was delayed until the next morning. That day, the 19th, was very misty; it was impossible to see anything through the periscope. Approaching Cumberland Bay, the edge of the Fortuna Glacier where it met the sea could be heard as a loud roaring noise in the headphones of the sonar operators. They were also running active sonar every ten minutes to locate broken glacier ice on the surface. Eventually, though, the fog and clouds did clear. Jonty Powis was on watch:

> I was on the periscope when we sighted land for the first time. There is a very tall mountain in the centre of the island, and I'd sort of worked out when we might see it. But weather conditions were never good and then suddenly there was a break, and there was this big mountain. I was able to call the captain and say 'Land Ho!' It's very satisfying to do this as a navigator.

*

Conqueror had arrived as the advance guard, tasked to perform the small operation of Task Group 317.9, to recapture the island of South Georgia: codenamed Operation Paraquet. On 12 April, while *Conqueror* was crossing the equator, a small, discreet group of officers had been set up in Northwood to control the operation. The destroyer *Antrim* and frigate *Plymouth* were on their way south along with the tanker *Tidespring*, which as well as its cargo of fuel oil was carrying M Company of 42 Commando Royal Marines. The commanding officer of the task group was Captain Brian Young of *Antrim*, and the commander of the assault forces was Major Guy Sheridan.

It was assumed that the Argentine forces that had landed on South Georgia and had precipitated the growing alarm about Argentina's invasion plans had not been reinforced. The island was far from the mainland of Argentina and would be beyond the range of most Argentine aircraft. Northwood assumed that the greatest air threat, that from the aircraft on the carrier *Veinticinco de Mayo*, would not materialize because the carrier would need to enter an area where it would be at a very high risk of possible attack from nuclear submarines. The greatest threat to the British warships was in fact expected to come from the Argentine navy, in particular the *Santa Fe*, the conventional diesel-powered submarine. The *Santa Fe* had been built in the United States and launched in 1944, one of the Guppy class. She was a big, fast submarine, with a speed of 20 knots when running on diesels on the surface, and 12 knots submerged. She had six torpedo tubes in the bows and four in the stern. After the submarine had been purchased by the Argentine navy in 1971 she had been modernized and was capable of firing sonar-directed, wire-guided torpedoes. British Intelligence had intercepted a signal ordering the submarine to sea on 9 April, with instructions for some unknown operations to be carried out on the 23rd. *Conqueror* was now on station, however, and should be able to neutralize the threat to the British surface ships. What Northwood did not know, and neither of course did Captain Young on *Antrim*, was that the *Santa Fe* had embarked forty Argentine marines on board to reinforce the Argentine troops in Grytviken.

The orders to repossess South Georgia were issued by Admiral Fieldhouse on 12 April, but when they were discussed the next day by the Chiefs of Staff, the Commander Imperial General Staff, Sir Edwin Bramall, head of the army, expressed concern that British troop numbers were not strong enough. The contradictory reasoning behind the decision to retake the island was quickly becoming apparent. This would be the first aggressive action taken by British forces as a response to an invasion of its territory, and as such it would have significance far beyond the strategic importance of South Georgia itself. Failure of this mission would jeopardize the success of the greater mission to retake the Falklands, and would be a humiliating defeat for the Prime Minister and the government. Margaret Thatcher and her ministers had already lost a considerable amount of support in parliament as a result of the Argentine invasion. They would probably not survive a bungled military campaign to reclaim South Georgia. However, making sufficient forces available for the operation could not be allowed to jeopardize the timetable of the main task force now steaming towards the Falklands.

The dilemma was solved, however, when the commanding officer D Squadron SAS, already in Ascension, told Captain Young that, in his view, it was essential to commit the whole of his forces to the operation, which would mean the addition of another seventy well-equipped soldiers to the 150 Royal Marines already on *Tidespring*. This was a comfort to Sir Edwin Bramall back in London, so the operation went ahead without further criticism from the Chiefs of Staff. The stock of the various Special Forces was riding high in Whitehall, particularly after their success in the Iranian Embassy siege, and with the 2SBS on HMS *Plymouth* and 6SBS on board *Conqueror* there were almost as many Special Forces aiming to land on South

Georgia as there were regular marines. Whether they would make a decisive difference only time would tell.

The fourteen members of 6SBS on board the *Conqueror* were there, it was assumed, to carry out reconnaissance of the possible landing sites on the island. They had therefore to make an assessment of whether the Argentine forces had in fact been reinforced, and where they might have established strong points overlooking possible beach heads, and then to work out how they were going to be disembarked from the submarine to make a landing.

Conqueror came to periscope depth and started slowly to make observations along the rocky coasts and inlets of South Georgia. On the Commanding Officer's Qualifying Course, Chris Wreford-Brown and Tim McClement had been expected to operate in extremely shallow water, but it was a rule of thumb that a depth of around 240 feet was desirable. Even here it was necessary to keep an eye on the speed, taking it quite slowly, and for the forward and after plane operators to have steady hands and steadier nerves. Both the surveillance and attack periscopes are remarkable optical instruments, producing highly magnified images of outstanding clarity. Both have a split-screen mechanism that can measure range and distance to within yards. At the same time, the radar operator, in his cramped little compartment at the side of the control centre, can immediately detect any hostile radar signals, and radio and signals traffic is also intercepted by a receiver on a mast projecting above the waves. An air of quiet intensity grips the control room as every piece of information is captured and processed, and everyone is alert for the first indication that the presence of the submarine has been detected.

It soon became clear to the captain and his first lieutenant that they were reporting back to soldiers on board the *Conqueror* who had a much better idea of what to look for than they had. A concealed machine gun or mortar emplacement, or camouflaged reinforcing to an abandoned whaling shed, would be far more apparent to David Heaver than to the submarine's crew. So Major Heaver was given some tuition on the periscope, and from then on it was his eyes that were monitoring the movements of the Argentine troops at Grytviken and Leith.

Conqueror cruised close inshore, and surveyed Cumberland Bay East, Stromness Harbour and Leith Harbour. On the next pass along the coast, photos were taken from the periscopes and panoramic mosaics of various beaches and facilities were assembled on the table in the senior ratings' mess so that the SBS troopers could plan their landings.

When the time came for the SBS to disembark, they would use either canoes or Gemini inflatable boats, depending on how close *Conqueror* could approach to the landing site and how extreme the wind and sea conditions were at the time. Once assembled in the boats, on the forward casing, the submarine would slowly submerge until the small craft were floating. When and how Major Heaver and his men would go into action, however, was not for him to decide. The overall planning for the mission had been carried out as the warships *Antrim* and *Plymouth* had steamed from Ascension to South Georgia. The final decision about the insertion of reconnaissance teams and then a full-scale landing would be made by Admiral Fieldhouse, with Captain Brian Young on *Antrim* in tactical control.

The plan that had been produced was essentially in three parts. A group from D Squadron SAS, the Mountain and Arctic Warfare Group, would land by helicopter on the edge of Fortuna Glacier, from where they would travel over the glacier and assess the state of Argentine forces in Leith, Husvik and Stromness. The marines of 2SBS would go by helicopter to Hound Bay, to the south, to assess the approaches to Grytviken. After these teams had made their assessment of the two Argentine garrisons, there would be a night landing of the Royal Marines five or six days later, and the SAS would make a daytime assault on Grytviken.

Antrim and *Plymouth* were due to arrive off South Georgia by 21 April and would start landing the Special Forces almost straight away. The SAS would be carried by Wessex helicopters from *Antrim* and the tanker *Tidespring* from 10 miles out, while *Plymouth* and *Endurance*, which had stayed in the vicinity of South Georgia, receiving radio messages from the British Antarctic Survey team that had remained at large on the island, would helicopter 2SBS to the shore, taking two inflatables out to them the next day. To the men on *Conqueror*, the plans were met with consternation. Despite their equipment, and their recent training in Arctic conditions, 6SBS figured nowhere in the operation. It was extremely frustrating.

The forecast weather was not good, with a predicted increase in winds and a consequent increase in wave height and drop in temperature. In short, a gale was on its way, and there was very little time left before it would hit South Georgia. *Conqueror* had now been given new instructions to operate an anti-shipping patrol to the north-west of the island to protect the small British task force under Captain Young from Argentine warships. Commander Wreford-Brown had also been sent the new rules of engagement allowing him to attack any Argentine warships, submarines or auxiliary vessels that he made contact with and authorizing him to assume that any non-nuclear submarine was Argentinian and could therefore be attacked without any further identification.

Conqueror was experiencing difficulty receiving signals from

Northwood, and also wasn't able to get confirmation that their situation reports were being transmitted successfully. Often the communications satellite would be below the northern horizon, and reception in the southern Atlantic was known to be poor because of this. The sea conditions had been rough as they approached South Georgia, with waves often breaking over the periscope, and Jonty Powis had thought that he had noticed some ice in the water. On 20 April nothing could be received on the high-frequency or very high-frequency channels and at sunrise the WE Artificer Charlie Foy was asked to come up to the control room and look through the periscope at the aerial. What he saw was dismaying. The 'Beehive' aerial on top of the mast was clearly damaged, but also the mast itself was bent at an angle.

The periscopes, aerials and snorkels of a submarine retract into the top of the fin when the submarine submerges, and to reduce the noise from turbulence the top of the fin is automatically covered by shutters that create a smooth, streamlined surface. One of the shutters was now badly distorted, and would neither open properly nor close, and the aerial mast wouldn't fully retract. This was extremely serious for the submarine, because the UHF (Ultra High Frequency) aerial was the main method of receiving the daily signals from Northwood. Moreover, the damaged shutters would cause a quite distinctive noise when the submarine was steaming at any speed.

There was no real alternative but to attempt to repair both the shutters and the aerial. This was easier said than done. The work could be carried out only on the surface and the submarine was in hostile waters, taking part in a secret operation. If they were spotted on the surface by an Argentine reconnaissance aircraft, not only would the presence of the submarine be noted and signalled to any enemy submarines in the area, but it could give the Argentine navy notice of Operation Paraquet and put the Argentine garrison on alert.

Any repairs would have to be carried out at night. *Conqueror* continued to move away from South Georgia to a patrol area to the west, where it would guard the surface ships in Operation Paraquet against a threat from Argentina. As the light faded, the order was given to surface and a young engineering artificer, Steve Mitchell, climbed up the ladder to the bridge, carrying a hammer and pulling oxyacetylene and connecting hoses behind him. He was followed by Charlie Foy. Halfway up, he unscrewed the watertight hatch and dogged it into place. He then had to turn through 90 degrees and grab hold of the next ladder that would take him up to the tiny bridge space 9 feet above. The submarine was rolling heavily now in the rough seas caused by the storm that had picked up the day before and Mitchell was flung against the sides of the hatch as he clambered out. The wind was severe and the temperature was below freezing. The antenna was bent and battered; it had probably been damaged at the same time as the shutters, so it was taken off by the two men. There was a lot of water inside the mast and it was taken down into the submarine. In the after end of the boat there was a lathe and a workbench, and the engineers went to work to see if they could either repair the antenna or build a new one. Meanwhile, Foy and Mitchell started to work on the shutters. The logical thing to do was to cut a hole in the deformed shutter so that the antenna could be properly retracted. Mitchell lay on top of the fin, holding the oxyacetylene torch to cut the hole. He had to work bare handed and was forced to stop every so often to regain the feeling in his hands. He clung on, the fin rolling and jolting in the rough sea like a giant bucking bronco. The weather was getting worse, and he struggled to keep the flame on the cutter alight.

Inside the boat the engineers had managed to rebuild the Beehive antenna, and the amplifier had been put into an oven to dry it out. Foy was attempting to replace it so that it could be reconnected in the fin. This work on the antenna was to take him almost sixteen hours. Despite the worsening weather and the threat of being blown or swept away, he clambered to the top of the fin in an obstinate and determined attempt to get the antenna and its mast working again. The weather was so bad that the watchkeepers had been brought down and Charlie Foy was told that he wouldn't need a life jacket: the sea was so rough that he would never be found if he was swept overboard. The upper lid was shut, and he was advised that if he heard the vents going he was to come down quickly.

There was the constant threat of discovery by Argentine aircraft, and possible attack, particularly as the dawn started to break, but with men working close to the radar mast it was impossible to use it to scan the sky for hostile planes. Commander David Hall, the senior engineer in charge of the operation, remarked that it is always a surprise how quickly people can climb down the fin when they have to, but the truth is that there would have been very little time for both men to re-enter the boat before it submerged, particularly cold and tired as they were, encumbered with their tools and welding equipment. Fortunately, as the repairs dragged on into the next day, snow-storms arrived, helping to reduce visibility and cloaking the presence of the submarine on the surface. The antenna was finally replaced and, although still bent, the repairs to the shutter would allow the mast to be retracted without fouling anything. However, the effects of the damaged aerial would continue to dog HMS *Conqueror* in the days ahead.

While *Conqueror*'s crew and the members of 6SBS were

being tossed around in appalling seas 150 miles to the west of South Georgia, the SAS were making preparations to start their insertion. Their decision to make a landing on the Fortuna Glacier, then to march across it and approach Leith from the rear, puzzled some people. During the planning of the reconnaissance operations, the spokesmen for the SAS were always anxious to stress the need for secrecy. It was true that the numbers of troops in the task group were not as overwhelming as conventional military planners would have liked, and there was still some uncertainty about what reinforcements the Argentinians might have in the area. An unforeseen contact with the enemy before the task force's plans were prepared might cause the whole operation to be aborted. The SAS wanted a landing spot where helicopters would remain undetected, and where the troops could make their own approach to the enemy garrison. Yet it would be hard to think of a more arduous route than a climb over the glacier followed by a long trek over two more high peaks before an approach to Leith Harbour was possible.

The journey had been done before – by the famous explorer Sir Ernest Shackleton. With his ship *Endurance* crushed by the Antarctic ice in the Weddell Sea, he and his crew managed to reach Elephant Island. In April 1916 Shackleton left Elephant Island with five others in an open boat just 22 feet long, heading for South Georgia 800 miles away to get help from the whaling stations that he knew were there. They landed on the south-western side of the island and Shackleton, with two of the crew who were still able to walk, set out to reach the whaling settlements. With just a length of rope and an ice axe they struggled across the ice and rock of the high central mountains. After three days they stumbled nearly dead from cold and exhaustion into Stromness.

The SAS troopers were much fitter, more experienced mountaineers, and much better equipped. After discussion via radio with other SAS members in their headquarters in Hereford, some of whom had recently been on expeditions in the Himalayas, they were convinced that their plan was achievable. The members of the Special Boat Service on *Conqueror*, however, when informed of the plan earlier, had expressed their disbelief. They had recently been on winter training exercises in Norway and had a healthy respect for glaciers and mountain weather generally. Moreover, the storm that had already made life extremely hard for the two members of *Conqueror*'s crew struggling to make repairs on the top of the fin was hurtling eastwards, and was about to bring disaster to Operation Paraquet.

On the morning of 21 April, Northwood had given the go-ahead for the planned reconnaissance landings, and *Antrim* and *Tidespring* were in position 15 miles off the coast. The weather was getting worse: there were clouds down to 400 feet and a gale was blowing from the north-east. Three Wessex helicopters were going to take the SAS troop on to the glacier. One of these, a Wessex 3 from HMS *Antrim*, was equipped with an automatic pilot, allowing the crew to fly it at night and in bad weather low over the ocean on anti-submarine patrols. The other two helicopters, Wessex 5s, were not intended for this type of operation, so the pilots had to rely on quite basic navigation instruments and their own 'mark 1 eyeballs' for judging altitude and drift. In the conditions that would be likely over the glacier, with low clouds, high winds and snow flurries being swept up by the gale, these two would follow the better-equipped Wessex 3, which was piloted by Lieutenant Commander Ian Stanley.

The SAS wanted to be flown to the highest point on the glacier, which entailed flying up its quite steep surface between high mountains on either side, where the helicopters would then enter the cloud base. To go higher might cause icing on the helicopter rotors, which would be fatal, and any deviation in the course could bring about a collision with the cliff face on either side. Landing would also be a risky business, because crevasses, which are created on the surface of the glacier by its downward movement, are often hidden by just a thin layer of ice and snow, incapable of bearing the weight of a helicopter. The insertion would test the flying abilities of the helicopter pilots to the utmost and would require considerable nerve.

After making a preliminary reconnaissance flight in the Wessex 3, Ian Stanley thought that the weather, although changeable, was an acceptable risk, so at 10.30 the three helicopters took off. By the time they reached the island, visibility had dropped like a stone and the helicopters were flying into a wall of snow. They turned back and landed once more on *Antrim* and *Tidespring*. The operation was stalled at this point and time was running out. The CO of D Squadron SAS, Major Delves, and Captain John Hamilton, leader of the Mountain troop, wanted to go to have another look at the insertion point, so, with the weather now slightly improved, Ian Stanley took them up the glacier to look for themselves. There were large numbers of crevasses in the surface, some very large ones at either side of the glacier as it met the cliffs. It was clearly a very difficult site, but time was pressing and Major Delves was anxious that nothing should delay the operation if it could be avoided.

By 11.45 the helicopters with their SAS passengers were in the air once more, their pilots fighting high winds and struggling to discern a horizon between the ice, snow and cloud that formed over the glacier. At times visibility shrank to as low as 50 yards. This time, however, the flight was successful and the sixteen

SAS troopers were landed on the glacier. The winds were severe, gusting to 60 knots, and the SAS men roped themselves together, checked their kit and prepared to pull their sleds loaded with food and ammunition behind them. They had to struggle against the force of the wind, but the major obstacle to progress was the hidden crevasses that they seemed to stumble into almost every 30 yards. They had covered only half a mile before the light started going, and Hamilton thought it wise to start looking for a place to dig themselves in for the night. In the hard ice they had to axe out shallow trenches large enough to hold two men; then they lay down in their sleeping bags, covered themselves with their tents and tried to sleep.

That night the weather got worse. The wind increased to gale force 11, reaching speeds of almost 100 miles an hour. It also brought heavy snow that covered the man-made trenches.

One hundred and fifty miles to the west, *Conqueror* had sent a situation report, received signals and submerged to 260 feet to continue her patrol. Nuclear submariners have an anxiety about conventional submarines that at first seems surprising. Nuclear submarines have an endurance and speed that far surpasses diesel submarines, yet nuclear submarines are far noisier. Whatever precautions are taken, the machinery of a nuclear power plant, depending as it does on pumps, turbines and reduction gears, can never be made completely quiet. The designers of British submarines had put a lot of effort into isolating the noisiest machinery from the pressure hull and help-ing to prevent the transmission of noise to the outside world; consequently they had made the nuclear boats of the Royal Navy much quieter than their Russian adversaries, but a conventional submarine, running on its batteries, was far harder to detect. If a conventional submarine was in the area, it had a good chance of knowing where the *Conqueror* was before the crew of the *Conqueror* could hear it.

The sound environment of a submerged submarine is monitored all the time by the sonar watchkeepers, who are located just off the left side of the control room. They sit in a row, earphones clamped on, mentally focused on the dark waters outside the hull. At the same time, there is a sonar indicator in the control room itself which on the *Conqueror* was like an old-fashioned seismograph, used to measure earthquakes. A stylus traces an ink line over a moving drum of paper.

Jonty Powis saw the trace before he had been told about it. He was convinced it was another submarine:

It was two pens high. In other words it was registering very loud in the high-frequency register. It was the high frequency that was telling me it was a submarine. And he was going fast, the rate of change in the bearing was quite significant. This thing swept past us, clearly relatively close.

The control room went to action stations quickly and *Conqueror* went rapidly to periscope depth, while in the torpedo room the SBS Booties got out of the way as Bill Budding and his team waited for orders of what torpedoes to arm and at what running depth to set them. At periscope depth, however, to the consternation of Jonty Powis, there was no sign of a target of any description.

The sea varies in temperature, salinity and pressure throughout its depth, and these variations affect the way that sound waves pass through it. In the water close to the surface sound can travel in a straight line and be picked up at a range of about

5 miles. But it can be dissipated by the effect of wind and waves on the surface of the sea and by the general turbulence of the sea at periscope depth. Below the surface layer, at various depths there is a layer of sea that is usually colder and denser, and this layer can reflect sound waves, acting as a transmission tunnel. Sound can also be reflected from the deep sea bed, and close to the depth where top and bottom layers meet there are what are known as convergence zones, where sound reflected from the bottom and from the boundary layers meet. At these points sound waves from many miles away can be detected. *Conqueror* dived deep in order to make use of this layer of sea and to chase after the suspected submarine, but the contact was still hard to find. In the torpedo room, Bill Budding was struggling to reload the torpedo tubes with modern Mark 24 torpedos. There was some quick discussion between Jonty Powis, the captain and Tim McClement. The target seemed clearly to be a conventional submarine, running on its batteries. It would be travelling at 7 or 8 knots and might well already have worked out where the *Conqueror* was. Commander Wreford-Brown had recently been given rules of engagement from Northwood that allowed him to fire at any conventional submarine they detected, safe in the knowledge that it could not be British. But with the target submerged and running quietly, the only weapons they could use were their modern Mark 24 torpedoes, which could be guided to the target using sonar location. They decided to make a short sweep with active sonar to locate the target. There was a considerable risk in this, because if the sonar operators on the Argentine submarine were alert it would reveal the position of the *Conqueror*, and the sonar signal might be sufficient for the Argentine submarine to target them and fire a torpedo from their after tubes. Various thoughts ran through Jonty Powis's mind:

You have to accept the fact that you are no longer covert. And you have to choose your transmission mode. There is a big switch in the control room to select a variety of transmissions – how much power you're going to transmit, your angle of search, the interval between transmissions, which affects how far you can see, and so on. When you do something like that and you make detection, you have to fire straight away. You've given yourself away – you can't give them the time to target you, or you're dead.

But to the consternation of everyone in the control room, the contact disappeared. Jonty Powis later discovered that they had made an error in their assumptions about the target. The Argentine submarine, the *Santa Fe*, was not running submerged on batteries, but was on the surface using diesels. Submerged, the *Santa Fe* could make a speed of about 6 knots, but on the surface it could probably travel three times as fast. Lieutenant Powis now thinks that the *Santa Fe* 'was probably three times further away and receding much quicker than we first thought. If we had perhaps come shallower we might, just, have been able to see him on the periscope, but that is just hindsight.'

This encounter was a shock to Powis. It scotched all thoughts he had harboured that it would all end in negotiations. 'It brought me up with a start. There we were, looking for a target, ready to fire at a moment's notice. I thought, this is serious. This is war.'

The *Santa Fe*'s commander, Captain Horacio Bicain, knew nothing of his close encounter with a British nuclear submarine. He wanted to get to South Georgia with his cargo of marines to reinforce the garrison as quickly as possible, but he was shortly forced to submerge and slow his speed, because he had hit the storm that was now centred on the island and making life very difficult for the British forces trying to recapture it.

Out at sea, the two ships *Antrim* and *Tidespring* rode the storm out, with waves breaking over *Antrim*'s bows, the seas too rough to try to get the Wessex helicopter into the shelter of the hangar. The ships jolted and reared throughout the night, with everything lashed down and crew movements kept to a minimum.

As the next day dawned, the SAS patrol clambered out of their snow-covered trenches and tried to assemble their kit, ready for another day's climbing on the glacier. But it was bitterly cold and hard to make headway against the wind. At –20°C the wind was like a razor, cutting through protective clothing and chilling the heart. Spending any time in these conditions without proper shelter would rapidly produce hypothermia. Hamilton signalled to Major Delves, his commanding officer on *Antrim*, that he needed to be evacuated.

The three helicopters flew off once more. Now the pilots were faced with the problem of locating the SAS men on the glacier but, like the day before, enveloped in thick cloud and snow-storms, it was impossible to find them and extremely dangerous for the two Wessex 5 helicopters without an autopilot to attempt the flight up the glacier. They had to turn back.

Two hours later they tried again. By this time the weather had cleared a little and the SAS troop heard the noise of the rotors. They lit orange smoke flares to help the pilots, who were able to land and retrieve the wet, freezing and by now exhausted soldiers. The wind was so powerful that the pilots had to keep their engines running and their noses facing into the 40-knot gusts. One of the Wessex 5s was loaded, so, wanting to waste no time, the pilot took off while the visibility was good – but, as he did so, the disaster that had been threatening the operation for days suddenly overtook him. The helicopter was engulfed in a snow squall and the pilot, flying low to stay underneath the cloud, was suddenly flying blind. Completely disorientated, the helicopter crashed into the glacier, turned on its side and smashed its way over ice, snow and rock for almost 80 yards. In the eerie silence that descended when the helicopter came to a halt, everyone seemed stunned, but, remarkably, they had all survived. Nobody had serious injuries. Kicking out the side windows, they managed to extricate themselves. The other two helicopters put down next to the crash site and everyone scrambled aboard them. There was no reason on God's earth why they should stay there a moment longer. The two remaining helicopters lifted off, at the limit of their take-off weights, and headed down the glacier, the Wessex 5 following the Wessex 3 with its autopilot.

After a few minutes, another snowstorm hit them. Ahead was a high ridge of ice which Ian Stanley managed to fly over because of his ground radar and automatic pilot. The pilot of the following Wessex, Ian Georgeson, could not see the ridge, and his first indication that something was ahead was when his altimeter showed him losing height. The undercarriage of the helicopter struck the ice and the helicopter was flipped on to its side by a powerful gust of wind. The passengers, some of whom had just crashed for the second time in an hour, were now in a state of shock, but eventually stumbled out. The pilot was struggling to free himself and had to be cut out of his harness. Again, remarkably, no one was injured. They knew, however, that they were not going to be rescued for some time, so, gathering together what equipment they could, they inflated the helicopter life rafts and used them as shelter, huddling together for warmth as they prepared to sit out another bitterly cold night.

On the remaining helicopter, they had no knowledge of the fate of their colleagues. What they did know was that the infiltration attempt had failed and they had lost two helicopters. This was the news that was sent to London, and was received by Margaret Thatcher and John Nott with an awful sense of foreboding. They feared that there would be considerable casualties. Nott recalled, 'This was the worst moment of the war for all of us.' The losses were considered to be so politically sensitive that details were even kept from a briefing of the War Cabinet, mainly, it seems, so that the Foreign Secretary should remain in ignorance.

The pilot of *Antrim*'s Wessex 3, Ian Stanley, now demonstrated remarkable courage. The version of the Wessex that he flew was equipped with only one engine, not two like the Wessex 5s, and it had a reputation for unreliability. He knew, however, that lives were at risk on the Fortuna Glacier, so with a load of blankets and medical supplies he flew back to the crash site. The weather was too bad for him to locate the wrecked helicopter and the survivors, but he was able to make contact with them on their radio and learned that everyone was still alive and not seriously injured. After a meal back on board *Antrim*, and with some maintenance on the Wessex, Ian took off again on what he thought was going to be his first rescue attempt. He managed to locate the wreck site visually this time and put the helicopter down. With the weather and the light going again, he decided that he would take everyone out in one go. All the equipment was left, but with the twenty passengers crammed into the helicopter he lifted off, and later made a heavy landing on the *Antrim*.

There was enormous relief at the successful rescue of everyone whose lives had been in such jeopardy just a few hours ago. However, for Captain Brian Young, commander of the task group on *Antrim*, the situation was serious. After a delay of two days nothing had been achieved, and he had lost two-thirds of his helicopter force.

The SBS reconnaissance team on *Endurance* had done just as badly. Their plan was to be flown from the *Endurance* to Hound Bay, then cross on foot to Cumberland Bay East. There the *Endurance*'s helicopters would drop inflatable boats, and the SBS troop would cross Cumberland Bay to make a landfall behind the high ground that overlooked Grytviken and King Edward Point, where the main Argentine force was stationed.

The helicopters on *Endurance*, Westland Wasps, were much smaller than the Wessex helicopters on *Antrim* and *Plymouth*; they could take four passengers, their personal kit and not much else. The Wasp was designed to be carried on small warships as a submarine killer. It didn't have any sonar equipment, but could carry several depth-charges or anti-submarine torpedoes, and was directed to the target from the control room of its parent ship. Subsequently the Wasp was fitted with French-manufactured AS-12 anti-ship missiles, designed primarily to attack small, fast patrol boats. The Wasp had largely been super-seded on Royal Navy ships by bigger and more powerful helicopters, but two were kept on *Endurance* because they were useful, strong and fairly easy to maintain – important consider-ations for a ship that spent most of its time in a harsh, remote location.

It would take several flights in the small Wasp to get all the 2SBS marines to their starting point in Hound Bay. The first flight took off at 17.30, landed two men and their kit, returned to *Endurance* and then flew two more on to the insertion point. By then the weather was starting to deteriorate, but there were still eight members of the SBS troop on *Endurance* and clearly the operation couldn't start until all the men were in place. The pilot of the Wasp made an attempt to fly two more men into the beach at Hound Bay at 03.00 hours, but was met with such fierce head-winds, turbulence and snowstorms that he abandoned the effort. In the dark, over a heaving sea, battered by gales, struggling to maintain course and altitude, with snow squalls suddenly obscuring any view forward or down, everyone on board the small helicopter must have wondered whether they would survive the trip. In a last attempt to get the reconnaissance mission under way, the remaining men of 2SBS on *Endurance* decided to make their insertion by inflatable, and they landed further down the coast.

The next day a Wasp helicopter with two inflatable boats slung beneath it in a net met the SBS troop on the eastern edge of Cumberland Bay East, and the men prepared to make their journey across the bay to land behind King Edward Point. The Nordenskold Glacier enters the sea at the foot of the bay, form-ing a massive cliff of ice that continually calves icebergs into the bay, the waters of which are littered with slabs of almost-submerged ice called 'growlers', the remains of pack ice and the large bergs that every so often crash into the sea from the top of the glacier. It is a hazardous location. To their dismay, the men of 2SBS found that one of the inflatables had been damaged in the flight from *Endurance* to the beach and was not seaworthy. Making a quick decision, the leader of the troop decided that half the troop were to remain on shore, while he and the rest attempted the journey to the landing point across the bay. They set out, but the prevailing winds were driving ice across the bay, threatening to crush the inflatable. The men struggled on, but made almost no headway against the wind. The gap in the ice was narrowing and they decided they had to turn back. On shore they signalled *Antrim* to be picked up, but *Antrim* had departed out of range of their radios and they were not picked up for another day.

HMS *Antrim* had moved out of radio range because the Argentinians had been making increasingly regular reconnaissance flights over the island and it seemed to Captain Young that they had clearly spotted *Antrim* and *Plymouth* and probably also knew that *Endurance* was to the south. Not only was there the danger that the Argentine troops on South Georgia would be fully prepared for any assault when it happened, but there was a very good chance that intelligence about his position was being passed to the submarine *Santa Fe*, which must by now be in the area.

The situation for the Paraquet task group was looking even more serious than it had just a day earlier. Captain Young had lost two of his three helicopters and had no intelligence about the disposition of Argentine forces on the island to show for it. His main force of marines was further out to sea on RFA *Tidespring*, which was waiting to meet another tanker, *Brambleleaf*, to transfer 7,000 tons of fuel, which his destroyer and the frigate *Plymouth* would soon need. An Argentine submarine was heading towards him, not only posing a threat to the warships and the two tankers with 150 troops on board, but also potentially able to reinforce the Argentine troops on South Georgia. Captain Young and the commanding officer of the landing force, Major Sheridan, had both received messages from Northwood asking why there were delays to their schedule. At the same time, Brian Young had had a conversation on the secure voice satellite communications system with the Chief of Staff at Northwood, Admiral Halifax, which stressed the need for Young to avoid shipping losses. How he was to invade an island without risking ships, particularly in his current situation and in the conditions he faced in South Georgia, was not addressed.

Operation Paraquet now started to eat into the resources of Admiral Woodward's task force, still attempting to make the best time possible to the Falkland Islands. There was only one way that the loss of the two helicopters could be made up, and that was to detach another frigate from the spearhead group moving in advance of the main task group and send it to join *Antrim* and *Plymouth*. HMS *Brilliant* was selected and steamed at full speed to join up with the ships to the north of South Georgia. Captain Young had considered a plan to make a frontal assault on King Edward Point, but the threat of being locked in by the approaching submarine *Santa Fe* made him abandon this option.

At roughly the same time as *Brilliant* was detached, *Conqueror*, with 6SBS still on board and apparently redundant in the fight for South Georgia, had by now received orders from Northwood to leave the South Georgia exclusion zone and make speed to the west to reinforce the submarine screen of the main task force.

The *Santa Fe* was now to become the bête noire of Operation Paraquet, threatening to undermine the whole adventure. The repossession of South Georgia had been conceived primarily as a political gesture, which would maintain Britain's momentum for war and put further pressure on the Argentine junta. The military value of recapturing the island was questionable, yet if it resulted in casualties, or failure, or both, it would call into question the wisdom of attempting to recapture the Falklands Islands themselves.

Captain Young decided that some Special Forces had to be

landed on South Georgia to provide the much-needed intelligence about the state of Argentine forces on the island, but once this was achieved he would need to organize his small group of ships to counter the submarine threat. Nothing else could be done while the *Santa Fe* lurked threateningly in the vicinity.

Captain Young took the *Antrim* close into Stromness Bay, and fifteen men of the SAS boat troop prepared to land on Grass Island, from where they could make observations of activity in Stromness. From there a small party would cross to the mainland and take up position on the hill overlooking Leith. Five inflatables were launched, but only three managed to land, and those did so with great difficulty. Two were swept out to sea, and the Wessex from *Antrim* had to travel down the coast to rescue three SAS troopers whose inflatable was being carried out into the South Atlantic. The soldiers on the other inflatable finally managed to restart their outboard and landed 3 or 4 miles along the coast from Grass Island. With a reconnaissance team now finally landed, Captain Young could devote his attention to the *Santa Fe*.

The Paraquet cell in Northwood had made their own calculations about the progress of the *Santa Fe* since she had left port on 9 April. They had calculated that the Argentine submarine would be in the vicinity of South Georgia around 24 or 25 April, and once it had achieved its objective of landing reinforcements would then seek deeper water in which to prepare for an attack on the British warships.

The Flag Officer Submarines now reversed his previous order. At 00.37 GMT *Conqueror* came to periscope depth and received signal COR 99, which instructed Commander Wreford-Brown to return to the area of South Georgia that he had left just twenty-seven hours ago and maintain a hunt for the *Santa Fe*. *Conqueror* duly changed course and started the 165-mile journey back to the island at 21 knots. Once on the previous day the sonar operators had picked up a noise that was taken to be a diesel-engine signature, but it had faded, and then again on the journey back to South Georgia a target was picked up with similar characteristics. Each time the signature was lost when *Conqueror* went deep to find a convergence layer. This may have been the *Santa Fe* running on the surface, but even if it was it was by now too close to South Georgia to be intercepted. Throughout the day Bill Budding, assisted by the SBS, struggled to reload torpedo tubes with wire-guided Mark 24 torpedoes for use against the *Santa Fe*, removing the Mark 8s that had previously been loaded. The effort to move the SBS equipment, to find room for the Mark 8s before the Mark 24s were loaded, and vice versa, had been going on for days with the change of tasking and different rules of engagement. Events, however, were to make all this effort unnecessary.

On the night of 24 April, the *Santa Fe* docked at Grytviken in Cumberland Bay and the Argentine marines were disembarked. Captain Bicain's orders were to leave Grytviken as soon as possible and head out to sea to attack the British force that was attempting to retake South Georgia. His rules of engagement were unambiguous: he could attack any warship that he saw. The aircrew of the Wessex helicopter on *Antrim* reasoned that Bicain would be taking his submarine into and out of Cumberland Bay on the surface, because of the threat of ice, and wanted to install a radar set and conduct some search operations. They were remarkably astute. Captain Young ordered the Wessex to be ready to fly at first light, armed with two depth-charges, and the Wasps on *Endurance* were to be ready in support, armed with their AS-12 missiles. *Brilliant*, which had by now arrived on the scene, would provide a Lynx helicopter carrying two torpedoes.

On the morning of the 25th, at around 6 a.m., the *Santa Fe* put to sea and the Wessex picked it up as it passed the headland. Captain Bicain assumed that the helicopter would be armed with torpedoes and decided to stay on the surface, which was his biggest mistake. The pilot of the Wessex, Ian Stanley, made a classic attack on the *Santa Fe*. Quickly estimating the speed of the submarine, he calculated his aiming point and the speed that he needed to achieve, and approached from the rear along the centre line of the submarine. He launched, and saw one depth-charge bounce high off the casing of the submarine before exploding in the water; the other landed close to the side. Two columns of water exploded into the air, and the stern of the sub-marine was lifted clear of the sea. The *Santa Fe* was damaged, its port ballast tank ruptured and an oil tank cracked. Captain Bicain could not submerge at all now even if he wanted to. He changed course, to head back to the Argentine garrison at Grytviken, but the Lynx from *Brilliant* now approached and confirmed the good fortune of Bicain staying on the surface. Nick Butler on the Lynx launched a torpedo designed to home in automatically on submerged submarines. The *Santa Fe* being on the surface, however, the torpedo passed harmlessly underneath. Captain Bicain and his crew must have been extremely shaken. The attack was sudden and unexpected, and they had no defence against air attack. They sent out an emergency Mayday call to the garrison saying that they had been attacked by a helicopter. They must have become even more frightened when the crew of the Wasp helicopter from *Endurance* was given their position and decided not to wait for orders but to go in. Tom Ellerbeck, the pilot of the Wasp helicopter from *Endurance*, got a fix on the submarine at 2 miles and fired one of his AS-12 missiles. It hit the *Santa Fe* on its fin, but because most of the fin was made of glass fibre it didn't explode. It hit a crewmember who was in the fin trying to fire a machine gun at the attacking helicopters, and he fell down the ladder into the control room, bleeding from a badly injured leg.

By this time the Wessex from *Antrim* had had a chance to re-arm, and another Lynx from *Brilliant* had taken off. The submarine was now being attacked by five helicopters. Captain Bicain managed to approach the jetty at King Edward Point but still the attacks went on.

The final assault was made again by the Wasp from *Endurance*, when the *Santa Fe* was tied up and Captain Bicain had already instructed his crew to disembark. The missile was launched and flew towards the fin, where this time it exploded, blowing pieces of pressure hull, aerials and periscope violently into the air.

The war had been brought immediately and devastatingly home to the Argentine marines and troops in Grytviken. Suddenly they were confronted with the presence of an apparently overwhelming force of British helicopters who had arrived from God knew where.

Major Sheridan on *Antrim* realized the impact the sudden return of the *Santa Fe*, damaged and defenceless, must have had on the Argentine troops, and argued that an attack should now be mounted with whatever forces were available before they had a chance to reassess the situation and take proper defensive measures. Captain Young agreed. The main force of marines was still on *Tidespring*, which had cleared the area and was still fifteen hours' sailing time away, but Young issued orders giving one hour's notice to all the forces that were immediately available to disembark and land on South Georgia. Altogether, with some elements of the Royal Marines on *Antrim* and some of the SAS troops, they could put together a force of seventy-nine soldiers. These would be put ashore south of Grytviken; meanwhile *Antrim* and *Plymouth* would start shelling the landing area and the high ground around it.

Antrim's Wessex helicopter and the two Lynxes from *Brilliant* landed all the troops in forty-five minutes, and they started to approach Grytviken. At 4 p.m. *Antrim* entered Cumberland Bay to improve her aim on King Edward Point. The naval bombardment, using the 4.5-inch guns on *Antrim* and *Plymouth*, was very accurate; it was directed by a naval gunnery support officer who had been landed by helicopter at the beginning of the assault. Shells were landing as close as 1,000 yards from the building on Grytviken, making an enormous noise and creating clouds of dust and debris. In all, the first naval gunfire of the Falklands campaign delivered 225 high-explosive shells on the area around the Argentine troops. Within minutes of the bombardment starting, Captain Bicain had decided to surrender. His situation was clearly hopeless: it was obvious that any attempt to fight would bring down the deadly gunfire directly on to him. The British troops approaching King Edward Point saw a white flag flying, and Bicain got on the radio to say that he wished to surrender. At 29 minutes past 5 in the afternoon London time, Young sent a signal to Commander-in-Chief Fleet: 'Argentine forces in Grytviken surrendered at 251715Z [25 April at 17.15 Zulu or Greenwich Mean Time] to British Forces.'

To Margaret Thatcher, John Nott and the other members of the War Cabinet, it can only have come as a blessed relief. Just four days earlier they had been confronted with the news that two helicopters had crashed and the lives of their crewmembers and the SAS troopers perhaps lost. Then for days Operation Paraquet seemed to be falling apart, needing reinforcements from the main task force. Now, in a complete reversal of fortune, victory had been delivered to them. Little wonder that Margaret Thatcher instructed the press that evening to 'Rejoice, just rejoice' – an indication, perhaps, of the despair she had felt at the possibility of failure.

There was only one other thing to do to secure the island of South Georgia and that was to deal with the garrison at Leith along the coast. This was headed by Lieutenant Commander Alfredo Astiz, the notorious torturer from the Navy Mechanical School in Buenos Aires that had been the centre of the torture and interrogations of the military junta. Astiz was wanted for questioning by the French and Spanish governments for the disappearance in Buenos Aires of their subjects. Now he was called upon to surrender, and at first he said that the civilian workers in Leith – the original demolition men who had landed as part of Señor Davidoff's salvage contract – would do so but that the marines were prepared to fight. This was clearly a delaying tactic, in the hope that the Argentine government might be able to mount some form of air attack, and indeed some Canberra jet bombers did take off to attack British shipping, but turned back because of bad weather and the difficulty of attacking the ships inside the bay. *Plymouth* was ready to start another bombardment by naval gunfire before the marines were landed, but at that point Astiz announced his surrender. Yet even then he was prepared to plant demolition charges on the helicopter landing pad and detonate them when Captain Barker of the *Endurance* landed there. Barker, fortunately, decided at the last moment not to follow Astiz's instructions for landing, and Leith fell without either British or Argentine casualties.

*

With the end of the fighting, and a successful conclusion to Operation Paraquet, Commander Wreford-Brown could look again to rejoin the nuclear submarine force. But first he had to disembark his group of 6SBS Booties, who had by now been on his submarine for more than three weeks. They were becoming jaded and out of condition, having been cooped up in the close confines of the submarine for so long. The submariners on board had a great deal of respect and liking for them, but whatever efforts the crew had made to give them space to train and practise, the Booties were wasted on the boat. They were there because orders had been issued without proper thought or preparation. They had carried out their reconnaissance of South Georgia, but isolated on the submarine they had been unable to influence or contribute to the plan to take the island and, given the weather conditions, may never have been able to make an effective landing directly from the *Conqueror*. In retrospect, it is clear that they should have been allowed to continue on their original mission and land on the Falklands. As Jonty Powis said:

> That was one of the things about the marines watching the SAS make a complete arse of themselves on the Fortuna Glacier – nobody seemed to realize that we had Arctic-qualified, Arctic-acclimatized marines on board who would have known that landing on a glacier was a pretty bad idea. They missed their opportunity, but, you know, there's a measure of luck in all these things.

On 26 April they received orders to disembark and transfer the SBS troop with its equipment by helicopter to HMS *Antrim*. *Conqueror* surfaced at the mouth of Cumberland Bay, where the crew started to unload the enormous amount of armaments, inflatable boats and other equipment that had been loaded so urgently at Faslane on to the forward deck of the submarine. The sea was rough and dotted with whitecaps, there was a force 8 wind blowing and it was close to darkness. Ten of the troop had been airlifted off when Wreford-Brown decided to call off the operation as it was becoming unsafe.

Conqueror's radio mast had failed again, with part of the fairing missing, so she stayed on the surface for more repairs. Wreford-Brown's only method of communication was by signal light to *Antrim*. Charlie Foy went up to the fin again and found the mast badly damaged. There were salt deposits in the connections and the mast was letting in a lot of seawater. He made contact, finally, with *Antrim* and used the destroyer's communications to forward a situation report to Northwood. *Conqueror* was in a bad state.

Next day, the 27th, the wind had eased slightly but the seas were still running high. There were still four more SBS troopers and the remaining stores to transfer. The outer casing deck of a submarine is flat for a width of about 6 feet and painted with anti-slip paint but, unlike on a surface vessel, there are no safety rails and no clear distinction between the deck, the hull and the ocean. Petty Officer 'Horse' Libby, the 'scratcher' responsible for the safe stowage and seagoing condition of the deck, was overseeing the transfer, organizing the deck party. The SBS troopers were issued with life jackets and were dressed in their own survival gear; Libby was wearing waterproof leggings and a white submarine sweater underneath a life jacket. The equipment was being brought up the conning tower and through the front hatch on the front of the fin to be laid on to the cargo net. Running down the side of the casing is a grooved channel so that anybody working on the deck can clip a safety line into it.

Libby was holding a long earthing pole, rather like a boat hook, with which he had to touch the approaching helicopter before anything else was attached because helicopters can build up a large charge of static electricity. The pole earths this charge to the boat or to the sea before anybody physically touches the helicopter. As Libby stood there, pole in the air waiting for the helicopter:

> The next thing I know, this wave has come from nowhere, the submarine dipped down, came back up and the next wave swept me, the cargo net and the SBS trooper into the sea. I had the weight of the cargo net on me and as it pulled me down the life-line broke. Which was lucky otherwise I would have drowned. The submarine just kept going – it's such a big beast it can't just stop.

Libby could see the helicopter in the air, but the ice-cold water was clutching him. He started to feel the heat flowing out of his body. The helicopter sent down only one strop, for both Libby and the SBS man.

> We sort of look at each other, and he's quite happy sat there in his dry suit, and I'm going blue, and he's sort of looking at me to say 'I'm going first,' and I'm thinking, 'I'm going first.' In the end we both went in the same harness. I was very close to collapse because of the cold.

Both men were taken to the *Antrim* and immediately put into a bath of cold water to try to get their circulation going. Libby spent six hours on *Antrim* recovering. He was officially classified as a survivor, and was given a survivor's kit – new clothes and plimsolls. When he was flown back to *Conqueror* later that day some of the crew were envious of his gifts, forgetting what he had been through to get them.

Conqueror remained on the surface, however, because the communications problems that the radio officers were experiencing were now severe. The submarine had made a cracking pace down to South Georgia, but had, at the end of the day, made little contribution to the success of the operation. The SBS had remained as passengers, and had now left on a surface warship to take part in the main effort against the Falklands. *Conqueror*, however, had never really recovered from the damage done on her initial approach to South Georgia over a week ago. Without adequate communications, there was a question mark over whether she could remain as part of Operation Corporate at all.

9

CONQUEROR ON STATION

Conqueror remained on the surface near Cumberland Bay throughout 27 April and into the next morning. Her officers visited *Antrim* and talked to the communications experts on the other ships to request advice, and also to get messages sent to Northwood.

The prospect that *Conqueror* might not be able to take any further part in Operation Corporate ignited once again the simmering conflict between Admiral Woodward and the commander of the task force, Admiral Fieldhouse, about the best way of controlling the submarine forces in the South Atlantic. Naturally, as the task group approached the Falklands and the 200-mile total exclusion zone, this question became increasingly pressing.

Woodward believed that he had the staff on board his flagship HMS *Hermes* to have a local submarine force coordinator.

Hermes had all the necessary communications facilities and, perhaps most importantly, it made more sense to Woodward that there should be local control to deal with a quickly changing set of circumstances with early and prompt action. Woodward also wanted to change the submarines' operating method. In the NATO area, in the North Atlantic and the Arctic, the main task of Britain's submarines was anti-submarine warfare against the Soviet navy, with large numbers of ships and submarines engaged in close proximity to the enemy and to each other. In order to control the submarines and prevent them attacking each other (known as blue on blue), each submarine was allocated a specific part of the ocean, and they were not allowed to trespass in other submarines' allocated areas. When submarines wish to move, or return to port, or are instructed to go to a specific location, they are allowed to do so only on a course that is specified or agreed to by the submarine controller at Northwood, in a signal known as a 'Subnote'. In this way the controller can keep track of all the submarines, including the nuclear-tipped missile-carrying 'bombers', and avoid any conflicts between submarines, or between submarines and surface warships and aircraft.

Woodward thought that this was unnecessary in the South Atlantic. Argentina possessed only four conventional submarines, one of which, the *Santa Fe*, had already been captured in South Georgia. As long as the nuclear submarines were prevented from attacking submerged targets until they were confirmed as conventional, they could be released from their patch and directed by Woodward to any group of Argentinian surface ships that was most threatening.

By 28 April the area around the Falklands had been divided up into three large areas and *Splendid* was patrolling in the north-west, closest to the threat from the Argentine navy; *Spartan* was patrolling to the north-east; and *Conqueror* was allocated to an area to the south of the islands, but was still, of course, in the area of South Georgia. Commander Jeff Tall on *Hermes* thought that Admiral Woodward's determination to gain control of the submarines was absolutely right. Moreover, he thought that the large area of water space that the submarines were being allocated was wrong:

We were subdividing the South Atlantic into just three areas. It took away all flexibility. I asked the question 'What if something happens over here and we need more than one submarine?' I didn't get an answer. So we began to understand at a very early stage that Northwood had no feeling for either the fight in hand or what was needed to fight a fast-moving scenario. I suggested that we could have a hot-pursuit scenario, where if one of our submarines was in hot pursuit of a high-value surface unit they could cross into the other sub's water. I got a reply saying that 'The Mark 24 [the new sonar-guided torpedo on the submarines] can't distinguish between friend or foe.' Well that was nonsense. What you do is the submarine in contact with a surface target sets a floor depth to the torpedo and the other submarine stays below it.

The other problem, as Woodward and Tall saw it, was that Northwood was setting the rules of engagement as well, 'so that effectively the Admiral [Woodward] had no retaliation capability'. He could not order his submarines to fire back at anything.

On the way down to the Falklands total exclusion zone, the British satellite communications system Gapfiller, which was in use by the navy in the North Atlantic, would often disappear below the horizon the further south the task group went. In order to avoid gaps in communication, Britain had leased two channels on the US Department of Defense's own Satcom satellites. Admiral Woodward was not prepared to continue the fight with Admiral Fieldhouse and FOSM over control of the submarines on a network on which the Americans might eavesdrop. He felt the dispute was a sensitive internal discussion and would only harm relations with the United States defence establishment if it became known. Jeff Tall, however, had made use of *Conqueror*'s dispatch to South Georgia, and the subsequent toing and froing, to make a formal request that *Conqueror* be placed under associated support – in other words, that Admiral Woodward could give instructions to *Conqueror*'s captain as long as they were sent via the Flag Officer Submarines. Northwood, to Commander Tall's surprise, agreed. He thinks that it may have been prompted by a desire to keep him quiet, 'To stop Tall jumping up and down again is what I've heard,' he says. Whatever the real reasons, it was a minor victory and was to prove extremely important. Intelligence which was passed to Jeff Tall from the captured *Santa Fe* emphasized that there was no reason for Northwood to fear a submarine-versus-submarine conflict. Embedded in the considerable amount of technical specifications and operational doctrine that was found on the submarine was the important information that the new wire-guided torpedoes, AST4, carried by the *Santa Fe* and the other Argentine submarines could be used only against surface ships. Intriguingly, Jeff Tall also learned that the Argentine navy had adopted a US navy doctrine about nuclear submarines:

Every time they'd operate with the Americans, in the planning document AX25 it specifically instructs planners not to task a nuclear submarine within the hundred-fathom line. In other words, they wouldn't expect a nuclear sub in water shallower than 600 feet. But we go much shallower than that. In training we'll go to 35 fathoms, not 100.

The importance of this last piece of intelligence was to become apparent later, but for now the more that Commander Tall learned about the Argentine submarines, the more angry he became at the inflexibility of Northwood's position. In a sense this was because he was frustrated at not being able to do the job he had expected to do when he joined HMS *Hermes* in Portsmouth. Captain Buchanan, the senior submariner on board, had been appointed Group Warfare Officer, as a deputy to Woodward, and Commander Tall was now not only the sole officer on the task force dealing with FOSM and the submarine controllers in Northwood, who were senior in rank to him, but was also bearing the brunt of Admiral Woodward's own frustration at his lack of control over the submarines in the task force.

The absurdity of the situation was also apparent to submarine captains, particularly those of *Spartan* and *Splendid*, who had been patrolling the area for almost a fortnight. Commander Roger Lane-Nott, the commanding officer of *Splendid*, felt that at times it was not clear who was in charge. He was highly critical of some of the intelligence he received in his signals, which in his opinion showed that the submarine controllers in Northwood did not understand the situation in the South Atlantic: 'They did not put themselves in our shoes.' The intelligence reports never had any weighting to them, essential for the submarine's commanders to assess their value, and consequently a great deal of time and possibly opportunity was lost. Various people, from the War Cabinet down, felt able to give orders for submarine movements. The Defence Secretary had ordered *Splendid*, via the Chiefs of Staff, to get into position for retaliation against the Argentine fleet in case the *Santa Fe* should sink a British warship off South Georgia. Lord Lewin, Chief of the Defence Staff, ordered *Splendid* to sail almost 1,000 miles to intercept the aircraft carrier the *Veinticinco de Mayo*, largely, it seems, for presentational reasons at a Cabinet meeting. When it was realized that *Splendid* had no rules of engagement that would allow her captain to take any action once he found the carrier, the orders were reversed. At one point *Splendid* was instructed to go to the mouth of Falkland Sound to prevent the Argentine aircraft carrier from taking up station there. There was not much depth of water in the Sound and there was nowhere for the submarine to escape to once they had fired torpedoes at the carrier, particularly as she would have been accompanied by several escorts. Nevertheless *Splendid* negotiated her way into the mouth of the Sound and waited. They saw nothing, and after twenty-four hours were told to abandon the position. Lane-Nott chafed at the tight control that Northwood attempted to exercise. There was also a constant demand for situation reports:

> an obsession with information feedback. I was being asked to send sitreps [situation reports] when I didn't have anything to say. I sent a hundred and three sitreps back to Northwood, and that was a hundred and two more than was necessary. But I had the ability to talk to *Hermes*, but was not allowed to.

The level of interference in the movements of the two nuclear submarines was quite absurd, and was to have serious repercussions when the fighting started in a few days' time.

Unlike the captain of *Splendid*, who felt oppressed by the demands that his communications channels placed on him, Commander Wreford-Brown on *Conqueror* felt extremely frustrated by the lack of communication he received and the difficulty he had in communicating with anybody. He had only once had the experience of a rapid reversal of orders and that had been when he had been sent away from South Georgia, then a day later sent back again.

Now there was the real possibility that *Conqueror* would have to return to Ascension Island for a mast change and repairs to her aerials. It looked to Wreford-Brown as if *Conqueror*'s war was over. He was extremely disappointed: the submarine had a reputation for running, in the words of her chief engineer, 'as reliably as a sewing machine. Wind her up and off she'd go like a clockwork mouse.' It was a potentially frustrating end to Wreford-Brown's first command, particularly as he had by now gained the respect of his officers and crew.

But the Commander Task Group had other ideas. Admiral Woodward was very unhappy at the prospect of losing one of his submarines. They were what allowed him to sleep at night, so having managed to get *Conqueror* under associated support, Commander Tall objected to any question of her returning to Ascension, arguing that Northwood had to demonstrate that she was not capable of carrying out the tasks that Admiral Woodward required of her. On board *Conqueror*, Wreford-Brown held a meeting in the wardroom with all the officers in charge of his various departments on the boat. He made it clear to them that he wanted a solution found to the communications problem and was determined not to have to go back to Ascension.

On the morning of the 28th, Wreford-Brown received a signal giving him instructions to proceed to the west, with coordinates for his patrol area to the south of the Falkland Islands. But reception was still extremely erratic, and messages had to be downloaded several times before they could be properly decoded and understood. However, *Conqueror* started to make her way slowly west through an area heavily infested with icebergs. On the 29th Wreford-Brown received another signal, this time sent on a high-frequency broadcast via New Zealand, telling him that he was now working with Woodward's task group in associated support. He also had new rules of engagement for the Falklands.

There was still the problem of communications to be solved, and the combined expertise of the task group and Northwood had come up with a fix that *Conqueror* could try. The submarine was fitted with a wire aerial about 300 feet in length. It was necessary to surface to deploy it from the rear of the fin, but they could then submerge to periscope depth while the aerial was trailed behind to receive very low-frequency transmissions sent out every four hours from Northwood. This aerial had a high-frequency connector, and it could be used with a modified end to pick up high-frequency broadcasts. There was some doubt about this plan on the submarine; Wreford-Brown was worried that trailing the aerial on the surface might increase his chances of being detected by Argentine anti-submarine aircraft. However, on 30 April, after the engineering and communications artificers had got to work in *Conqueror*, she surfaced at 11.25 and streamed the wire. It worked. Reception of all the signals was greatly improved, and they continued to get better as the *Conqueror* steamed west. The modification was an excellent decision. It seemed that the communications problem, while it had not been solved, was at least containable.

*

Conqueror's orders were to operate an anti-surface vessel patrol to the south and south-west of the Falklands, operating inside and outside the 200-mile total exclusion zone. In particular she was to locate and remain with the Argentine task group TG79.3. This was the cruiser *Belgrano* and two destroyers, *Hipólito Bouchard* and *Piedra Buena,* with an oil tanker, the *Puerto Rosales,* and an oceangoing tug, *Gurruchaga.* The assessment given to Wreford-Brown was that this force was conducting operations in shallow water 40 miles to the north of the Isla de los Estados. He was particularly instructed to report if there was any indication that the group was heading towards South Georgia.

Admiral Woodward's main concern, on the other hand, as his ships steamed ever closer to the total exclusion zone and what he knew would be the start of the fighting, was the location of the Argentine navy's flagship, its aircraft carrier the *Veinticinco de Mayo.*

This was the ship that Woodward knew could cause serious havoc to his plans, and he had to deal with it sooner rather than later. Woodward knew that the Argentine air force had overwhelming superiority in aircraft numbers. The key question of their effectiveness was the extent to which they would be able to use the runway at Stanley. If they couldn't, their range from the mainland would limit the amount of time they could spend attacking the task group and would give his Sea Harriers a fighting chance. The aircraft carrier was another matter, however. It was mobile and could operate with fighter protection to give the Skyhawk bombers a range that exceeded the eastern limits of the total exclusion zone. Woodward's only protection against the carrier was the submarine screen that was in place around the Falklands. If they couldn't find the carrier and deal with it, he could not take his task force close to the Falklands and risk losing either HMS *Hermes* or *Invincible*.

Woodward's second problem with the Argentine carrier was not only finding it and trailing it, but convincing his political masters that, once found, it should be attacked immediately. What he needed were rules of engagement for the submarines that allowed their commanders to sink the *Veinticinco de Mayo* as soon as they had positively identified it. The submarines, however, did not have such rules. They were restricted to attacking warships outside the total exclusion zone only in self-defence. Woodward knew that the first sign of an act of aggression from the Argentine aircraft carrier would be a group of aircraft, perhaps armed with Exocet anti-ship missiles, making a determined attack on one of his ships and sinking it. By then it would be too late.

The rules of engagement that existed might be satisfactory to deal with a surface warship that would need to approach to within 25 miles before it could launch its Exocet missiles, but the carrier had a range of perhaps 500 nautical miles from its port, and its aircraft had a range of about 400 nautical miles on top of this. It was therefore always a threat, at whatever distance it was sailing from the task force.

Woodward made his views felt, but the War Cabinet was worried about Britain being cast in the role of an aggressor if it appeared to sink the Argentine carrier miles from the exclusion zone and without any warning. The politicians were worried not only about world opinion, and pressures to negotiate that were coming from the United States and the United Nations; they were also worried about maintaining a fragile consensus for war in the British electorate. At a Cabinet meeting on 23 April, where the issue was discussed, William Whitelaw wondered if public opinion was ready to see a carrier sunk. Margaret Thatcher argued that this might be preferable to attacks on mainland Argentine airfields, which might be seen to be threatening civilians' lives.

As the task force approached the exclusion zone around the Falklands and the prospect of battle grew ever more imminent, these issues of presentation were increasingly irrelevant to Woodward. The discussions about changing the rules of engagement seemed as though they were taking place on another planet, where time and men's lives were of no importance.

In London, making the running for the argument to sink the carrier were the old sea dogs Sir Henry Leach, the First Sea Lord, and Lord Lewin, the Chief of Defence Staff, neither of whom needed any reminding of the danger of carrier-borne aircraft to warships at sea.

Sir Henry Leach was the most determined, hardly wavering from a position that would allow the submarines to sink the carrier without warning. He argued that the existence of the carrier was a permanent threat to the security of the Falkland Islands, and that it should be sunk. Lord Lewin argued also that the carrier was a serious threat to the amphibious forces and that it had to be dealt with by 3 May, the date that it was expected the British task force would be in the exclusion zone and attacking Argentine forces. But they did not win over some of the objectors from among their own members on the Chiefs of Staff Committee, and so the issue had to be reviewed further. As part of this process, various intelligence assessments were produced to inform ministers about the capabilities of the carrier and its aircraft. There was considerable room for speculation. There were questions about the mechanical reliability of the carrier's engines, the numbers of aircraft it could carry and how the

Argentine navy would choose to deploy them. There were even uncertainties about the types of aircraft that could operate from the flight deck of the *Veinticinco de Mayo* and what level of training had been carried out. One paper that was passed to the War Cabinet said that:

> Argentina has one old carrier. However she can carry seven to nine Skyhawk aircraft and up to five Super Etendard aircraft. Both types of aircraft are capable of mounting air to air and air to surface attacks at a distance of about 400 miles from the carrier. The six Tracker aircraft can carry out radar surveillance operations up to 500 miles from the carrier, giving her the ability to direct other air and naval units into attack positions as well as using her own offensive aircraft.

By 1 May the assessment had shifted. It was now considered that the French-supplied Super Etendard, supersonic aircraft capable of carrying Exocet anti-ship missiles had not previously been flown from the carrier, and it was highly unlikely that the Argentine navy would attempt to do so. Furthermore, problems with the flight deck, in particular its arrester gear, might affect its ability to launch its Skyhawk A-4Q aircraft, which were elderly American jet aircraft armed with anti-aircraft missiles and conventional freefall bombs.

By the time this assessment was issued, the rules of engagement had been changed. This was largely due to the persistence of Sir Henry Leach, backed up by Lord Lewin. They were perhaps the best people to understand the problems now immediately confronting Admiral Woodward. Shifting assessments from the Joint Intelligence Committee about the nature of the threat from the carrier would cut no ice if an error of their judgement cost the lives of British sailors or the loss of ships. Lewin forcefully argued to the War Cabinet that if the carrier could sail 500 miles in a day and launch aircraft with an operating radius of 400 miles, it was always going to threaten the task force. The War Cabinet was also influenced by the realization that the shooting war was imminent. Plans were under way for the RAF to bomb the runway at Stanley in order to deny its use to Argentine fighters and bombers. This would make little sense if the task force could be threatened from any direction by aircraft taking off from the flight deck of the *Veinticinco de Mayo*. In the face of these arguments the War Cabinet finally acquiesced to Lewin's demand and accepted a change in the rules of engagement for the carrier. All forces would be allowed to attack the carrier outside the total exclusion zone even if there had been no previous attack on the task force. The only limits to aggressive action would be if the carrier was within the 12-nautical-mile limit of the Argentine mainland, or was north of Buenos Aires.

Woodward had achieved what he wanted. He could now sleep slightly safer in the knowledge that the *Veinticinco de Mayo* would be torpedoed as soon as it was located by one of the two nuclear submarines searching for it. But this turned out to be a much more difficult task than it should have been.

By the time that the rules of engagement had been changed, *Splendid* or *Spartan* should have been in a position to locate and trail it. They had been on station for over two weeks and *Splendid* had in fact been directed to search for the carrier, albeit fruitlessly and with constantly changing information, since 21 April, nine days previously. As we have seen, Commander Roger Lane-Nott was becoming very frustrated by his lack of success and his contradictory orders. On 26 April the sonar operators on *Splendid* had obtained a contact with a group of Argentine warships, provisionally identified as two destroyers and three frigates. The original contact was made when the targets were at a range of 14,000 yards. They were doing very little, not transmitting a great many signals nor running their active sonar. Closing on them, Lane-Nott positively identified them and transmitted a critical report to Northwood saying that an Argentine task force had been sighted.

Lane-Nott, after so many fruitless directives, had located what he believed to be an escort group waiting for its flagship, which could only be the carrier. He was euphoric, believing that these ships would lead him to the *Veinticinco de Mayo*. He realized that he had no current rules of engagement to attack, but he believed that sooner or later they would come. After twenty-four hours, however, he was instructed to leave the group and head north because it was believed in Northwood that the carrier would be found there. For Lane-Nott this was sacrilege. It was a cardinal principle that 'you attack what you see'. The weather was good, there was a bit of swell but it was very easy to keep track of the group of warships. Lane-Nott felt that everything he had been taught was being ignored; he could not understand why he was being instructed to abandon so promising a target. He decided that he would turn a Nelsonian blind eye to the signal and ignore it. Six hours later, he again received the signal to leave the group and head north to search for the carrier. Again, he chose to ignore it. His First Lieutenant was becoming rather anxious at this refusal to obey orders, but Lane-Nott stuck to his guns. Perhaps if he had not been sent on so many fruitless missions in the previous days he would have been more prepared to obey the instruction, but he was utterly convinced that the targets that he had located were the best leads to the carrier that he could find. The third signal was received and again it instructed him to leave the targets he was trailing. Again he ignored it. Six hours later he was sent a personal signal from Vice Admiral Herbert, Flag Officer Submarines, ordering him to 'go now'. In the face of this, and increasing disquiet from his senior officers, he at last reluctantly left the group of ships: 'We started chasing shadows again.'

Splendid had in fact found what was to become the basis of the Argentine Task Group 79.1, which was indeed waiting for the *Veinticinco de Mayo*. The nuclear submarines in the South Atlantic would never come so close to finding the carrier again.

Roger Lane-Nott had one other close encounter, and this time its failure could not be attributed to a wrong direction from Northwood. The sonar operators on board *Splendid* thought that they had located the carrier acoustically, travelling south along the 12-mile limit of Argentine national waters. After trailing the contact during the night, everyone went to action stations to prepare to attack at sunrise. The contact was moving slowly, but *Splendid* came to periscope depth, only to discover, to Lane-Nott's chagrin, that visibility was 10 yards. The target was in solid fog. Without visual identification he could not attack. The target turned and headed north again, but Lane-Nott was prevented from following it.

Conqueror had been relatively free of these frustrations while attached to Operation Paraquet. Commander Wreford-Brown was now in a fairly ambiguous situation, however. He was theoretically under the direction of the Commander Task Group, though his communications with him were via Northwood. At the same time, Woodward still had no power to set any rules of engagement for the submarines.

Nevertheless, *Conqueror* was assigned a patrol area and a target, and Wreford-Brown was sent some intelligence information to help locate it. The *General Belgrano* had been patrolling in the area off the Isla de los Estados for some days, the purpose of which had not become apparent to Northwood, nor to any of the intelligence agencies. Some days before, however, two destroyers and a tanker had joined her. It looked as though the small force was preparing for some operation, perhaps to recapture the island of South Georgia. *Conqueror* steamed towards the last-known position of this group of ships.

10

THE TRAP

The long hull of the ARA *General Belgrano* had passed slowly down the Beagle Channel and her bow had started to meet the heavier seas of the South Atlantic. The whole crew could feel the ship respond to the long swells of the open ocean as the engines slowly increased speed to 13 knots and they moved to reach the patrol area known as Miguel. There they would rendezvous with the two destroyers that, together with the *Belgrano*, would make up the task group TG79.3.

These destroyers, sailing down the coast from their position in the other naval task group, were the ARA *Hipólito Bouchard* and the *Piedra Buena*. Both were former United States navy destroyers, commissioned in 1944. Driven by steam turbines, they were 370 feet long, weighing around 3,000 tons. Originally they had been armed with six 5-inch guns, but when they were sold to Argentina in 1972 they were modernized with the addition of four Exocet anti-ship missile launchers, modern search and fire-control radar and variable-depth sonar to improve their anti-submarine performance. Accompanying them was a tanker, the *Puerto Rosales*, carrying fuel for the destroyers and the *Belgrano*. The *Bouchard* was delayed by a technical problem, but the *Piedra Buena* reached area Miguel, to the north of the Isla de los Estados, on 28 April and the destroyer's captain was then flown by helicopter to the *Belgrano* to discuss orders for the forthcoming mission. Commander Galazi, the executive officer of the *Belgrano*, was the most senior officer after Captain Bonzo and would become second in command of the small task group. He knew that there was little time for working the ships up together, or for any training in anti-aircraft manoeuvres or anti-submarine operations before they might be in action.

The mood on the *Belgrano* was becoming sombre. It had begun with the departure from Ushuaia; now, with the rendezvous with the task force, people knew that another stage in the war had started and that the British task force was on its way. Down in the ratings' mess decks even ordinary seamen were capable of making informed guesses about how long the British might take to reach the Malvinas, especially if they were coming from South Georgia. It couldn't be long before things came to a head.

At 22.00 hours, the *Hipólito Bouchard* arrived and took up a position 15 miles to the north-west of the *Belgrano*. The *Belgrano* was now around 25 miles to the north of Cabo San Juan on the Isla de los Estados. According to Captain Bonzo, his biggest concern was that he was in range of the Sea Harriers carried by the British aircraft carriers; although the surface-to-surface armament of the *Belgrano* and her destroyers was good – they could attack warships both with Exocets and with the *Belgrano*'s

6-inch guns – her ability to shoot down attacking aircraft was not good. The Harriers were modern, fast aircraft and would not be deterred by the Sea Cat anti-aircraft missiles on the *Belgrano*.

The deception plans that Admiral Woodward on the British task force had carried out had paid off. The Argentine junta believed there was a clear possibility that the initial arrival of the task force would be the start of a concerted effort to land on the islands. It was unclear where, but for the junta this represented the best opportunity to inflict damage on the British forces, and they started to make their plans to prepare for offensive action. On the afternoon of Thursday the 29th Captain Bonzo received a signal with orders to move the task force from area Miguel to another area, Julián, which was south of the shallow waters of the Burdwood Bank, an area to the south of the Falklands that rose up from the sea floor to a depth of around 160 feet in its shallowest part. A nuclear submarine can operate in these depths, but at speed there is a danger that its bulk will create sufficient turbulence for surface disturbance to reveal its presence. This area of shallow water would therefore provide a possible safe area for the task group. The destroyers and the *Belgrano* were ordered to depart from Miguel at noon on 1 May.

Before this, on 30 April, the doctor on board the *Belgrano*, Lieutenant Commander Levene, had two more patients: one was another emergency appendicitis case, a senior rating who was operated on just in time before his inflamed appendix burst; and the other was an armourer who had fallen a great height down the shaft of one of the 6-inch gun turrets and had suffered a severe concussion. Both patients were recovering after their treatments.

*

On the same day, at 08.25 local time, HMS *Conqueror* came to the surface. The buoyant low-frequency wire had been modified, and a high-frequency tail had been added to the end. This needed to be streamed out from its attachment to the rear of the fin, although once this had been done it would remain as a permanent fixture. It was bad enough having to come to periscope depth every day to flush the atmosphere in the boat; Commander Wreford-Brown certainly didn't want to surface every time to trail an aerial for his signals. The replacement UHF aerial, put together by the engineers in the back end of the boat and perilously welded on to the mast by Charlie Foy, was also going to be given a test. In the radio room everyone waited anxiously, the operators as well as Charlie, to see if their work had been successful. Then the signals started arriving, three of them from all sources – high frequency, UHF, satellite – all started delivering their orders and intelligence.

The intelligence was, in the words of Commander Wreford-Brown, 'excellent'. It seemed that there was little about the planned movements of the Argentine navy that British Intelligence didn't know. Wreford-Brown was quickly told that he was expected to intercept an Argentine task force that was composed of the *Belgrano*, the two destroyers *Hipólito Bouchard* and *Piedra Buena* and the oiler *Puerto Rosales*. Britain had even been able to intercept signals from the Argentine navy and could easily decode them. Even the coded patrol areas were known to the British; on *Conqueror* one signal, COR 153, told Wreford-Brown that the *Belgrano* group was in patrol area Miguel and gave the coordinates for it.

At the start of the day Commander Wreford-Brown gave a brief outline to the crew, telling them that they were going to the west of the Falklands, looking for the *Belgrano*. The submarine was still trailing its towed array sonar receiver, which gave the sonar operators the advantage of a sonar receiver separated from some of the boat's self-generated noise and was a useful detection device if the boat was making a certain amount of speed. It paid off. At 16.45 GMT – 13.45 local time – on 30 April, Petty Officer Libby was on sonar watch. 'The first contact was a heavy – it was a heavy ship. A heavy oiler makes a lot more noise than a warship does.' Graham Libby heard the steady beat of the propellers of a slow-moving ship, and he could hear the clatter of the diesel engines that were driving it.

> We had to investigate every single contact that we came across. With experience, you can listen to a vessel and know immediately that it was not what we were looking for. We had various fishing vessels as contacts, but as soon as we heard the tanker, we knew this was of interest. I reported it to the control room, the control room told the captain, and we investigated it further.

The contact with the oiler was made at a range of over 50 miles. Commander Wreford-Brown thought that it was a good point for the *Belgrano* to operate from, as it had a depth of water of about 210 feet behind a shallow patch of 95 feet. It was under Argentine air cover and only 35 miles from the British total exclusion zone. He made a decision to go closer. *Conqueror* headed on a course of 268 degrees. If a submarine moves at speed through the water, the sensitivity of the sonar decreases. The noise of water flowing over the hull masks other sounds, and the sonar's range diminishes to 1 or 2 miles. So on its voyage to the designated patrol area, and the contact that Commander Wreford-Brown believed would take them to the *Belgrano*, the

Conqueror would travel deep and fast for several miles, then reduce speed to 5 knots and attempt to take another accurate bearing on the target. So through the night *Conqueror* headed towards area Miguel and the heavy sonar signal that Libby had identified.

The oil tanker *Puerto Rosales*, whose thudding diesel engines and reverberating propeller blades had filled 'Horse' Libby's earphones 50 miles away, had a lot of work to do before the *Belgrano* and her accompanying destroyers could head out on their mission. The oil tanker manoeuvred to come alongside the *Bouchard* to refuel, starting at 09.00 local time on 30 April. One hundred and twenty-five tons of fuel were transferred to the destroyer's bunkers, and the process – known as replenishment at sea – was finished by 10.00. Then it was the *Piedra Buena*'s turn. The hoses were attached and the two ships rode the heavy swell side by side as 142 tons were pumped over and the destroyer was once more at full capacity.

Finally the *Puerto Rosales* had to refuel the *Belgrano*. At 16.00 local time the pumping began, but the wind had started to increase throughout the day and the waves became higher and higher. It was hard to keep the two ships on station with each other, so refuelling was frequently interrupted. After an hour, during which only 90 tons had been transferred, the operation was abandoned and the two ships separated, with Captain Bonzo deciding that they would start again the following morning. They had until tomorrow afternoon to reach area Julián, so there would be time for another refuelling attempt. For the rest of the evening there would be enough work in final maintenance and briefings before the *Belgrano* went into action.

The *Conqueror* was now barely 30 miles away.

*

Next morning, 1 May, at 08.34 the sun rose on a bleak, grey-black sea, capped with foam-crested waves driven by a force 3 wind from the west, with temperatures of just 3 degrees centigrade.

This morning the fighting on the Falklands had already started in earnest, although the crews on the *Belgrano*, her accompanying ships, and also on the *Conqueror*, hadn't yet realized it. Admiral Woodward's plan was to create in the minds of the Argentine junta the illusion that landings were going to begin in earnest, so encouraging the Argentine forces into battle. This would start the process of attrition with the Argentine air force and also, most importantly, lure the Argentine aircraft carrier out to sea, where Woodward's submarine screen would be able to attack it. Admiral Woodward's view about the success of this plan differed from that of Admiral Leach and Admiral Fieldhouse, both of whom thought that the Argentine navy would never dare risk their ships once they realized that the British nuclear submarines were in position. In Woodward's mind this was unsatisfactory, because while the Argentine ships remained in port they would always present a potential threat to a possible invasion force. Better to solve the issue sooner rather than later.

It wasn't that difficult to create the illusion of a decisive moment in the battle. There were several actions that needed to be carried out to reduce the danger to the task group, and to improve British reconnaissance and intelligence capabilities on the Falklands. If they took place at the same time it would be hard, initially, for the Argentine forces in the Falklands to be certain about what was really happening.

The battle group had approached the total exclusion zone in an anti-aircraft formation, with the Type 42 destroyers *Glasgow*, *Sheffield* and *Coventry* 'up threat' – that is, further to the west of the two carriers and the frigates, where the first indications of air attack would be detected. Early in the morning of 1 May they crossed the unseen line that had been drawn on the waters of the South Atlantic. The battle for the Falkland Islands had officially started, although the loss of the submarine *Santa Fe* in South Georgia a few days earlier had not gone unnoticed by the *Belgrano* crew.

However, the first casualties among Argentine forces on the Falklands since the invasion were caused not by the Royal Navy but by the Royal Air Force. The question of whether adequate air defence for the task group and any amphibious landings could be provided by the navy had been a major concern to members of the Joint Chiefs of Staff Committee at the very beginning of Operation Corporate. It was a serious issue for Admiral Woodward and his amphibious commanders Julian Thompson and Mike Clapp. To a large extent the size of the Argentinian threat was unknown. There were still unanswered questions about whether or not the new Exocet-armed aircraft, the Super Etendard, could be launched from the aircraft carrier *Veinticinco de Mayo*. It was unclear whether the aircraft could be refuelled in the air, and whether the range of other mainland-based aircraft could be extended by air-to-air refuelling. What was clear was that if the modern jets of the Argentine air force and navy could use the airstrip at Stanley, then their range would be increased enormously, and the Sea Harriers carried on *Hermes* and *Invincible* might be overwhelmed.

Admiral Woodward wanted to see the Stanley runway put out of action, so when the RAF came up with a plan to attack it he readily agreed. The plan was to use aircraft from the former atom-bomb force of V-bombers, the delta-winged Vulcan. This aircraft wasn't ideal for the task of precision bombing an airstrip over 8,000 nautical miles from Britain. In its last incarnation the Vulcan was intended to be a low-level bomber carrying nuclear weapons to strategic targets in Eastern Europe and Russia. The Vulcan crews had developed a technique called 'toss bombing', which allowed then to aim an atomic bomb on a ballistic flight path, releasing the weapon some way away from the target. This was out of the question on the Falklands. Air Ministry studies showed that to get even a 50 per cent chance of damaging the runway, a stick of twenty-one bombs had to be dropped in a straight line across the target; this could be achieved only by a plane flying straight and level, no lower than 8,000 feet. The plane and its crew would then be a perfect target for Argentine anti-aircraft fire and missiles. If the bombing could be done it had to be done at night to lessen the risk of being shot down, but this would increase the problem of actually hitting the runway. The next obstacle to overcome would be actually getting the planes to the Falklands. But the RAF persisted, and with a refuelling probe fitted to a Vulcan bomber, one might be able to make the 3,000-mile round trip from Ascension Island to the Falklands and back. The downside was that this would need the support of eleven Victor tanker-aircraft, with ten refuelling rendezvous during the flight. There were some initial reservations about this from the American commander of Wideawake airfield on Ascension, but these were fairly quickly overcome.

Late on 30 April the first flight of Victor tankers had taken off, to their intercept points, then two Vulcans followed them into the sky. One Vulcan had a problem with its cockpit window and could not adequately pressurize, so one lone Vulcan, piloted by Flight Lieutenant Martin Withers, flew above the battle group in the dark, and at 04.40 local time the first bombs hit the runway at Stanley, exploding in a long line across the airfield. Three

Argentinians were killed – a member of the marine anti-aircraft battery and two members of the air force. Buildings were damaged and the windows of the control tower were smashed out by the blast. One bomb hit the runway: this was sufficient to break up the tarmac and cause problems for any aircraft landing there. Even with local repairs, the surface was never considered safe again, although Hercules transport planes continued to land and take off during the war.

When the coded signal sent by the Vulcan was received on the *Hermes*, the battle group steamed into the British exclusion zone around the Falklands and headed south-west towards Stanley. Woodward intended to persist in his tactic of making the Argentinians assume that he was going to attempt to make a landing on the main settlement of East Falkland.

The next phase in the concerted assault on the Argentine positions in the Falklands was an attack by twelve Sea Harriers on the runway and buildings of the airfield at Stanley, and on a smaller airstrip at Goose Green. The Sea Harriers were loaded with bombs, missiles and full tanks of fuel, and needed the assistance of the ski-lift at the end of the flight deck to get airborne. Even with this they dropped alarmingly before gaining their maximum lift and climbing away into the sky. At 08.00 they flew low over the islands, splitting into two forces. One group dropped anti-personnel bombs on the anti-aircraft positions around the airstrip, while five Sea Harriers flew low, dropping cluster bombs on the runway, on parked aircraft and on buildings. While this attack was taking place, another three Harriers made a low-level pass down Falkland Sound, the stretch of water dividing East and West Falkland, and attacked the runway at Goose Green, hitting a Pucara ground-attack aircraft as it prepared to take off, destroying it and killing the pilot.

Apart from one Sea Harrier which had been hit by a 20mm cannon shell over Stanley airfield, punching a hole in the tail fin, none of the Harriers suffered any damage; they all made it back to the *Hermes*.

It was now daylight, but Woodward intended to keep up the pressure on the troops at Stanley, and HMS *Glamorgan*, with *Arrow* and *Alacrity*, were sent to bombard the airfield with their 4.5-inch guns. Nothing saps the morale like the relentless explosions from the continual fall of shell that artillery can keep up for hours. In addition to this, HMS *Brilliant* and *Yarmouth* were deployed to the north-east of the Falklands to start a search for any Argentine submarines that might be on patrol.

The Argentine forces had been on the islands for almost a month now, often cold, with constant supply problems caused by the presence of the British nuclear submarines. With the announced deployment of HMS *Splendid* and *Spartan*, the Argentine junta had abandoned regular supply ships, relying instead on flights from the mainland to bring food and ammunition to the troops.

The sudden violent eruption of hostilities on 1 May was a shock, particularly as it had immediately called into question the defence of the extremely important runway at Stanley. It took some time for the junta to respond, and initially just two French-built Mirage 111 fighters came in from the west and attacked two Sea Harriers on a combat air patrol over Stanley. The Mirages fired two air-to-air missiles, but both missed. This was the only contact from a mission of four Mirage fighters and four Daggers – Israeli-built versions of the French Mirages – which had flown from the mainland at Rio Gallegos and escorted a group of US Skyhawk bombers to attack the three British ships on the gunline bombarding positions around Stanley. Once they entered the islands' air space they were put under the control of the local Argentine air force at Stanley, but in the control tower they had not accurately assessed the situation and failed to direct the bombers on to the three British destroyers. The ships' gunfire was being directed by helicopters, observing the fall of shot, and these were fired on by anti-aircraft missiles, which missed; they were also attacked by two small Turbo-Mentor, propjet training aircraft, which were driven off by the arrival of two Sea Harriers. As well as providing forward gunfire direction, the helicopters inadvertently added to the illusion that troops were being landed on various parts of the islands, and signals stating this were sent back to the mainland.

As the day progressed, the Argentine air force started to gather its resources to assess the situation. Aircraft had been at readiness all morning but only now were targets properly identified. A coordinated attack on the battle group was planned, with around fifty aircraft from airfields on the mainland taking part.

Three Daggers from the 6th Fighter Group took off from the Argentine air force base at San Julián with the intention of mounting an attack on the warships *Brilliant* and *Yarmouth*, which were carrying out the anti-submarine operation with Sea King helicopters to the north-east of East Falkland. They missed their intended target, but came instead upon the three warships – *Glamorgan*, *Arrow* and *Alacrity* – bombarding Argentine positions around Stanley with their combined force of four 4.5-inch naval guns. The Daggers, supersonic delta-winged aircraft that carried cannon, missiles and bombs, attacked at a height of more than 900 feet, approaching the line of ships from the landward side, giving them little time to react. The pilots fired their cannons and rapidly dropped their bombs, which were parachute-retarded, and then they were past, rapidly climbing into cloud, the thunderous, ear-splitting roar of their engines competing with the deafening explosions of their bombs.

The British warships were lucky, two of the bombs exploding on either side of *Glamorgan* and two more falling astern of *Alacrity*.

Meanwhile, two Mirages were attacked by two Sea Harriers at 12,000 feet, and one of the Mirages was hit and destroyed by a Sidewinder missile. The other was badly damaged; it tried to make a landing at Stanley, but was shot at by Argentine anti-aircraft defences and crashed. Both pilots were killed. There was another fight in the air over Stanley when two more Daggers were confronted by another two Sea Harriers. Again, one of the Daggers was hit and destroyed by a Sidewinder missile, killing the pilot.

The next encounter with the British fleet was with a group of Canberra bombers, jet bombers built in Britain which had first entered service in 1951. Six of these took off from a base at Trelew, in Argentina, the most northerly air force base to mount an attack. They failed to find any targets, but even so one flight of three was located by a pair of Sea Harriers and one of them was shot down, exploding in flames as it was hit by a Sidewinder missile.

The major part of the Argentine effort that day was an operation of twenty-four Skyhawk bombers that flew out of both San Julián and Rio Gallegos airfields. Again there was no co-ordination between the Argentine mainland and Argentine forces in the Falklands who could direct the aircraft on to any targets. Only one flight of Skyhawks succeeded in launching an attack, and that was against one of Argentina's own merchant ships, the *Formosa*, which was sailing from Stanley in an eager effort to leave the danger zone. Two bombs hit the ship, but luckily for the crew of the *Formosa* and Captain Gregorio they didn't explode.

By the end of the day, the result of the opening of hostilities had not been good for the Argentine junta. The British battle group had received no damage, but the Argentinians had lost one ground-attack aircraft, damaged in the attack on Goose Green; there had been several deaths on the airfield at Stanley and in the troop positions around it; the airstrip had been damaged; and the air force had lost two Mirage fighters, a Dagger and a Canberra bomber, with their aircrew. Woodward knew it was going to be a long war of attrition against the larger number of Argentine aircraft, so the first day's results were better than he might have expected.

The Argentine navy had not yet showed its hand, however. The only ship whose whereabouts he thought he was certain of was the cruiser *Belgrano*. Despite excellent signals intelligence and the presence of two nuclear submarines to the north of the Falklands, the aircraft carrier *Veinticinco de Mayo* and a group of Exocet-armed destroyers were at sea, perhaps already steaming straight at him.

While the sound of exploding bombs and the scream of jet fighters filled the air over Stanley, a few hundred miles away to the south-west the *General Belgrano* was making final preparations to move east. Half an hour after sunrise the refuelling tanker *Puerto Rosales* had once again closed up to cruise parallel to the *Belgrano* and pump over the remainder of the fuel that the cruiser needed. When the ships were about 20 yards apart the hoses were passed across, but after only thirty minutes the alarm was suddenly sounded in the operations room of one of the destroyers. The electronic counter-measures screen had picked up the radar signal of an approaching aircraft.

On the *Belgrano* the response was immediate. The cruiser and the tanker were in no position to take evasive action joined so closely together by the oil hoses, so the *Belgrano* executed an emergency breakaway, raising steam and turning to starboard. In the alarm, the anti-aircraft guns were manned and the diesel generators for the Sea Cat missiles by the bridge were started up. Anxious lookouts scanned the sky, and on every ship below decks eyes were glued to the radar screens for another telltale blip. Had the Argentine task group been spotted? Were they about to be attacked by Sea Harriers armed with 1,000-lb bombs? But there was nothing. It had to have been a false alarm.

Or had a Sea Harrier spotted the group of Argentine warships and immediately returned to one of the British Aircraft carriers, *Hermes* or *Invincible*, to report their position? Was an attack being planned even now on board the flagship of the British task force? Captain Bonzo didn't know, but had no choice. He needed to refuel before heading to his next position, so once again the two ships steamed side by side and by noon 390 tons of heavy fuel oil had been transferred to the bunkers of the *Belgrano*. But the false alarm was a wake-up call in one respect. From now on the closer they got to engaging with the British task force, the greater the air threat would become. The crew were closed up to action stations, and they were not stood down.

The young ship's doctor, Lieutenant Commander Alberto Levene, who had carried out the two appendectomies in the *Belgrano*'s operating theatre in the preceding two days, found himself in an emergency casualty station below the water-line. He could hear the sea against the side of the ship and was suddenly filled with very morbid thoughts. After the ship had left Puerto Belgrano he had reflected that, in all the stories he had read about war at sea, there were always very few survivors. He thought,

'If a torpedo hits us now, I will not even notice.' Dressed as he was, he knew anyway that in the water he would die in minutes.

HMS *Conqueror* had been heading towards the *Belgrano* overnight, and at 09.49 the captain had ordered the submarine to rise to periscope depth, making the first visual identification of the cruiser. So good was the British ability to intercept and decrypt Argentine signals that the wardroom on *Conqueror* knew more about the movements of the *Belgrano* than did most of the crew on the cruiser itself. At midnight *Conqueror* had come to periscope depth and received its packet of signals, one of which, numbered 160, told Commander Wreford-Brown that the *Belgrano* was expected to leave area Miguel at 16.00 hours GMT and head east. He steered a course for Miguel. At sunrise, again at periscope depth, he checked his horizons, and saw nothing. Then he ordered a change of course to 275 degrees, went to a depth of 210 feet and set a speed of 15 knots. He was going to area Miguel for a search.

At this time, the rules of engagement for the nuclear submarines working as part of Operation Corporate stated that inside the maritime exclusion zone warships, auxiliary vessels and submarines could be attacked, while outside the maritime exclusion zone surveillance was to be carried out on the *Veinticinco de Mayo* and only this ship and submarines could be attacked.

At 09.54 local time, *Conqueror* had once more come to periscope depth and slowed to 4 knots. At a bearing of 285 degrees, just over 5 miles away, were the ships of TG79.3. Wreford-Brown originally thought there were five ships, but was probably confused by the mast of the oil tanker. Now he could identify the ships and recognize their individual sonar signatures.

The *Belgrano* was refuelling when the ships first appeared in the eyepieces of the periscope, and Wreford-Brown could easily see the white king posts of the tanker. Its sonar signature was at a frequency of 645 Hz, and showed six-cylinder two-stroke engines. The radar operator, deep in three deck, could tell that one of the destroyers was making an occasional sweep with its radar, but generally the radar and sonar on the destroyers and the *Belgrano* were in passive mode. The course of the Argentine task group would take it into the centre of area Julián. The *Conqueror* was going to shadow the group, keeping a distance of around 5–8 miles from it. A white signal flare was fired from the *Belgrano*, and one of the destroyers emitted some black smoke. They were heading out of area Miguel.

Conqueror tried to send a signal to Northwood on the SSIXS satellite link to say that the Argentine task group had been located, but no contact with Northwood was possible. At 12.14 local time *Conqueror* went to a depth of 200 feet and set a course of 130 degrees. With all three warships topped up with fuel, the tanker *Puerto Rosales* had finished her mission and steamed back to the mainland. Throughout the afternoon *Conqueror* continued to trail the *Belgrano* and its accompanying destroyers south-east. Almost hourly, she would rise to periscope depth for a visual sighting and to check that the plot that was being maintained in the control room was correctly measuring the course of the Argentine task force.

A permanent sonar contact was being maintained by *Conqueror* as well. An accurate measure of the Argentine ships' bearing in relation to the submarine was maintained by the sonar operators. Each operator had a bearing indicator, which was a dial in front of him with a needle moving across a scale, which could point to the bearing where the sonar signal was at its most intense. By marking this indicated position on the plotting table, an accurate track of the course and speed of the targets could be maintained. But experienced sonar operators like Graham Libby could tell what was happening just by listening through their headphones:

> You did have a paper trace that was very slow moving and gave you a hard copy over a period of, say, half an hour. Then the bearing rate might change, so you use the indicator. We used to have a little button to press that would tell you if you were at the loudest point. If you were to the right of it the needle swung to the right. But you can hear the change. You can hear the change in propeller speeds, there'll be a slightly different engine tone, or a turbine noise. The majority of the bearing will be done by the ear and the meter, and the ear is the predominant tool.

11

SAILING INTO DANGER

The atmosphere on board the *Belgrano* was now tense, as everyone on board realized that they were sailing towards the exclusion zone and there was the possibility of imminent action. The crew were closed up at action stations, with all the watertight doors shut.

At 14.30 local time, Captain Bonzo called a planning meeting in the admiral's cabin to make preparations for the action that everybody expected to take part in the next day. The Alouette helicopter took off from the stern of the *Belgrano*, flying to each destroyer in turn to pick up the commanding officer and second in command. Landing back on the *Belgrano*, they joined the senior group of officers around the big table in the admiral's quarters. In total, eighteen men gathered to discuss the coming fight. They all realized that they were approaching a situation for which their training and their doctrine had not prepared them. In the words of Commander Galazi, executive officer of the *Belgrano*, 'The situation bore absolutely no relation to anything that we could find in our textbooks. But we had our orders, and we had to do the best we could.'

Those orders were to head towards the position of the British battle group and in coordination with the other Argentine units to the north of the Falklands, principally the aircraft carrier and its Skyhawk aircraft, to attack surface ships with Exocet missiles launched from the *Hipólito Bouchard* and *Piedra Buena*. These had a theoretical range of around 35 miles, but in any event had a greater range than the *Belgrano*'s big 6-inch guns. If any British ships were hit and damaged by these missiles, only then would the *Belgrano* move into battle and attempt to sink them with artillery fire.

The first problem for Captain Bonzo was being able to pinpoint the location of the British battle group. The only resources that were available were two Lockheed Neptune aircraft based in Rio Grande, which had the range and radar necessary but were tasked with assisting other units of the Argentine navy. They were slow aircraft, and if they used their radar in a search mode they could easily be spotted by the British battle group and attacked by Sea Harriers. Against these the *Belgrano* group had very little defence, and there was no fighter aircraft based in Rio Grande that had the range to provide protection from air attack.

But all agreed that the biggest threat was from the nuclear submarines that they believed were on station around the Falklands. They were all aware that the warning issued by the British government to the junta via the Swiss Embassy – that any units steaming towards or threatening British forces would be considered a threat and be subject to attack – had come into force on 30 April. They were also aware of the 200-mile total exclusion zone that the British had imposed around the Falklands, though Captain Bonzo's view was that entering it would not increase the threat to them from the enemy and shouldn't influence their assessment of the danger from submarines. Steaming east as they were doing could become a greater risk than heading into the exclusion zone over the Burdwood Bank, because the submarines would be constrained by the shallow water found there. In fact, within the exclusion zone there were areas where the depth of water was only 160 feet, whereas on their present course, skirting the exclusion zone, there was nothing to restrict the movement of submarines, so the risk factors were equal. For Bonzo and Galazi the problem wasn't where the submarine threat would be likely to come from but what could be done to prevent it.

Their tactical handbooks and training were solely concerned with the threat from conventional diesel-electric submarines. In this case there was a standard set of anti-submarine defence tactics. Conventional submarines had to prepare an attack on a surface ship from ahead, because the submerged speed of a submarine wasn't enough to catch and overtake a surface ship that was zigzagging at a speed of anything between 12 and 15 knots. A calculation was recommended in the training manuals to produce something called an 'approach limit angle', which was an area in front of the ship where a submarine had to position itself to make a torpedo attack. If escort vessels were positioned in that area their sonar would be able to detect any submarine. But these calculations were based on a submarine speed of 12 knots. Everyone in the meeting in the admiral's cabin was aware that a nuclear submarine could go at least twice that speed. In other words, it could approach from any angle.

Even if the nuclear submarine were approaching from astern,

it would have no problem overtaking the *Belgrano* and its destroyers. With the destroyers at top speed, it would still take only about sixty-five minutes for the submarine to overhaul them and be in an attack position. The figures for conventional submarines suggested that after the submarine had fired a torpedo, the escort ships had a 5 per cent chance of detecting the submarine within the first half-hour, and this chance receded to 2 per cent an hour and a half after the attack. With a nuclear submarine, however, there was no scenario that produced any success rate whatsoever. Realizing also that the new modern Tigerfish torpedo carried by the British submarine had a range of 15,000 yards, they knew the situation was hopeless. 'Even with ten escorts, there was no anti-submarine formation that we could think of that could provide any defence. A nuclear-powered submarine can detect a ship up to twenty-five kilometres distant, but our destroyers' hydrophonic capability was much less.'

The sonar system on the two destroyers (*Belgrano* was not fitted with one), the SGS 39/42, had a low performance in passive mode. It might hear and pick up the sound of an approaching torpedo. In active mode the sonar should be able to pick up the echo of a submarine or torpedo 3,000 yards away – but by then it would probably be too late.

Against this rather bleak prospect there were some basic measures that would be followed. The ships would adopt a very flexible formation and keep separation from each other of 10,000 yards, following a random course, sometimes zigzagging, sometimes not. The ships would not use active sonar, unless there was a very strong contact, and the radar would be used extremely intermittently. There would be radio silence, and the communications between the ships would be by an Aldiss signal lamp with a red filter. The ships would keep at a cruising speed of

TEMPUS OMNIA VINCIT

CONQUEROR

OPERATION CORPORATE

The cover we produced for the Patrol Report

(CONQUEROR's crest has a Raven on it normally)

MOTTO: "TIME CONQUERS ALL"

(Above) *In her previous incarnation as the USS* Phoenix, *the Belgrano steams out of Pearl Harbor after the attack by the Japanese.*

Modernized and newly painted, the ARA General Belgrano *steams into the South Atlantic (above).* (Right) *The* Belgrano *refuelled at sea the day before she was sunk. Those on board were unaware that Conqueror had already sighted her.*

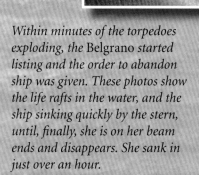

Within minutes of the torpedoes exploding, the Belgrano started listing and the order to abandon ship was given. These photos show the life rafts in the water, and the ship sinking quickly by the stern, until, finally, she is on her beam ends and disappears. She sank in just over an hour.

Survivors from the Belgrano show their life jackets to the press (right). *The Sun's* notorious headline (below right) reported only that the Belgrano had been hit. It took some time for the Argentine navy to realize that the ship had been sunk.

THE Sun

Tuesday, May 4, 1982   14p   TODAY'S TV: PAGE 12

QE2 IS SET TO SAIL FOR WAR

Liner may be turned back from a cruise

We told you first

NINE days ago The Sun said that the QE2 was to be called up. Every-body denies it. Yesterday, the Ministry of Defence confirmed it. If you really want to know what's going on in the war say the Sun. We try harder. See Page 5

GOTCHA

SUNK   AN Argie patrol boat like this one was sunk by missiles from Royal Navy helicopters after first opening fire on our lads

Our lads sink gunboat and hole cruiser

From TONY SNOW aboard HMS Invincible

THE NAVY had the Argies on their knees last night after a devastating double punch.

WALLOP: They torpedoed the 14,000-ton Argentine cruiser General Belgrano and left it a useless wreck.

WALLOP: Task Force helicopters sank one Argentine patrol boat and severely damaged another.

The Belgrano, which survived the Pearl Harbour attack when it belonged to the U.S...

BATTLE FOR THE ISLANDS

Troops surround the Sea Harriers on the hangar deck of HMS Hermes, as dawn breaks in the South Atlantic.

The process of moving equipment and thousands of troops from ship to ship prior to the landings was done after the threat from the Argentine navy was removed.

The vulnerability of the navy to air attack never went away. The first British casualty was HMS Sheffield (right), hit by an Exocet missile. Her commander, Captain Sam Salt (below) survived.

(Below) Finally, on 16 June, the Union Jack was raised by Royal Marines on the Falklands.

(Left) Conqueror *returned home to an unexpected media storm, with a bearded crew, a battered and ice-damaged fin and a Jolly Roger, the symbol of piracy, flying from her mast. It was the first time a Royal Navy submarine had flown a flag like this since 1945.*

Tuesday
22 June 19

'The Bear

10 week:

(3rd in the Com

THE REPLY !!!

RECEIVED FROM ZIPPO

"We do appreciate that you may have received the lighters just before you were summoned to the defence of the Empire. However, if in between confronting hostile forces you do find a moment to send us a cheque we would be extremely grateful!!"

One of the letters in the Mail-Drop!

LRO(SM) LUDGATE with the 'JOLLY ROGER' he made for HMS CONQUEROR - the first to depict the Nuclear Symbol. Dagger - Special Ops (SBS)
Ship - G.BELGRANO Torpedoed.

Tuesday
29 June 1982

1st Prize in
the Moustache
Competition !!

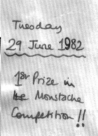

Pictures from a scrap book (above and right) *show the Jolly Roger in the torpedo room, bearing crossed torpedoes, a dagger for the SBS mission, the Belgrano, and a symbol of an atom. A more light-hearted memento is Lieutenant Commander Tim McClement's winning entry in the moustache competition.*

The government celebrated the victory in the Falklands with a parade through the City of London, a flypast and a service at St Paul's Cathedral.

Ordinary people found more direct ways of celebrating. Friends and families gathered in Portsmouth as the British warships returned home bringing sons, husbands and lovers.

HMS Conqueror *was decommissioned in 1990. On her last voyage, on the way to being scrapped, she found more controversy and publicity, this time from protesters against nuclear energy.*

Margaret Thatcher, her status bolstered by a British victory in the Falklands, urges decisive action after Iraq invades Kuwait in August 1990. George Bush looks on.

A statue stands in front of the Royal Marines' Eastney barracks in Portsmouth, a memorial to those who died on the Falklands and who never returned home.

around 14 knots, which should help to prevent any cavitation caused by the propellers, a phenomenon that occurs when the impact of a fast propeller blade against the water creates bubbles and areas of low pressure. This can create a great deal of noise, and increases the range at which a ship can be detected by sonar by as much as five times. It was more important for the *Belgrano* to remain undetected than to make a fast passage to the patrol area.

Finally they talked about what to do when they came into contact with British surface ships. They decided that the destroyers would take up a position ahead and with a separation of about 20,000 yards. They would launch their Exocet missiles, then break away to either side, allowing the *Belgrano* to steam ahead and unleash its artillery fire on any ships that had been disabled in the first attack. The *Belgrano* group was vulnerable to air attack, so they had to coordinate the timing of their advance with the aircraft from the *Veinticinco de Mayo*, which they hoped would divert any Sea Harriers that were mounting an air patrol. Also, the results of such an attack needed to be decisive. There would be no second chances.

The meeting broke up, and Captain Bonzo and Commander Galazi went back to the bridge. Before the officers from the destroyers left the *Belgrano* their commanding officers sought another brief meeting with Captain Bonzo. Commander Galazi stood next to him. 'What', they wanted to know, 'is the best action to take if one of us is hit by a torpedo?' It was Galazi who answered. 'The rest must escape immediately. There can be no question.' They all looked at each other, saying nothing more.

Later on that day Conscript Fernando Millan was on duty in the radio room close to the bridge. He remembers, 'It was a serious mood. There were a lot of long faces on the bridge. I was very nervous. I think everyone was.' Galazi summed up the mood, or at least his feelings about the day ahead: 'We had been dealt a hand of cards. Now we had to play them.'

At the time Galazi, Bonzo and everyone on the *Belgrano* were completely unaware that 5 miles behind them, 200 feet below the surface of the South Atlantic, was HMS *Conqueror*. Patiently trailing the group of ships, Commander Wreford-Brown or Lieutenant Commander Tim McClement would occasionally raise the periscope, checking the course and speed of the targets, plotting on the attack computer and in their heads the 'fire control solution' – the distance and angle at which a torpedo could be fired to rip open the sides of the ships successfully.

Around 20.30 hours an urgent message was rushed to the bridge and handed to Captain Bonzo by one of the cipher clerks. It was an order from the commander of Force 79 for the *Belgrano* group, TG79.3, to move during the night to a new position where they could better coordinate their actions with that of the carrier group and their aircraft. Captain Bonzo knew that this course would now take them into the exclusion zone. They were around 200 miles away from the British task force and would have to make their maximum speed to be in range of the British ships in order for the Exocets on the Argentine destroyers to hit their targets in Admiral Woodward's battle group. Captain Bonzo made an announcement over the loudspeaker system to the ship's crew, saying that he had received orders to attack the British fleet. Everyone on the ship knew what this meant. A group of junior officers went to Commander Galazi's cabin and asked him to take a message to Captain Bonzo. He walked up to the bridge and told the captain that all the officers wanted him to know that they would be loyal to the end.

The crew were very aware of the danger that they were sailing into. Conscript Millan had two hours free at a time between his watches during action stations, but could not sleep. Conscript Oscar Fornes, a radio operator, thought that he could smell war as they got nearer to the British task force; he grew more and more anxious. Conscript Juan Heinze had made a decision a few days earlier that during his off-watch period he would sleep as close to his Sea Cat launcher as possible. His bunk was on four deck and it took him several minutes to reach his action stations – minutes that he knew might be a matter of life and death for himself and the ship if there was an air raid. 'You are going into the unknown at this point. You don't know what will happen, and you don't know how you will behave. It is a very unpleasant feeling.'

So the *Belgrano* and her escort steamed on into the darkness, with her crew of over a thousand souls heading for a battle that they had never trained for and never imagined they would take part in. God knows what they would have done if they had known that beneath them was the dark bulk of a British nuclear submarine, the *Conqueror*, her sonar operators patiently listening to the *thwump, thwump, thwump* of the *Belgrano*'s propellers.

Several hundred miles to the north, the main force of the Argentine navy was preparing to launch the key attack against the British forces in the total exclusion zone. The senior commanders of the Argentine forces still believed that the British task force was preparing to land troops on the islands, and that they would be at their most vulnerable.

The aircraft carrier *Veinticinco de Mayo* had put to sea on 28 April and had met up with her escort of two Type 42 destroyers,

Hércules and *Santísima Trinidad*, and two former US destroyers, *Comodoro Py* and *Segui*. The *Veinticinco de Mayo* was a 20,000-ton monster. Built originally as a Colossus-class carrier for the Royal Navy, and launched as HMS *Venerable* in 1943, like the *Belgrano* she saw service in the Pacific against the Japanese in the Second World War. At the end of the war she was transferred to the Dutch government and renamed *Karel Doorman*. While serving in the Dutch navy she was modernized with an angled flight deck and steam catapults so that she could operate modern jet aircraft. Bought by the Argentine government, she was commissioned into the Argentine fleet in 1969, when she replaced the *Belgrano* as the navy's flagship.

The *Veinticinco de Mayo* could take up to twenty-one aircraft, but normally carried a squadron of Skyhawk A-4Q fighter bombers, a section of four Tracker anti-submarine and reconnaissance aircraft and Sea King helicopters. The Argentine navy had recently purchased its squadron of French Super Etendard aircraft, to be equipped with the air-launched Exocet anti-ship missiles, five of which had already been supplied by the French manufacturer, but, as we have seen, British Intelligence was unsure whether these aircraft could be launched by the *Veinticinco de Mayo* or not. If they could, then the carrier would be able to target the British task force from as far away as 400 miles, and Woodward's positioning of his air-defence ships would have to be able to cover a circular area of 360 degrees. The threat that the *Veinticinco de Mayo* posed was the reason why so much time had been devoted by the Joint Chiefs of Staff and the War Cabinet to discussions about whether the nuclear submarines' rules of engagement should be changed to allow an attack on the carrier outside the maritime exclusion zone.

The truth was that the Super Etendard aircraft could not be

flown from the carrier, and the Skyhawks that were now being worked on in the ship's hangars could not carry Exocet missiles. But they could carry 9,000 lb of bombs for over 500 miles. On the morning of 1 May the carrier was less than 300 nautical miles from the British battle group. However, while it had been relatively easy for British Intelligence to locate the *Belgrano* group and feed this information to the *Conqueror*, the location of the *Veinticinco de Mayo* task force had eluded them. Similarly, although the British battle group's progress had been followed by overflying Boeing 707s, its precise location was still unknown to the Argentine high command. On 1 May the majority of the air force sorties had failed to locate a target.

The Argentinian carrier did have on board three of the Grumman Tracker aircraft, however: twin-engined propeller planes equipped with search radar that were designed to locate seaborne targets. While they would be vulnerable to attack from Sea Harriers, and from long-range anti-aircraft missiles carried by the British ships, they could detect the radar emissions from the British battle group. If the Tracker reconnaisance missions were flown cautiously, they might give Admiral Allara on the carrier an accurate position for the British ships without revealing to Admiral Woodward the fact that the Argentine ships were closing on him.

At 08.30 on Saturday 1 May a Tracker, its engines at full throttle, was catapulted from the flight deck of the *Veinticinco de Mayo* and flew on a course to the south-east searching for the location of the British ships. However, although it picked up some transmissions from the British battle group, it failed to come up with any accurate direction or range.

Four hours later a second Tracker flight was launched, and this time the pilot, Lieutenant Commander Dabini, went sufficiently close to the British battle group to receive a warning in his cockpit that their radars had picked him up. Nevertheless, he still went in to get an accurate fix, flying to within 55 miles of the battle group. Turning, and flying low, he made his way back to the carrier, radioing the position that he had identified.

12

'THEY WON'T MAKE IT'

On board the *Veinticinco de Mayo* they now had the information they needed to launch a strike, but Admiral Allara waited. Whether he was concerned about the threat of submarines or wanted to see what the other air attacks from the mainland would achieve isn't known. It wasn't until after dark on 1 May that another Tracker took off to update the position of the British ships. This plane also located the battle group, and flew to within 60 miles of them before returning. It too had been picked up by the battle group's radar, on both *Coventry* and *Invincible*, but unlike the previous incident it had not been ignored and a Sea Harrier was flown off to investigate the intruder. It failed to find anything, but the battle group had been alerted and a second Harrier was flown off an hour later. The pilot of this Harrier in turn was picked up and illuminated by the radar of a Sea Dart tracking radar, the missile system carried by the Argentine Type 42 destroyers. Now each combatant knew the location of the other, and the advantage of surprise had slipped from Admiral Allara's grasp. Nevertheless, he ordered the air group on the *Veinticinco de Mayo* to prepare for an attack in the morning. The Argentine navy was still worried about the ability of the British Sea Harriers to carry out bombing attacks on their ships, although it is unlikely that Admiral Woodward would have risked losing any of his precious fighter cover in that type of mission. Sinking the Argentine carrier was what he thought his submarines were there to do.

The Argentine assessment of the Harrier threat, however, meant that they wanted to launch their attack on the British task force from as great a distance as the range of their Skyhawks would allow. The aircraft were assembled on the carrier's flight deck and fuelled with their maximum load, primed with two 500 lb bombs each and armed with Sidewinder missiles. There would be no other Argentine aircraft to provide cover against the British Harriers, so the pilots would have to defend themselves as best they could. Only six of the Skyhawk aircraft were serviceable, so a total of eighteen bombs would be carried to be aimed at the British warships. The pilots' briefing started at 23.00 and continued for some time. They were most worried about the effectiveness of the British anti-aircraft missiles; the leader of the attack, Lieutenant Commander Philippi, was told by an intelligence officer on board the carrier that in his estimate only two planes might survive the assault. This was extremely uncomfortable news, and Lieutenant Commander Philippi admitted that he became frightened when he was told it.

But other events were intervening. The Skyhawks were heavily loaded with fuel and weapons, so needed a strong wind over the flight deck for take-off. Bizarrely, the area in which the carrier was cruising was experiencing a dead calm. The aircraft could not take off. In addition, it became clear to Admiral Lombardo in Puerto Belgrano, who was coordinating the whole of the naval operation, that the British task force had started to withdraw to the south-east and was not after all going to attempt a landing on Stanley. He made the decision to abandon the attack on the British battle group and signalled this to Admiral Allara. The *Veinticinco de Mayo* and her destroyer group set a course for the west, heading towards the mainland.

On board HMS *Hermes*, the news that Argentine Tracker aircraft had managed to locate them was causing consternation. Earlier that night Woodward had received an intelligence summary based on an intercepted signal from Admiral Allara to Puerto Belgrano. It told him that a major Argentine attack was being planned on his battle group for 2 May. It gave him the position of the *Belgrano* to the south, but gave no specific details about the location of the Argentine carrier group. He was aware by now that *Conqueror* was trailing the *Belgrano*, although he knew that Commander Wreford-Brown did not have rules of engagement that would allow him to fire torpedoes while the cruiser was outside the exclusion zone. What he was most incensed about was that two submarines to the north had been unable to locate the carrier, despite searching for several days. Confidence in the arrangements for managing and directing the nuclear submarines had dropped to a very low level among the admiral's staff on *Hermes*. On the evening of 1 May they were passed intelligence from a US electronic surveillance satellite that a radar transmission from a Type 42 destroyer had been identified, and this was taken as evidence that the Argentine carrier was at sea with an escort, and was approaching from the north-west. Lieutenant

Commander Jeff Tall contacted the submarine controller in Northwood and made a request that they direct the two northern submarines, *Splendid* and *Spartan*, to positions where at least one of them would be able to make contact with the Argentine carrier task group. He also requested that the submarines should make radio contact every six hours to receive updates of the situation, which clearly could start to change rapidly if the two opposing naval groups came into conflict with each other.

But the signal that was subsequently sent from Northwood to the submarines only gave the flagship's request for movement of the submarines as one option in a series of possible scenarios. *Splendid* moved on a course opposite to the one that Commander Tall had requested, and in his view, 'In that minute Northwood had exposed our north-west flank to the carrier. Had we been sunk it would have been down to one submarine controller.' For Lieutenant Commander Tall it was one of his worst moments of the war.

The flagship was still receiving indications of the approach of the Argentine carrier, and the failure to communicate properly with the submarines was becoming acute. *Hermes* made another request to Northwood to release *Spartan* from its water-space limits and allow it to cross into *Splendid*'s area, but this was refused. It was at this point that Captain Peter Woodhead, on *Hermes*, ordered the Sea Harrier into the air to find the *Veinticinco de Mayo* in a last attempt to locate what was now the biggest threat to the battle group.

Admiral Woodward was furious that the two submarines had failed in their primary mission, to guard the battle group against the most potent threat from the Argentine navy. He immediately instructed Lieutenant Commander Tall to send a direct order to the *Conqueror* to sink the *Belgrano*.

In fact, Woodward did not have the authority to change the rules of engagement for the submarines, even though *Conqueror*'s relationship with the battle group was in the form of associated support. Admiral Woodward, however, was in no mood to put up with any dissension. As Lieutenant Commander Tall remembers: 'I said to him, "Well, you haven't got the ROE, Admiral." And he said, "Are you disobeying an order?" It was getting serious. I said, "No." ' Tall sent the signal, but delayed it by four minutes so that *Conqueror* would not receive it on the scheduled 06.00 broadcast of signals to submarines. He then spoke to Northwood and asked the Staff Officer Operations to read the signal, but to make sure that it was deleted before *Conqueror* downloaded it later. He then asked the officer to inform Admiral Fieldhouse straight away that Woodward was making a very urgent request to change the rules of engagement for the *Belgrano*.

The request was taken that morning, Sunday 2 May, to the daily Chiefs of Staff meeting at 09.15 in London. Lord Lewin said that he would take it to a meeting with Cabinet ministers at Chequers, the Prime Minister's country residence, at lunchtime. Here, told that a decision was urgent, Margaret Thatcher gathered a few ministers together and sought their views as Lord Lewin explained the situation. Two issues helped to resolve the question fairly speedily. One was the risk of losing the *Belgrano* again if *Conqueror* was not allowed to attack. The other was what the politicians would say if, having refused permission, the *Belgrano* and other units continued their mission and inflicted British casualties or sank a British ship? So the *Belgrano*'s death warrant was signed and sealed. Officially, the decision was minuted as having been made on 'the latest intelligence about the movements and intentions of the Argentine fleet, and that of the new situation created by the military events of 1 May.'

*

On board *Conqueror*, travelling at 200 feet below the surface of the South Atlantic, almost nothing was known of this crisis on *Hermes* and its repercussions in the War Cabinet. Equally, on the *Belgrano*, Captain Bonzo was unaware of the problems that Admiral Allara was having in launching his attack. Late in the evening of 1 May, as the *Belgrano* was still steaming on her easterly course, her radio room received a signal from the army commander on the Falklands sent to Admiral Lombardo in Puerto Belgrano summing up the situation and reporting that the attacks on Stanley had ceased. As far as Captain Bonzo was concerned, this seemed to indicate that the British had decided that their first strike was enough, and that they were retiring to replenish their ammunition, stand their crews down from action stations and regroup for the next day:

> This immediately put the usefulness of our pincer movement into question, and I was not surprised at 05.00 hours [on 2 May] to receive a message ordering us to return to a patrol area midway between the areas Ignacio and Julián. At 05.00 hours, with the dawn light arriving and on a course of 250 degrees, we started for area Ignacio at a speed of 16 knots.

The area they were being directed to lay directly to the south of the Burdwood Bank, the area of shallow water to the south of the Falkland Islands.

In the *Conqueror*, meanwhile, Wreford-Brown had signed off his report at the end of Saturday 1 May, recording that he had been in the trail for the last eleven hours: that the Argentine task group TG79.3 had maintained a constant line of advance; and that because they were not showing any lights he would maintain the trail using sonar, ready to employ a Tigerfish torpedo should the Argentinians head into the maritime exclusion zone. 'A good day – in contact with the enemy at last!' he recorded. In fact, compared to the problems of locating the aircraft carrier in the north, *Conqueror*'s interception of the *Belgrano* group had gone remarkably well. They had picked up the sonar trace from a long way away and were now ensconced behind the ships, hidden and capable of making an attack at any time. In comparison with the frustrations of South Georgia, the serious problems they had had with their aerials and the doubts about their ability to continue as part of Operation Corporate, Commander Wreford-Brown and his crew had good reason to be pleased with what they had achieved.

The submarine continued to trail the *Belgrano* through the night, keeping track of her position on the plot. The submarine, however, steered a course to intercept the Argentine cruiser when she entered the maritime exclusion zone, which was predicted in the intelligence briefings that *Conqueror* had downloaded earlier. At this point everyone on the submarine knew that the *Belgrano* might be attacked, and a provisional firing solution was being continuously updated.

The change of course that the Argentine cruiser implemented upon receiving the signal from Admiral Lombardo to abandon the attack on Woodward's battle group took the *Conqueror* by surprise. At 06.00 GMT, which was 03.00 local time, *Conqueror* had downloaded signal 171 which was still informing Wreford-Brown that the *Belgrano* would move to a position at 54 degrees south and 60 degrees west with the aim of attacking Royal Navy units. Wreford-Brown commented, 'They won't make it.'

However, by 09.00 GMT the change of course of the *Belgrano* had been noticed, and it was realized that she was not going to venture into the exclusion zone, to the disappointment of

Commander Wreford-Brown. The Argentine group had changed its positions as well as its course during the night, placing the two destroyers to the north of the cruiser. At first Tim McClement thought that the navigator, Jonty Powis, had made a mistake on the plot. McClement looked at the track of the sonar targets that Lieutenant Commander Powis had kept during his watch: 'I said you must have got confused during the night. There's no way the capital ship will be on the wing – it's got to be in the middle.' Jonty Powis was adamant: 'No, sir, I've been on watch all night and that is what has happened.'

Jonty was emphatic because during the night the *Conqueror* had practised a manoeuvre that had been developed for nuclear submarines in their spying missions against the Soviet navy. It was a practice called underhulling: sailing underneath the hulls of Russian warships to take photographs and inspect any new additions to their sonar equipment, or anything else mounted underwater that could affect their performance. The manoeuvre was practised on the Submarine Commander's Qualifying Course and was almost routine, but still required cool nerves, great skill from the planesman and an aggressive audacity on the part of everyone on the boat. Lieutenant Commander Powis had done this before on a Russian cruiser. 'Nothing prepares you for the shock, your first time,' he says. 'Your heart, your liver, everything leaps into your mouth when you look through the periscope and you see this propeller going round.' That night the *Conqueror* got close astern to the *Belgrano* at safe depth:

> We knew the distance between his cruiser and the top of our fin
> was fifty feet, perfectly safe because you don't go up or down,
> and we kept the sonar trace to a deflection so that we knew we
> were two hundred yards behind him.

While the *Conqueror* was in this position, the two destroyers crossed over the *Belgrano*'s course, both moving on to the port side of the cruiser, the position that Jonty Powis had recorded on the constant plot.

On board the *Belgrano*, Captain Bonzo was still worried about the possibility that with the start of a new day they would be spotted by renewed Sea Harrier patrols and then they could be subjected to an air raid, so he kept the crew at action stations. The sea state had deteriorated as they travelled west, with wind speeds of over 30 knots and heavy waves coming from the west. In an effort to turn the head of the ship slightly more into the wind, thus easing the battering of the sea on the bows, the *Belgrano* changed course at 09.00 to 270 degrees. The accompanying destroyers were finding it hard to keep up this speed in the face of the strong waves and were pitching heavily, so they eased their speed a little to conserve fuel and improve conditions on board the small escort ships.

Belgrano, *Bouchard* and *Buena* continued to battle westwards through the steep seas. Nobody on board thought that the approaching battle had been delayed for long. But at 10.00, Captain Bonzo believed that they had left the immediate radius of action of British aircraft from *Hermes* or *Invincible*, and ordered the crew to stand down from action stations so that some of them could eat and get some rest. So the crew reverted to the three-shift system, with some of them staying at their posts until midday, while others, who were due on duty again at 16.00, went to eat or to try to sleep. Some went to the Sunday morning church service, which was more crowded than usual. Prayers were said for the families of crewmembers and for those who had been captured in South Georgia. Commander Galazi went to get some rest, Lieutenant Commander Bernasconi went to his cabin on the second deck and Conscripts Bellozo and Otero went down to their mess on the second deck to rest. The Sea Cat operator, Juan Heinze, stayed at his action stations, but lay down on his bedroll on the table on the bridge wing and closed his eyes.

Throughout the day *Conqueror* trailed very close to the *Belgrano* and the two destroyers, keeping a distance of between half a mile and 2 miles astern, were confident of remaining undetected. Petty Officer 'Horse' Libby was on the sonar watch during the day:

> A ship has a blind arc behind it, where all the machinery and propeller noise is, and that's where you hide, in that blind arc. You are reducing the chance of detection but still maintaining contact. So if you're in close and the contact you're following alters course, you need to alter course with it to stay in the blind arc. A submarine will do a 'Crazy Ivan', a manoeuvre where you suddenly change course to get a quick look at what's behind you. It's called clearing your arcs. The Russian subs do it, we do it, but I've never known a surface ship to do it. There's nothing secret about it – it's just good practical seamanship.

Beyond the concentration of maintaining a trail, the atmosphere on the *Conqueror* had not, according to Petty Officer Libby, altered perceptibly: 'Up to this point it's just like a normal patrol for us. Surveillance, report back on the ship's position, what they're up to, where they're going.'

The trail continued, with the *Belgrano* group heading west at a course of 270 degrees. At 14.10 GMT the *Conqueror* fell back from its close position, went to periscope depth and reduced speed to 5 knots. It was time to receive more routine signals, but there were still problems receiving signals on the Fleet Satellite Communications UHF aerial.

Some of the signals added to the confusion. Signal 174 was a cancellation of the signal from Admiral Woodward to sink the *Belgrano*, which, of course, Lieutenant Commander Tall had ensured was never received by *Conqueror*. Signal 177, however, appeared to give Wreford-Brown permission to attack. The message was garbled, and it was downloaded six separate times. No single message was complete, so Wreford-Brown gave Tim McClement the task of constructing the complete message from the six fragments, ensuring that the carbon copy from the telex was not cut or broken. He wanted the paper audit of this order to be unambiguous, recalled McClement. He was absolutely correct.

While Lieutenant Commander McClement was trying to make coherent sense of the signal, there was a meeting in the ward-room with the captain, the senior engineer, the weapons engineer and the navigator, Jonty Powis:

> There was a period, well, we think we have been told, but we are just going to get another run of the signal to make sure, and the question was, what torpedo to use? And we all sat around this table waiting for the signal, and we thought we've got a ship that was built in 1936 and a torpedo that was used in 1943 that we know works, and we've got weapons that were built in 1980 that we are a bit worried about. Let's use the old ones.

Conqueror had loaded two types of weapon before leaving Faslane. There was a torpedo called the Mark 8, which, as Jonty said, was designed in the 1930s and introduced into service in the Royal Navy in 1936. The Mark 8 was powered by a piston engine that burned a fuel mixture of compressed air and oil. It had a speed of around 45 knots and a range of around 5 miles at that speed. It carried a warhead of 365 kg of an explosive called Torpex, which was a mixture of the explosive RDX, TNT and aluminium granules, designed specifically for use underwater. It was very powerful, and the aluminium increased the duration of the explosion, maximizing the effect of the blast wave on a ship's hull. The Tigerfish was the modern replacement for the Mark 8, approximately the same size with a length of 21 feet and a diameter of 21 inches. The Tigerfish was powered by batteries and had a greater range. Moreover, it could be guided to its target by signals sent down a very narrow flexible wire that remained attached to the launching submarines. In contrast to the Mark 8, which went in a straight line after it left the torpedo tube, the Tigerfish could be launched from different angles, and could follow its target even if the ship started to try to evade the torpedo. But the Tigerfish torpedo had proved to be very un-reliable once it was introduced into service, and *Conqueror* had never been able to fire one successfully. Everybody sitting down around the table thought that using the Mark 8 was the most intelligent thing to do. The detail that clinched the matter was that the *Belgrano* had a belt of 6-inch armour plating along the waterline, and the Mark 8 torpedo had a much bigger warhead than the Tigerfish. They were quite confident that they could hit the target.

When Tim McClement had finally deciphered the six separate signals, it was clear that Wreford-Brown had permission to attack the *Belgrano*. They were now going to close once again on the cruiser and work out a final firing position.

Conqueror increased her speed to 21 knots and approached the *Belgrano* and her escorts, coming to within 2½ miles before going to periscope depth. Both the destroyers were on station on the starboard side of the cruiser, their positions having shifted from the morning. Wreford-Brown decided that he would get an unobstructed shot from the port side of the *Belgrano*, and would also be shielded from the destroyers while he made his escape.

Sunday lunch had been served while these manoeuvres were going on; Tim McClement remembers that it was a traditional Sunday meal of roast pork followed by apple pie. He lay on his bunk, going over the firing calculations in his head. Although the final decision was the commanding officer's, as first officer he was responsible for working out the solution for the captain. In the control room was a fire-control computer, an analogue system with dials that were used to enter the course and speed of the target relative to the submarine, the range and the speed setting of the torpedoes; it would also calculate the certainty of a hit. Every officer on the submarine was trained to work out these calculations in his head, and it was the most natural thing in the world for Tim to treat it as a problem of mental arithmetic.

By now the crew on the *Conqueror* were aware that there was more to the day's activities than the routine trailing of a ship. Then the captain made an announcement over the loudspeaker. He said, 'This is the captain speaking. We'll be going to action stations in half an hour to attack the *General Belgrano*. The rules of engagement have been confirmed.' Petty Officer Libby said there was still an air of disbelief:

Loads of us were in the mess – you couldn't sleep with what was going on – and we all sat around having a drink of coffee before we went to action stations. You're thinking, 'That's never going to happen – we'll never fire.' Even up to the point of firing no one thought we would do it.

Conqueror dived to 380 feet and passed to the east of the *Belgrano* at 21 knots, heading south-west to come on to *Belgrano*'s port quarter. Wreford-Brown's original intention was to fire three torpedoes at an angle of 100 degrees to the *Belgrano*'s course, but while setting up for this position the group of ships started zigzagging.

The *Conqueror* was approaching close to the *Belgrano* now, but the two destroyers were still maintaining a passive sonar watch. Captain Bonzo wanted to test their sonar reception, and ordered the *Hipólito Bouchard* to move away to test the passive sonar range. *Bouchard* moved away to the north and sent a signal to the *Belgrano* that, because of the surface sea conditions, the maximum range at which she could hear the *Belgrano* propellers was 4,000 yards. There was no other sonar contact; even during the closing hours of the attack on the *Belgrano*, no sonar warning was ever detected by the operators on either the *Bouchard* or the *Buena*.

By 18.22 *Conqueror* was manoeuvring to get into a position to make an attack. The *Belgrano*'s course and speed were being plotted all the time, and fed on to the contact-evaluation plot, which was a handwritten record of the course of the target and the submarine's position. It was fed into the fire-control calculator, which was the analogue computer mounted forward of the plotting table, and calculations were constantly being done in people's heads.

It was essential to remain at periscope depth now; the captain measures the bearing of the target from the angle of the periscope to the bow of the submarine. The commander will then tell the navigator he's 30 degrees on the port bow, and the navigator will draw a point on the paper plot. Over a period of time, the angle on the bow is measured at regular intervals, so that a course or a mean line of advance for the target can be established. The sonar operator is informing the captain of changes in the engine note – is it maintaining the same speed?; every thirty seconds the sonar angle is read out to the captain; and the control room is becoming noisier and noisier as information is passed to and fro.

Lieutenant Commander McClement was in the control room:

> The captain's looking through the periscope – he spent years being trained to assess visually the course and range; the sonar are saying it's doing so many revs; and then the navigator is saying, 'Actually he's not doing the course you're saying.' There's always a slight difference, and as second in command and the attack coordinator it's my job to put them all together and come up with the best possible solution. The whole team is helping you to refine the solution.

Once the course and speed of the target is established as accurately as possible, then the firing point and angle have to be calculated from the speed of the torpedo and the angle of the submarine to the target's course, what is known as the angle on the bow. The Mark 8 torpedo can be set so that it fires at an angle after it leaves the submarine, but this increases the risk of a malfunction. Commander Wreford-Brown was about to give the order to fire when Tim McClement stopped him.

> The first time he was going to fire he was going to fire on a seventeen-degree right shot. I said, 'Do not fire.' That was my job as the attack coordinator, although Admiral Herbert did tell me afterwards it was a pretty gutsy call for the first ever torpedo attack since the Second World War. Wreford-Brown came over and said, 'Why not?' I said, 'The angle is reducing.' And then we

had a solution for three torpedoes, one at one degree right, one at zero angle, and the third two degrees left. You can't get better than that. And the reason you have three is because you have a fan of weapons, all fired at slightly different intervals. Even if he sees them coming there's nothing he can do.

The patrol report recounts the last few minutes. At 18.54 GMT the captain records a last all-around look, then thirty seconds later sets target speed 10½ knots. The order to stand by 1, 2 and 6 tubes has already been given; then 1, 2, 6 tube bow caps open; then the final set-up and then at 18.56 and 45 seconds the order: 'Fire!'

The order of firing was 6, 1 and 2. The navigator, Jonty Powis, remembers it was a familiar sound. 'There's a click, then the groan of the water rams that push the torpedo into the water, the shudder and thud through the boat as the ram reaches its limit in the cylinder and the noise of the torpedo's engines starting, then the whirring noise as they run out.' And they were on their way.

Even up until the very last minute, there was nothing out of the ordinary, nothing that would take this moment out of the banal daily routine of practices, exercises and perfected procedures.

It's a funny feeling [Libby recalls] because you weren't nervous because this is all you'd ever trained to do. As time went on, you were constantly passing to the captain the bearings and updating the captain on its position – it was constant updates and the chatter back and forth was tremendous. And even then we were still going, 'It's never going to happen.' Then I thought, 'Fuck me – we are going to fire.' And people looked at each other and went, 'Fucking hell.' I'll never forget it, never forget it. And then the boat vibrated, the first one went, you're moving your cursor around and you hear the fish running away, there's two, there's three, all three are running. And you can hear the captain asking, 'How long to run?' So the periscope goes up at the last minute and as the scope goes up and he puts his eyes to it, *bang*.

In the radio room down on three deck Charlie Foy was listening to the events from the control room that were relayed around the boat. He shared the air of disbelief that affected Libby: 'It was what we were trained to do. It didn't register really, and then there was a feeling of "Bloody hell, it's real now." Then we heard the bangs, and everybody was shouting their heads off, "Bloody hell – got him!"'

In the control room Wreford-Brown put his eyes to the periscope and watched one weapon hit. Then for the report Jonty Powis asked him, 'Well, where did you see the weapon hit, sir?' The captain looked at him as if he was mad: 'Pilot, do you know something? I don't sink a cruiser every day.'

*

The Attack

10 May
Deseado
Puerto San Julien
Puerto Santa Cruz
7 May attacked by aircraft
6 May
1 May
4 May
3 May
Ushuaia
Rio Grande
CHILE
Magelan Straits
Cape Horn
ARGENTINA (Patagonia)
Falkland Islands
30 April
5 May
2 May a.m.
2 May p.m. General Belgrano *torpedoed*
ATLANTIC OCEAN
29 April
28 April
South Georgia

On the *Belgrano*, the time was just approaching the 16.00 hour watch change (local time). Lieutenant Commander Levene was walking up a companionway, and realizes now that, as he was doing so, the first torpedo was heading towards him. As he reached the top, ready to turn on to the main deck, he was thrown violently into the air and fell back down the steps.

Radio telegrapher Fernando Millan was walking to the bridge to start his watch when he heard an enormous explosion, like the main guns firing, and a noise like a giant car crash. He felt a massive wind and the ship shook from side to side. Then the corridor filled with an acrid smell.

On the second deck, Conscript Ruben Otero was in his mess area just about to start shaving when he felt the ship shudder as if it had hit a wall, and heard a huge explosion. The lockers burst open and the fluorescent tubes exploded. The chains supporting the collapsible bunks snapped and they all crashed to the deck. There were no lights, but Ruben remembers shafts of light coming through the broken deadlights, illuminating clouds of dust just hanging in the air, and a moment's silence. Then there was another massive impact and the ship started listing.

Oscar Fornes was on watch in the communications room, waiting for his relief to arrive. He was ten minutes late. At the first impact Oscar's head smashed against a radar screen and he blacked out, then roused sufficiently to hear a second explosion and smell the bitter scent of explosive and burnt metal.

Captain Bonzo was just leaving the communications room on his way to the command deck on the bridge. At the first impact he knew at once that it was a torpedo. The ship came to a dead halt, as though it had run aground. It immediately started listing to the left. He made his way to the command deck, then the second torpedo exploded and he saw a column of black smoke and water, mixed with flying debris, climb 80 feet into the air.

The first torpedo hit the *Belgrano* underneath the middle engine room, located just aft of the second funnel. The warhead exploded, creating a violently expanding ball of gas that ripped open the hull of the cruiser and burst upwards through four decks, creating a ferocious blast of unbearable heat, killing everyone. Above this machinery space was the senior ratings' mess and above that the petty officers' mess. Then on the main deck was the dining hall and the relaxation area, the 'Soda Fountain' where the barmen, the two civilian brothers Heriberto and Leopoldo Avila, worked. As the explosion and fireball ripped through these decks, everyone in them was killed. Just behind this area were the magazines for the rear main armament in the two 6-inch gun turrets. They didn't explode, but the initial blast from the torpedo killed in the first instance 272 crewmembers and caused severe burns to scores of other sailors.

The second torpedo hit the front of the ship 50 feet from the bow, just before the first main gun turret. The whole of the front of the cruiser was destroyed and fell into the sea, but the main bulkhead didn't fracture. There were no crewmembers here; so this destruction caused no casualties.

The *Belgrano*'s second in command, Commander Galazi, was asleep when the first torpedo struck. His immediate reaction was that there was an exercise with the main guns firing. Then he realized the ship was listing, and then there was an almighty crash and it felt that the ship had run aground. He knew then that they had been torpedoed. He went to the bridge. Both he and Captain Bonzo started to get damage reports but found it was impossible. There was no electricity and no light. The first explosion had smashed the generators and destroyed the electrical switchboard. Lieutenant Commander Bernasconi was sleeping above the port-side boiler room, and was fortunate that the explosion from the first torpedo had travelled upwards. It was so loud that he thought one of the boilers had exploded. He rose and went to assess the damage and organize damage control. He tried to reach the main engine rooms, but they were on fire. Everybody was killed, because of the lethal effects of fire and high-pressure steam. The bulkhead to the seamen's mess had been broken and many were killed there also. The dining room on the main deck was smashed and many had been killed there by exploding fuel. There was no light, no power for pumps, the engine room and lower deck were filling with oil and seawater, and the smell of fire, explosive and oil made breathing difficult. Bernasconi realized it was hopeless. The old-fashioned voice pipes still worked, and gradually the severity of the situation was communicated back to Captain Bonzo and Commander Galazi on the bridge. The ship was listing, at a rate increasing by one degree every minute. Steam was pouring from fractured pipes, and oil and water was reaching the upper decks. By 16.21 the ship was listing by 30 degrees: it was clear that she was lost. The captain gave the order to abandon ship.

There was no panic. Everyone went to their evacuation stations. Life rafts were thrown into the sea and inflated on contact with the water. They were large, covered rafts that could hold on average twenty-five survivors. As the rafts inflated, orders were given to the men queuing up and they jumped in, some of them managing to land on the rafts, others landing in the freezing water and struggling to safety.

The wind was strong and the seas were picking up. The rafts started to drift and, as they reached the side of the hull where the bows had been torn off by the second torpedo, they hit jagged pieces of steel plating and were ripped open. Lieutenant

Commander Levene went to the operating theatre, but the only casualties were those with burns over their hands and backs who were being treated by two nurses. But everything was falling off the walls as the ship listed and he ordered the operating theatre to be evacuated. He then went to his 'abandon ship' position.

By 16.40 almost everybody had left the ship. Captain Bonzo walked down to the main deck. He was in a daze, shocked by events, shocked by the loss of his ship and the deaths of his crew. He was close to mental collapse. He heard a voice behind him: '*Vamos, commandante!*' He stared and thought he was going mad. Then he saw a young petty officer, walking along the sloping decks, who told Bonzo that he would not leave without him and dragged him up to the main rail, where they walked down the side of the ship into the sea. They swam for about 100 yards to where three life rafts were clustered. The captain was too tired and cold to hold a rope, but he was hauled over the side into the packed raft. At 17.00 he was told 'The boat is sinking, sir.'

There were heavy explosions when the *Belgrano* disappeared beneath the sea, so severe that several survivors standing in the rafts were knocked off their feet. No one knew what caused them. After that there was silence, save the howl of the wind and the crash of the waves, and the groaning of injured men. Night fell.

On board the *Conqueror*, the momentary euphoria and excitement of what seemed like a successful torpedo attack was rapidly replaced by an awareness of the need to escape any counterattack that the Argentine destroyers might try to mount. Graham Libby felt that adrenalin was just everywhere: 'Everybody was on a high because of what we'd done, but it's momentary. We've got

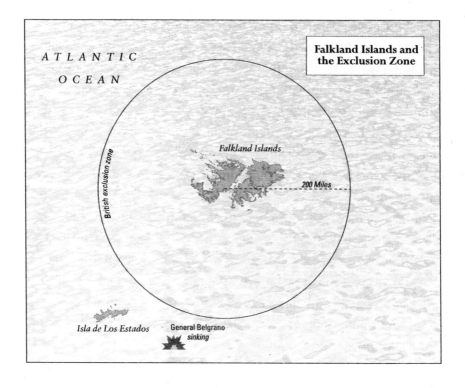

ATLANTIC

OCEAN

Falkland Islands and the Exclusion Zone

British exclusion zone

Falkland Islands

200 Miles

Isla de Los Estados   General Belgrano
sinking

to get our heads back on. The threat's now what else is around us, update the skipper on everything so he can plot a way out safely without getting caught.'

The periscope was lowered, and rapid orders for a change of course and depth were given. The *Conqueror* went to 500 feet and a speed of 22 knots, heading south away from the wreck of the *Belgrano*. The crew became tense when explosions were heard shortly after the attack, and the *Conqueror* remained deep at 500 feet, changing course to head to the east. Then Wreford-Brown gave the order to head north, intending to make a large circle to approach the target area again. Throughout the period of evasion from the *Belgrano*, the sound room kept reporting loud bangs, which it was assumed were anti-submarine weapons being dropped either from the destroyers or from Argentine aircraft. These noises may well have been the sound of the *Belgrano* breaking up as she turned over and sank, the boilers and other spaces imploding under intense water pressure, and finally the impact of the wreckage with the sea bed, some 10,000 feet deep at this point. Wreford-Brown commented that the noises were like gunfire, but these sounds continued into the night, long after the *Belgrano* would have reached the bottom of the sea. At 21.05 a series of loud noises was heard which were estimated to be within 5,000 yards, although neither of the two destroyers launched any anti-submarine weapons.

Conqueror moved south and west, distancing herself from the *Belgrano*'s position by 50 nautical miles. The apparent attacks stopped, and the submarine reverted to routine operations, returning to periscope depth to receive further signals from Northwood and sending a report of the successful attack on the *Belgrano* – the first torpedo attack from a nuclear submarine, and the only submarine attack since the Second World War.

The crew had been shaken out of their euphoria by the evasion manoeuvres and the fear that now they too were a target and might die. And through the night, in various parts of the boat at different times, people reflected on what they had done. It had been a perfect attack, faultless in its preparation and execution, but a ship and its crew had been sunk. The men on board the *Conqueror* were sailors as well, and knew what the survivors, if there were any, were going through.

Throughout the evasion manoeuvres, Graham Libby returned to the frequency and direction of the *Belgrano* on his sonar and listened to the ship breaking up. There was one sound he still remembers:

It was a noise we'd never heard before, and we couldn't understand what it was. It was a tinkling noise, like someone wafting their hand through a big glass chandelier. And it wasn't until the analysis of all the tapes afterwards that they realized, following the explosion and the fires and all that hot metal, it was like dousing a piece of hot metal in a bucket of water. That's what it was as it was going down.

The next morning the *Conqueror* headed back to the attack point, aware of the noises of the destroyers that had returned to search for survivors. These had been joined by a tug that gave a heavy diesel sonar signature and *Conqueror* also detected the radar signature of the Neptune aircraft that were quartering the ocean searching for survivors. Wreford-Brown identified the destroyers *Bouchard* and *Buena*, but did not have rules of engagement to attack them or any ship involved in the search and rescue operation. So *Conqueror* left and continued her patrol.

13

THE RESCUE

The first torpedo that hit the *Belgrano* at 16.01 on the afternoon of Sunday 2 May exploded against the hull at frame no. 106, just forward of the two rear 6-inch gun turrets, almost level with the keel. The second torpedo hit the front of the cruiser at frame 15, effectively removing the bows of the ship. The first torpedo caused all the initial deaths on board, as the explosion smashed its way through the rear engine room and the second and third accommodation decks. The officers of the *Belgrano* believe that 272 sailors were killed in the blast, although many others suffered burns, either from the heat of the initial explosion or from the fires that started immediately after. Many survivors described helping sailors with badly burned hands and feet, as well as other burn injuries.

The order to abandon ship was given quickly after damage-control reports revealed that electrical power and all communications had failed, and that the ship was severely holed, was going down by the stern and was listing to port. There was almost no panic, the crew quickly moving to their 'abandon ship' positions, or at least to those that were not already becoming submerged. The emergency drills had been regularly practised on the voyage from Puerto Belgrano to Ushuaia, and the ship's command structure remained intact despite the damage to the boat and the deaths of nearly three hundred seamen.

The *Belgrano* carried seventy-two self-inflating life rafts mounted along both sides of the main deck, contained in large fibreglass drums connected by rope to the ship. When they were pushed over the side the tightening rope would detonate a gas generator, breaking open the drum and inflating the raft. They had all been fitted and inspected before leaving port. The rafts varied in size and could carry between twenty-two and thirty people. They were well equipped with water, fishing lines, small packs of emergency rations, emergency lights, and had a roof that could be sealed against the weather. These were quickly thrown into the water, but the ship was rapidly listing and the wind was picking up. Many survivors struggled to climb into the rafts.

People found it hard to survive the cold water. Captain Bonzo swam into the water, but the rafts were being blown away from the side of the ship and he had to swim more than 100 yards. He was weakening and quickly losing energy when he was pulled aboard.

Fernando Millan had prepared a waterproof bag of dry clothes wrapped in a blanket, as had a lot of crewmembers, in case of any emergency. These helped to save many lives. Acting automatically, almost in a state of shock, Millan managed to jump into a life raft from the side of the ship, fully clothed. But, he says, 'It was a very extreme situation and if you jumped straight into the water you knew that you were going to die. People were jumping into the water without shoes and in their underwear. Without the clothes and blankets they would not have survived.' There was food in the life rafts and a signal pistol, and dye to stain the sea yellow.

The second torpedo, which had blown the bows off the ship, had left tangled wreckage and torn metal. Several of the life rafts were blown against it and punctured.

Santiago Bellozo went into his assigned raft, but that was then snagged by the wreckage on the front of the ship and it started sinking. He went into the sea to swim to another raft but then got his feet caught in the rope that circled the raft to provide hand holds; it started to drag him under. He was saved by a lieutenant who grabbed hold of him, helped him untangle himself and then pushed him into another raft.

Ruben Otero also jumped 20 feet from the deck into a raft that was already punctured; he then clambered into a second one, then a third. He would spend forty-one hours altogether in his raft. Even in this extremity he never lost hope, believing that he would be rescued and would return home safely, as he had reassured his mother on his last unauthorized leave. He remained calm because, 'When you are in the middle of it, you don't think.' However, when he saw the ship sinking and disappearing beneath the waves, he realized the finality of what had happened and the precariousness of his position. He had served on the ship for some months and it had already become home to him. Now it was gone. 'When you see the ship sinking it is like you want to pull it up, to stop it in some way.'

Oscar Fuentes jumped into his raft at 16.23. It was raft no. 8, the one formally assigned to his 'abandon ship' station. There ought to have been very many people at this raft position, but there were a lot missing because they were in the other watch and had been asleep in the area above the explosion. Nobody had survived. When Oscar was in the raft a burned sailor, too badly injured to move, was lowered down to him from the side rails. There were sixteen people on board the raft altogether, and the wind that had now started to pick up began to blow them towards the ship and the bow wreckage. Then, to the relief of all on board, a large wave took the raft away from the ship. Oscar was 500 yards from the ship when it finally went down. They felt the large underwater explosion that followed; it hit the bottom of the raft and was so severe that people were knocked over by it. They had no idea what it was, but assumed that the ship's boilers had somehow exploded as it sank.

Earlier in the day Lucas Ocampo had been anxiously assuring some of the younger conscripts that it didn't matter if they couldn't swim; the only important thing they had to be sure of was that they kept their life jackets close to hand. Now he was making sure that they got into the life rafts, urging them forward one by one before he too jumped into a raft that was bumping against the deck of the listing *Belgrano*. That raft was over-crowded, so he moved to another, then saw that the long barrels of the 6-inch guns were slowly coming down on top of the raft and threatening to sink it. He too was saved by a wave that pushed the raft further down past the stern of the *Belgrano*, away from the wreckage. On his raft there was also a badly burned man, in severe pain, constantly groaning.

Juan Heinze had to abandon ship down the upturned side of the boat. He walked down a rope that had been secured to the rail, but lost his footing on the wet, oily hull, and slid, banging against the side, cutting himself against the barnacles and rivets.

Even now he still remembers the cold, and the fear he felt as he slid into the freezing water.

The medical doctor, Alberto Levene, jumped into the water and went down by as much as 6 feet. The cold was a brutal shock, and he nearly drowned there and then. It seemed ages before he started rising back to the surface. 'I rose up and saw all this steel in front of me. I thought it was my last moment.' He was already beginning to suffer from exposure when two conscripts grabbed hold of him and struggled to pull him over the side, where he collapsed on the floor of the raft.

In all, it now seems that another twenty-eight sailors died in the water, either from drowning, from the cold, or both, and never made it to the safety of a life raft.

Dr Levene's raft was stable but had been flooded and was half full of water. He watched the cruiser sinking. Within an hour, a storm started to build up. As the waves increased and the wind cut through their wet clothing like knives of ice, Alberto and the others in his raft realized that they were in danger of dying quickly from exposure. But they knew they had to keep going. They started to bale out the water with a boot, and shared out what dry clothing they had. The doctor, who was twenty-five years old, was the only officer on the raft, with ten young conscripts and a nineteen-year-old petty officer. He knew that they had to keep awake if they were going to survive the night.

The waves were getting very high. To start with, people had tied life rafts together, five at a time, so that they would be easier for searchers to locate. Some of the rafts had a radar reflector; others were fitted with yellow dye and signal pistols to help rescuers. The high waves put great tension on the ropes that tied them together, and threatened to help overturn the rafts. Reluctantly, the survivors severed the ropes and the rafts scattered in the dark and the gale-force winds. As night fell the cold got worse, and conditions became severe. With some life rafts carrying as many as thirty-two people they generated enough heat to keep everyone warm. Oscar Fuentes had broken open the medical kit on his raft and used some of the antiseptic cream and painkillers to treat their badly burned passenger. They told each other stories and jokes to keep up morale, but as the storm increased it became very uncomfortable. They tried to keep a watch system going, but in the rough weather 'it was like being in a giant washing machine.' As the temperature dropped, on those rafts where there were only one or two survivors the cold became too much and people succumbed to exposure and hypothermia.

At the time of the attack on the *Belgrano* the two destroyers *Hipólito Bouchard* and *Piedra Buena*, hearing a loud noise on their sonars, steamed 30 miles to the north at high speed, as they had previously agreed they would do if there was an attack from a submarine. They regrouped and attempted to contact the *Belgrano* on the radio, but received no reply. At 16.35 they reported to the commander of task force 79, Rear Admiral Allara, that they had lost contact with the *Belgrano* and, fearing that she had been disabled, requested air support and further assistance to tow her to Ushuaia. At this time the worst that they expected was that the *Belgrano* was damaged. The two destroyers then returned to the *Belgrano*'s last position, but saw nothing; neither did they see any sign of any wreckage, or life rafts.

The warships continued to search in the area, but were hampered by the rough seas and the onset of darkness. At 03.00 on Monday 3 May a Neptune anti-submarine aircraft arrived to join them, but its searchlight was broken so it could only conduct a survey of the area with its radar. It carried out a patrol for two hours, then had to break off because it was running out of fuel, and at 05.00 it headed back to the mainland.

At 08.00 the destroyers started a square-pattern search from the last known position of the *Belgrano*, looking for rafts or anything that would indicate the fate of the cruiser. The two ships could make only 8 knots because of sea conditions. The temperatures in the early morning were as low as −10°C, visibility was low and the sea was still extremely rough, with waves reaching heights of more than 20 feet.

At 06.45 a second Neptune aircraft arrived and started searching to the east and south of the last known position of the *Belgrano*. As the light improved, at 09.10 one of the Neptune search aircraft saw a large oil slick. It was to the south-east of the *Belgrano*'s last position and was 11 miles long. This was the first indication that a tragedy had occurred, and as news of the sighting was signalled back to the mainland and the circling aircraft, it was becoming plain that the ship would not be found. There was also still no sign of life, and the awful possibility that not only the ship but all of its thousand crewmembers were lost began to crush the spirits of all those engaged in the search.

The search continued, with the Neptune aircraft dropping sonar buoys at regular intervals in order to detect the presence of any submarines. At 10.40 the radio operators on the *Bouchard* picked up a distress signal from a group of life rafts, but it was intermittent and the operator was unable to fix the location of the transmitter. The transmission was repeated twenty minutes later, but again it was too short to locate. By this time other aircraft had become involved in the search, but the Neptune aircraft that had spotted the oil slick now spotted a yellow object floating just beneath the surface of the water, disappearing altogether in the rough seas, then slowly rising to the surface again. This was clearly a damaged and capsized life raft. If there had once been any occupants, there was no sign of them now, although their bodies might be trapped beneath the rippling rubberized fabric. The pilot continued on the course that had led him to this ominous piece of flotsam.

Calculations carried out on the *Piedra Buena* confirmed that the oil slick and the submerged life raft were consistent with a current and the wind direction from the last known position of the *Belgrano*. At 13.15 on the day following the sinking the first inhabited life rafts were seen from the cockpit of the Neptune aircraft. It had been almost twenty-one hours since the order to abandon ship. The surface ships were still over 30 miles away, and the sea was not good. The wind speed had dropped considerably since the storm during the night, but was still blowing at 30 knots, and there were only a few hours of daylight left. The Neptune circled the location until the rescue ships, now joined by the seagoing tug *Gurruchaga* and the ice-breaker *Bahía Paraíso,* could fix a course and head for the position. Then, once again running low on fuel, the plane returned to base.

The *Gurruchaga* had been dispatched from Ushuaia at 21.30 on the night of 2 May to assist in towing the *Belgrano*, but at 08.30 that morning they had been assigned an area to search that was 17 miles from the Isla de los Estados. The tug then changed course after the signal from the Neptune and at 17.30 made contact with the first life rafts. The crew had to make rapid changes to the boat, because they realized there would be nothing to tow, but they hoped they would have a lot of survivors to deal with.

During the night the survivors on the life rafts had endured extremely difficult conditions. The seas had been mountainous and the cold bitter. During the first twenty-four hours after a shipwreck survivors do not experience thirst or hunger, and the emergency rations had been untouched. On most of the life rafts there were people with injuries and the fit ones did their best to help them get through the night. The raft bearing Dr Levene and his young conscript companions had survived intact and they had managed to keep contact with an accompanying raft all night by holding on to a rope. As dawn came their spirits rose slightly and they manoeuvred themselves over to the other raft. There they found the bodies of two dead crewmembers, who had died of exposure in the night. They emptied the raft of its rations and equipment, then let it go.

Fernando Millan had lost all sense of time during the night and the next day. The crewmembers they had pulled out of the sea the day before had managed to survive the night and now they waited for rescue. In the afternoon they heard the noise of an aircraft, then twenty minutes later they saw a Neptune search aircraft. Fernando was absolutely certain that they had been seen, as the aircraft waggled its wings – but it didn't return. Neither did they see any sign of other ships. As evening fell and it started to get dark once more, he was hit by a sudden overwhelming sense of despair. He felt that all he could do now was pray. Rescue was no longer certain, and the young man who had believed that the world was at his feet could no longer be certain that he would live much longer. One of the crewmembers on the raft became hysterical when he realized that no ship or plane was coming; he was punched in the face to keep him quiet.

The destroyers *Bouchard* and *Buena* were making their way slowly to the point where the Neptune aircraft had spotted the first group of life rafts. They were limited to a speed of around 8–10 knots because of the heavy weather, and both vessels were showing some signs of damage from the mountainous seas they had encountered the night before. The *Piedra Buena*'s fuel tanks were beginning to develop splits along the seams; the *Bouchard* had problems with her engines and could not come to a dead stop.

The tug *Gurruchaga* was also heading for the rafts. This boat had powerful searchlights and a low freeboard at the stern, both of which were to prove invaluable in the recovery. By the time that the three vessels arrived in the area night was beginning to fall, but they started at once to hail the life rafts and rescue their occupants.

On the raft carrying Commander Bernasconi and the *Belgrano*'s second in command, Commander Galazi, they had been using a steel helmet as a urinal. Galazi was emptying it into the sea when he saw the grey shapes of vessels approaching. Bernasconi was exhausted, utterly drained of energy. He didn't care whether the ships were British or Argentine – he just wanted to be rescued. He picked up a torch and waved it frantically to be noticed. In its beam he could see other rafts tossing in the seas. The *Piedra Buena* approached, and suddenly Bernasconi realized that they were in danger of being ploughed into the sea by the bows of the destroyer, which towered more than 15 feet above them. But it slowed, and they climbed wearily up the rope ladders that were thrown down. They were safe.

Many other survivors lived through a second night on the stormy sea, hugging each other for warmth, holding on to the vestiges of hope, greeting the second dawn with increasing lack of energy, cold and wet, their universe reduced to an insanely tossing raft, an empty bleak horizon on a dark ocean, with companions who were burned and cold, sometimes lapsing into unconsciousness.

Later that day Fernando Millan and his companions were rescued by the *Hipólito Bouchard,* and Captain Bonzo was also rescued, so cramped and cold that his legs were paralysed and he had to be lifted on to the boat.

At 16.00 on the afternoon of Tuesday 4 May, Dr Levene heard the sound of aircraft engines. On his raft, they too had begun to despair. One of the conscripts was deteriorating physically, despite being wrapped in blankets and clothes from some of the other men in the raft. The sight of the aircraft was 'an absolutely fantastic feeling. A reprieve, from death.' The tug *Gurrachaga* steamed towards them. This vessel had saved an enormous number of people, over 365 in total, and the twenty-one on board Dr Levene's raft would be some of the last survivors of the cruiser to be rescued. They had spent forty-eight hours adrift and were still alive. They were hauled over the low side of the tug's rear deck and taken down into the crowded cabins and mess deck. But tragedy struck at the very last minute. The conscript who had been so affected by the cold, his body unable to cope with the sudden change of temperature, had a heart attack and died in the saloon of the tug that had rescued him.

By the time the search for survivors was called off on 5 May everybody on the *Belgrano* had been accounted for. Twenty-three corpses, dead from exposure, were recovered from the life rafts, but 770 crewmembers had been rescued alive and were eventually landed on the mainland at Ushuaia.

In the aftermath of the rescue the survivors had an intensely difficult time coming to terms with what had happened to them. Fernando Millan was hit by a wave of depression on his return to Puerto Belgrano when he realized that so many of his shipmates were dead. He felt surges of anger and powerlessness – feelings that were exacerbated when he realized, during a week's leave with his family, that the military junta was telling lies about the conduct of the war and that the general population still believed victory was possible. He was in fact extremely disturbed, and his mother told him how at night he would shout and talk in his sleep.

This was common to all the survivors. Ruben Otero would wake in the middle of the night, totally disorientated, in a state of absolute dread, believing that he was back in his bunk on board the *Belgrano*. Even now there is not one day of his life that he does not know that he was on the *Belgrano*. 'Once you have been torpedoed,' he says, 'you remain torpedoed. It is never possible to forget that it has happened to you.'

Today Argentina has been a democracy for twenty-five years. The country and the people, however, are still trying to recover from an economic crisis of epic proportions that created mass unemployment and galloping inflation. With the military defeat in the Malvinas and the subsequent fall of the junta, the reputation of the armed forces, and the navy in particular, was at an extremely low ebb. As the senior figures behind the invasion and the repression have grown old and died, and less senior ones have avoided prosecution for their crimes, the Argentine armed forces have sought a new role for themselves, taking part in exercises with NATO countries and contributing to United Nations peacekeeping forces.

Monuments to the dead of the *Belgrano* have been erected in Buenos Aires and Puerto Belgrano, and the Asociación Amigos del Crucero General Belgrano now organizes annual reunions and conferences. In 2006 I attended a public meeting in the capital of Argentina where over a thousand people, veterans and relatives, packed a lecture hall to listen to details of the rescue operation, many of which were being revealed for the first time. It is true that the recovery of 770 survivors was an impressive operation and – rather like the British story of the evacuation of the army from Dunkirk in 1940 – an attempt is being made to snatch some glory from the jaws of defeat. But defects in equipment, even the facts of the *Belgrano*'s mission itself, are now openly discussed in a way that would have been impossible twenty-five years ago.

One thing has not changed, however, which is that everyone I talked to, young or old, knows, in the way that they know their left foot from their right, that the Malvinas belong to Argentina. I doubt if that will ever change.

14

Conqueror Steams On

On the morning of 3 May *Conqueror* headed first towards the Isla de los Estados, where a more detailed report of her attack on the *Belgrano* was sent back to Northwood. Not permitted to attack ships engaged in rescue operations, she continued west and passed to the south of the area where they had torpedoed the cruiser. Although from the sonar events after the torpedo hits it seemed likely that the *Belgrano* was sunk, there was still no real confirmation. Their information about the success of the attack was based on intercepted reports that had originally been sent by the Argentine destroyer *Hipólito Bouchard* to the mainland immediately after both *Bouchard* and *Piedra Buena* had lost contact with the cruiser. At that time they had signalled that there had been an attack, and that the *Belgrano* was drifting. These signals were intercepted and retransmitted to the *Conqueror* as part of the regular intelligence update from

Northwood, although this information appeared to contradict the sonar evidence of events immediately following the explosions of the torpedoes that hit the *Belgrano*. One signal did, however, provide evidence of the fate of the third torpedo fired by *Conqueror*, which had hit the keel of the *Bouchard*, damaging its sonar and starting leaks, although the warhead hadn't exploded.

At 04.00 GMT on 4 May the submarine was 58 miles northwest of the *Belgrano* attack position and had detected the searching Neptune aircraft, which those in the control room of the *Conqueror* assumed were searching for them, not for survivors of the *Belgrano*. Six hours later the sonar operators detected another faint ship contact entering the area from a position to the south of the Isla de los Estados and the *Conqueror* went at 10 knots to investigate it. At 08.45 the submarine had moved into a position directly under the hull of the target, as though the ship were a Soviet warship and *Conqueror* was on a spying mission. The reason for this manoeuvre, of course, was not to photograph the hull of the ship, but because this was the safest place for the submarine in an environment where there were likely to be several ships and aircraft searching for it. The noise of the target's engines and propellers would mask the *Conqueror*, and if she were detected, the assumption would be that it was a spurious echo or signal coming from the ship she was underhulling. Commander Wreford-Brown was planning to continue like this until sunrise, when he would move ahead and visually identify the ship before firing a torpedo. When he looked through the periscope, he saw that the ship had a red hull with a pennant number painted on the side: B1. There was a helicopter landing pad to the rear of the second superstructure, and there were large red crosses painted on a white background. *Conqueror* had been trailing the *Bahía Paraiso*, which had now

257

been turned into a hospital ship and was part of the rescue mission for the *Belgrano* survivors. The submarine followed the ship into the search and rescue area and took a photograph of it. *Conqueror* then identified various aircraft, the *Bouchard*, the tug *Gurruchaga* and the hospital ship as all being involved in the search. Any one of these ships could become a target, and this covert view from *Conquereor*'s control room of the aftermath of the attack on the *Belgrano* showed how vulnerable the Argentine vessels were.

Elsewhere, proper assessments of the outcome of the attack had still to be made. The news was first announced in the UK on the morning of Tuesday 4 May, when the front page of the *Sun* news-paper had two stories of Argentine naval casualties next to its banner headline 'GOTCHA'. The first was a small patrol vessel, the *Sobral*, which it said had been sunk by a Sea Skua missile fired from a Lynx helicopter; the other was the *Belgrano*, which the paper claimed was holed, but not sunk, by torpedoes fired from the *Conqueror*. In fact, the *Sobral* was badly damaged but managed to make its way back to port, while of course the *Belgrano* had been sunk.

Official confirmation of this came when John Nott, the Defence Secretary, made a statement in the House of Commons later that same day. He said: 'At 8pm London time one of our submarines detected the Argentine cruiser *General Belgrano* escorted by two destroyers'. This, of course, was wrong. He then went on to say that the *Belgrano* was 'close to the exclusion zone and was closing on elements of our task force which was only hours away', which was also, at the time of the incident, untrue. By then estimates of the loss of life were being published, and the enormity of the attack was beginning to sink in. It gave even those who supported the war pause for thought, bringing home to people in Britain and around the world what the men on the

Conqueror and the *Belgrano* had already known: that the war over the Falklands was a matter of life and death; ships were going to be sunk and men would be killed.

But what the outside world was saying or thinking did not affect the crew of the *Conqueror*. They had made their own immediate adjustment to the fact that, after years and years of training, they had, shockingly, fired a torpedo in anger and evaded what they thought was a determined attempt to sink them. Admiral Woodward had wanted the Argentine aircraft carrier to be hit, rather than the *Belgrano*, not only because it was a threat, but also because he thought that if it had been crippled by one torpedo and limped back to port, it might cause a political revulsion against the war, ending it before it became even more bloody. This was a naïve belief, although genuinely held. The loss of the *Belgrano* and the deaths of 272 men did not bring about any alteration in the Argentine junta's policies. They intended to prosecute the war as best they could. The problem for the Argentine navy and air force was the same as it had been on the night of 1 May. They knew that the British battle group was somewhere to the east of the Falklands, but the aircraft that took off from the mainland were at the limits of their endurance, and they needed pinpoint locations for the British ships in order to make an effective attack. As we have seen, two of the new Super Etendards, the supersonic bombers equipped to carry Exocet missiles and able to be refuelled in flight, had taken off from the airbase at Rio Grande on the morning of 2 May to attack the British task group, but developed mechanical problems with the air-to-air refuelling system and had to turn back.

The search and rescue operation for the survivors of the *Belgrano* continued through the night of the 3rd and into the morning of 4 May. Taking part were two Neptune aircraft, which were equipped with maritime surveillance radar and which *Conqueror* had already identified. One Neptune, however, picked up a radar contact to the north-east and, while continuing the search for the survivors at low level, surreptitiously gained altitude to track the targets. It was not the *Conqueror* that the radar operator on the Neptune had identified, but three ships, *Sheffield*, *Glasgow* and *Coventry*, all Type 42 destroyers which were forming an air-defence screen about 18 miles to the west of the main body of the battle group. The three destroyers were actively employing all their electronic sensors, so the radars were working; they were using active sonar and were trans-mitting on high-frequency radio, ultra-high-frequency and super-high-frequency wavelengths. They were highly visible and relatively easy to locate once the Neptune had come into range. The Argentinians now had what they needed: a precise location of suitable targets.

By 09.45 two Etendards were ready to take off, armed with an Exocet missile each. They met their tanker plane, a converted Hercules transport aircraft, over the sea and this time the refuelling operation was successful. They passed south of the Falklands and climbed to get their own radar fix on the targets, then dropped low again. The planes were flying through rain showers and low cloud, travelling very fast at about 500 knots, and they launched their missiles 20 miles away from the target.

Although the three destroyers were an anti-aircraft screen for the battle group, the overall control of the operation was the anti-air weapons controller in the operations room of *Invincible*, 18 miles to the east.

The radar operators on *Glasgow* had detected the two approaching Etendards when they first popped up to search for the ships, and had issued a warning to all ships in the battle group. The crew of *Glasgow* then went to action stations and fired chaff to confuse the homing radar on any Exocet missiles the two intruders might launch. The radar on *Invincible* had picked up the contacts at 50 miles out and 30 miles out, which correlated with *Glasgow*'s report. Sea Harriers on a combat air patrol were told to investigate but they saw nothing, and the anti-air warfare officer refused to accept *Glasgow*'s classification of the attack, saying they were spurious contacts, and so didn't take any action. By now the Etendards were heading towards *Sheffield* and ready to launch. *Sheffield*'s own radar was not working because the ship was transmitting on the SCOT satellite communications system and the systems were incompatible. There had also been no back-up from *Invincible* to the warning from *Glasgow*. To compound the vulnerability of the destroyer, the *Sheffield*'s anti-air warfare officer had left the operations room, as had three of his staff. *Glasgow*'s repeated warnings on the radio were either not picked up in *Sheffield*'s operations room, or not given any credence.

The crew of *Sheffield* were totally unprepared for the impact of the Exocet missile that struck them on the starboard side of the hull. The second one, fortunately for them, missed and went into the sea. The warhead of the Exocet that penetrated the second deck did not explode, but it started fires that spread rapidly through the ship, issuing toxic fumes and smoke. Men in the galley were killed instantly by the impact, and five operators in the computer room who stayed at their post were quickly killed by the fumes and the fire. The water main for the fire-fighting system had been broken by the missile, and after an hour the fire was still spreading throughout the ship. The captain, Sam Salt, ordered the *Sheffield* to be abandoned.

Scenes on the deck of *Sheffield* mirrored those on the *Belgrano* two days earlier, as badly burned men were helped by their comrades off a stricken ship. The *Sheffield* had a crew of 281 men, and of those twenty were killed and twenty-six injured. HMS *Sheffield* remained afloat for some days, but she was lost to the task force, and the twenty dead were lost for ever.

If the sinking of the *Belgrano* had brought home to the world that in war at sea ships are sunk and men are killed, then the *Sheffield* brought home that nobody had seen the end of the killing yet. For people in Britain, happy with the loss of the *Belgrano*, it was a sudden shock to find that Royal Navy ships were also vulnerable and that victory was by no means certain. In the words of Admiral Fieldhouse, the *Sheffield*'s loss 'was an expensive warning, and a foretaste of the real Argentine capability.' Admiral Leach remarked after the war was over that 'Ships are there to be sunk. I knew we would see many more casualties.' While old wartime admirals like Leach and Lewin had no illusions about the necessity to take casualties if one were to have any chance of success, they were more nervous about the reaction of the politicians in the War Cabinet. Ministers were deeply shocked; for many this was their first real awareness of what being at war meant.

It was a shock too for the men of the battle group, and an opportunity for Admiral Woodward to remind his masters back in Northwood what exactly he had to deal with. He was unhappy that the *Conqueror* had not been allowed to sink the two destroyers involved in rescuing the survivors of the *Belgrano*. They were warships armed with more Exocet shipwrecking missiles, and would be a dangerous foe if they came close to the task force when British troops were trying to land on the Falklands:

Each of them is likely to return with four Exocet in due course and ruin another day. What with my limited surface surveillance and the winter weather ... I request early political recognition that there is a war going on down here and that this is no time to allow ARG [Argentine] warships to start being treated as hospital ships.

Woodward still wanted the Argentine aircraft carrier *Veinticinco de Mayo* to be put out of action for good, as well as the destroyers. In the immediate aftermath of the loss of the *Belgrano*, units of the Argentine navy were staying very close to the mainland, but there was the continual argument that the carrier presented a very special problem, being mobile, with aircraft that might be able to carry bombs up to 500 miles from where they were launched. There was a repeat of the argument about what rules of engagement should be given to the nuclear submarines about attacks on the carrier. This was precipitated by the fact that *Splendid* had made contact with a large target on 4 May and was following it. In all, as well as the large target, there were three other sonar contacts, and it was supposed they might be the carrier and an escort. The difficulty was that the carrier was inside the 12-mile limit from the mainland of Argentina and moving north. As usual, there was pressure from Admiral Leach and Admiral Lewin that the carrier was a permanent threat while she remained afloat, but the War Cabinet did not believe that either public opinion or international support would put up with an attack on another Argentine ship, no doubt causing heavy casualties, unless she was an immediate threat to the task force. On the table was a diplomatic initiative from Alexander Haig, the US Secretary of State, that might lead to a ceasefire, and Francis Pym, the Foreign Secretary, was particularly vociferous about not being seen to jeopardize the chance for peace. This should take precedence, said Pym, who went on, 'The instructions to the submarine concerned should be modified, at least until we know whether the Argentines are going to accept the Haig proposals.' The rules of engagement were not amended, but it didn't matter, because poor visibility prevented *Splendid* from making any positive identification of the ships that she had been following.

A few days later, under continued pressure from the Chief of Defence Staff, John Nott again raised the issue of rules of engagement in the War Cabinet. After discussions, a new proposal was worked out: that a message should be sent to the Argentine junta via the usual channel of the Swiss Ambassador in Buenos Aires. The new rules that were transmitted said that any Argentine warships or military aircraft that were more than 12 nautical miles from the Argentine mainland would be liable to attack.

These new rules of engagement were not in reality that significant, because since the attack on the *Belgrano* most units of the Argentine navy had stayed within the 12-mile limit any-way, for fear of another encounter with the British nuclear submarines. That made vigilance on the part of the submarine screen all the more necessary, however. The day that *Sheffield* was hit, *Conqueror* was ordered to break off its patrol between the Falklands and the Isla de los Estados, where they were track-ing the destroyers and other ships engaged in the *Belgrano* rescue mission, and head for the position of the *Sheffield*. The British destroyer, although completely crippled, hadn't sunk and Admiral Woodward believed that Argentine warships might move in to finish it off, or to attack British frigates engaged in the salvage effort. *Conqueror*'s task was to act as a barrier to any

Argentine ships that might seek to do that. By the evening of 4 May the submarine had set up a patrol line. There were no enemy ships in the offing, however, nor any indication that they were going to approach.

At the beginning of the voyage, on Easter Sunday, *Conqueror*'s nuclear reactor had been shut down to investigate what turned out to be an electrical fault in the monitoring instruments. Now the chief engineer, Commander David Hall, notified Commander Wreford-Brown that there was a potentially more serious problem with the reactor, and indications were that it was inside the reactor containment shield. The control rods were lowered, with a thud, and the reactor was shut down. Two engineering artificers went through the double-sealed hatch in the side of the air lock to attempt to see what was causing the alarm. Everything was now running on batteries and the crew were alert, waiting for the reassurance of the announcement 'Reactor critical.' There is a very limited amount of time that anyone can spend inside the reactor containment, so once the problem – a leak in the steam generator circuit – had been identified, the engineers quickly exited while they worked out what to do about it. The control rods were slowly raised and the reactor started to produce power once more. A barely perceptible sigh went through the boat.

Wreford-Brown decided that *Sheffield* was not going to attract Argentine warships and left to the south, searching for the Argentine destroyers again. At 02.00 GMT he received a signal that the destroyers were now valid targets. But the main contact that *Conqueror* was now trailing was a very large, modern super tanker, carrying its massive cargo of crude oil halfway around the globe, with a big five-bladed propeller that made her sound like a warship.

The next day the submarine's reactor was shut down again as engineers made a second entry, this time to place a collar, which had been fabricated in the small workshop, around the leaking pipe and joint. This time it took forty-five minutes before the reactor went critical again, but David Hall hoped that the problem had been solved. Two hours later, the *Conqueror* was at periscope depth, downloading more signals and using the snorkel to ventilate the boat, when the alarm was raised that an active radar was targeting the raised periscope, snorkel and masts. Visibility was good and, as well as the electronic warning, an aircraft was spotted through the periscope at a range of 2,000 yards by the officer of the watch. A flash signal had just been received that a Neptune anti-submarine aircraft was in the area. The *Conqueror* immediately went deep to 600 feet and a speed of 21 knots, and the boat was closed up for action stations. The aircraft was flying low and on a parallel course to the submarine – so low that the noise of the aircraft engines was picked up by the towed sonar array.

As the submarine dived, a warning sounded in the control room that a fast-moving contact was in the water and Wreford-Brown knew the chances were high that they had been seen by a Neptune which had dropped an anti-submarine torpedo. He ordered full ahead, and everyone on board looked at their watches. They knew that they might be in extreme danger, perhaps minutes away from death. The last time they had looked at their watches so intently was when they were counting the fifty-seven seconds it took for the torpedoes to leave the *Conqueror*'s torpedo tubes and hit the *Belgrano*. This time they had far longer to wait for an explosion, and they were the target. The Argentine Neptune aircraft carried modern German-made sonar-guided torpedoes. They were fast, but their power cells had a life of just six minutes. The hands on the clock in the control room ticked away, as the depth, dive angle and speed were read off and reported back to Wreford-Brown. The sonar trace followed, but got no closer. After seven minutes, when the torpedoes' batteries must have been exhausted, everyone allowed themselves a moment of hope, and then they were certain they had survived.

It was time now to go over the evidence. In retrospect, nothing was certain, not even that the plane had spotted them, or that it was a Neptune. With time to think, it could have been an Argentine blockade runner, more worried about evading British Sea Harriers and getting home safely than about spotting the feather of a submarine's snorkel in the water. If this was the case, had there been a torpedo at all? Was the sea playing tricks on them? But Wreford-Brown could take no chances. If it had been a Neptune, and if the pilot had spotted them, then a search would be set up around the point where they had dived. Trying to out-fox any pursuer, he headed for shallow water and stayed just off the 100-fathom line, putting 50 miles between him and their last position on the surface.

There were no more alarms that day, but problems were building up. The electronic surveillance aerial was not picking up the most important radar frequencies – those of aircraft – and Commander Wreford-Brown was unwilling to spend time at periscope depth ventilating the submarine until this could be fixed. By 11 May *Conqueror* had been moved north, then east, and there had been a recurrence of the communications problem. Satellite communications were down, and all that was working was the high-frequency trailing aerial that had been deployed when they left South Georgia. Signals were still getting through, but *Conqueror* was still being moved north and, with the arrival of other nuclear submarines, *Courageous* and *Valiant*, she had less sea space to monitor.

On 16 May a sound was detected which swiftly brought the control room to an extremely alert state: the noise of a submarine's hydroplanes. The sonar was quickly prepared for active transmissions and torpedoes were brought to readiness. Twenty minutes later a very strong sonar signal indicated another submarine, and *Conqueror* went to 425 feet to see what could be heard below the surface water layer. But nothing was picked up by the towed array, and the signal was fainter below the thermal layer, which was currently at 240 feet. *Conqueror* rose to 200 feet, but nothing became clearer. It was extremely unlikely that it was another nuclear submarine, because there was no other sonar confirmation: it could be a conventional submarine, but there was no intelligence that there was one in the area, and British signals intelligence had always accurately detected an Argentine submarine deployment in the past. The other possibility was that it was something biological, but it was unlike any other whale in the *Conqueror*'s sonar library. Options were limited. The control room could continue to monitor the situation; they could go to active sonar, which carried a lot of dangers; or, finally, they could try to close on the target, which was also risky given its unknown quantity.

Over the next three hours *Conqueror* changed course and depth to isolate the strange noise, which was still being detected but had none of the associated characteristics of a nuclear or conventional submarine. There was a fleet of Russian trawlers some way away, which *Conqueror* had positively identified some days ago, and whether the ocean was playing tricks with acoustics it was impossible to tell.

This was the day that Flag Officer Submarines signalled to *Conqueror*:

As we come up to the landing phase, I want to congratulate you all on an excellent performance. Despite long spells of inactivity for you, your presence has persuaded the ARG navy to stay well away from the operational area. I feel pretty sure you will get another crack at them. Your success on *Belgrano* completely changed the Args' plans and enforced a very protective attitude which has aided our operations enormously. Good Hunting.

*

In the days after the loss of the *Belgrano* and the *Sheffield* there was a brief interlude of relative quiet, but Admiral Woodward still had to accomplish his most important tasks before the arrival of the amphibious landing force. Almost nightly, British warships mounted a bombardment of Argentine positions on the Falklands, Special Forces were inserted by helicopter to carry out reconnaissance and sabotage, and various attempts were made to provoke the Argentine air force into combat, hopefully to start reducing their numbers. The loss of the *Sheffield* had exposed some problems with the anti-aircraft missiles carried by the destroyers and frigates in the task force, and Woodward wanted to find a combination of warships in which the different missile systems might complement each other. On 12 May, *Glasgow*, a Type 42 destroyer, was sailing off the Falklands in company with *Brilliant*, a Type 22 frigate. *Glasgow* carried the long-range Sea Dart, while *Brilliant* was armed with the modern and very fast Sea Wolf, designed, it was hoped, with the ability to shoot down low and fast targets like Exocet missiles.

Glasgow and *Brilliant* had been shelling positions close to Stanley with their 4.5-inch guns, but had stayed in position well into daylight – an obvious and attractive target for the Argentine air force. Four Skyhawks carrying free-fall bombs appeared over the Falklands, and made their attack on the two ships. *Glasgow*'s Sea Dart missiles failed to launch, and it was up to *Brilliant* to take on the four aircraft. The Sea Wolf radar picked up the targets, and two missiles streaked from the decks of the frigate, hitting two of the approaching Skyhawks. A third aircraft was hit by the debris and also disintegrated, while the fourth pilot ploughed on, and managed to release his bomb, which bounced harmlessly over *Glasgow*.

Twenty minutes later, another four aircraft appeared and went into the attack. This time the Sea Wolf fire control computers rejected the targets, the Sea Dart missiles on *Glasgow* also failed, and the four Skyhawks flew over the ships, all releasing their bombs. By this time, *Glasgow* and *Brilliant* were travelling at high speed, both desperately manoeuvring to evade the aircraft. One bomb hit *Glasgow*, penetrating the engine room, but, miraculously, it didn't explode and continued on through the other side of the ship, leaving two neat holes in the hull. The Argentine air force lost four aircraft that day (the fourth Skyhawk was shot down by Argentine anti-aircraft fire over Stanley), but it was an extraordinarily lucky escape for *Glasgow*, and emphasized once again the vulnerability of the warships to air attack.

By 18 May, the assault ships *Fearless* and *Intrepid*, with the giant troop carrier *Canberra*, had rendezvoused with *Hermes* and the other warships of the task group. There were several other store ships in the fleet that was assembling, including fleet auxiliaries, landing ships and escort vessels. The *Atlantic Conveyor*, a huge container ship, had also arrived, carrying RAF ground-attack Harriers and twin-rotor Chinook helicopters destined to transport troops from the landing site at San Carlos to the outskirts of Stanley. The next day, troops from Canberra were transferred to *Fearless* and *Intrepid*.

Time was running out, the southern summer was coming to an end, and a landing was now inevitable. On 21 May nearly five thousand troops were set to land on the Falklands.

While final preparations for the landing were taking place, the crew of *Conqueror* were wrestling with their own troubles.

*

Over the next two days *Conqueror* experienced further problems with her trailing aerials, and discovered that water was entering them. Despite repairs and changes, they never worked very well for long. As a result, she moved east and took up a longstop position behind *Valiant*. On 19 May, Petty Officer Charlie Foy and two of his artificers rebuilt and repaired another trailing aerial, made the high-frequency connection and then the submarine surfaced at 23.44 GMT. The old wire was released and jettisoned overboard. *Conqueror* returned to periscope depth, but the new wire didn't appear to improve reception of signals on the high-frequency wavebands.

However, when the submarine dived and speeded up there was a very strong noise coming from the propeller; it seemed that one of the two wires had become wrapped around it. They tried several manoeuvres, even going into reverse to see if the wire could be freed, but it was to no avail. At any speed above 6 knots it sounded, according to Wreford-Brown, as though *Conqueror* was trailing a metal dustbin.

Throughout the whole patrol, the crew of *Conqueror* had been encountering and fixing defects. They had had to make reactor entries, the oxygen-making electrolyser had failed, recently one of the carbon-dioxide scrubbers had broken down and, above all, the problems with communications had persistently dogged them since leaving Faslane. Now a trailing aerial was seriously jeopardizing the submarine's safety. *Conqueror* was patrolling an area on a direct route from Puerto Belgrano, the Argentine navy's main base, to the Falkland Islands, and it was the submarine's responsibility to shield the task force and the amphibious group from any threats from the Argentine fleet, whether that was Exocet-carrying destroyers or conventional submarines. The rattle from the *Conqueror*'s propeller made them an easily identifiable target for an Argentine submarine and meant it was almost impossible for them to trail a destroyer or other surface ship. The cavitation that was being produced by the tangled aerial increased by over 400 per cent the range at which they could be detected. As soon as the weather was calmer, a diver would have to go into the water and attempt to investigate.

The landings had already been made on the Falklands, and *Conqueror* was coming to periscope depth for signals traffic every six hours to be kept informed of the fast-changing situation and the latest intelligence updates on movements of the Argentine navy. At 07.53 GMT, 04.35 local time, the officer of the watch thought he saw through the periscope an aircraft with a bright white light coming straight towards the submarine. The *Conqueror* immediately went to 700 feet and increased speed to 21 knots, assuming the worst. At action stations, a series of fast and deep evasion manoeuvres was carried out, but the crew were unable to do anything about the appalling noise emanating from the cable around the propeller. Nothing was detected and after two and a half hours the crew fell out of action stations. What they had seen might have been a maritime patrol aircraft with a bright searchlight, or more likely the officer of the watch had seen the planet Jupiter low in the night sky. The experience of sinking the *Belgrano*, and the perception that they had been attacked immediately afterwards, had created an extremely heightened sense of awareness. They would react first, and take no chances. But the noise from the propeller had to be fixed!

On Sunday 23 May, Commander Wreford-Brown approached Petty Officer Graham Libby. 'Horse' was one of the ship's divers. 'I was in the control room and the captain came out and he looked at me and I knew what he was going to say – "Is the diving gear ready?"' Sure enough, Commander Wreford-Brown looked at Libby and said exactly what Libby expected: 'Is the diving gear ready?'

I was a single man, I was quite happy to go out there because I was pumped up. We had just sunk a blooming great warship – this could be the icing on the cake, you know. It's just something exciting that I might never ever get another chance to do.

He said, 'We won't be at full buoyancy in case we need to do a quick dive if something comes up.' I knew what he wanted to say and I pre-empted him. What he wanted to say was, if you can get back on board all well and good; if not, you're on your own. I knew that. You're not going to risk a submarine and ninety-nine men for one man if we were detected.

Conqueror went to periscope depth and checked that there was nothing in the vicinity, no surface activity, sonar contacts or radar warnings. The weather seemed slightly better than the previous day, and the submarine surfaced. On the top, the weather appeared at best marginal. The boat was rocking and rolling; it was dark and cold. Petty Officer Libby had already experienced how cold the South Atlantic could be when he was washed overboard in

Grytviken Bay off South Georgia. Second officer Lieutenant Commander Tim McClement was the senior diver, and he went up to the top of the fin with a lookout. If there was an emergency contact, like an aircraft, or any danger that the submarine had been detected, McClement would give the order down the voice pipe: 'Press the Klaxon twice.' The crew would immediately go to their diving stations, and the order would be given to open main vents and shut the top lid. Graham Libby would never make it back, and everybody knew it.

Horse got into his diving gear inside the fin, then opened the fin door and walked on to the rear casing. 'A wave came and took me straight into the sea, and I was loaded up with hacksaws and anything I might need. The water was absolutely freezing and I didn't have gloves on because I needed the dexterity of being able to try to unpick this thing by hand.'

Libby's first problem was how to get to the back of the boat without his lifeline being cut by the slowly moving propeller. The engines had been stopped, but the propeller still slowly rotated. 'I was getting thrown around all the time and found it very difficult to get to the back of the boat. The propeller's creeping round, so I've got to move my lifeline to a safe position for the next blade coming round, and I'm getting thrown violently in the sea.' The submarine, like an enormous black whale, was wallowing in the huge waves of the South Atlantic, powerless to manoeuvre, and Libby was alternately being dashed against the submerged hull and tossed by the waves 30 feet away from the submarine. He had to drag himself hand over hand on his lifeline back through the pounding waves each time. It was dark, and the men on the fin could neither see him nor tell whether his lifeline had parted, whether he was attached to the ship, or whether he was gone for ever. Libby started to cut the tangled aerial wire into sections, so that it would just fall off when the propeller was started. 'I persevered for probably twenty minutes, just cut strategic pieces then struggled back on board.' His strength had gone completely, and he was beginning to develop hypothermia. 'I was told to ditch the gear, but I didn't: I thought I might need it again, you never know. I was absolutely done in, totally exhausted. I slept for eight hours straight after that.'

Conqueror dived; the noise was vastly improved. As Wreford-Brown wrote in the patrol report, 'I now feel happier about closing an SSK [conventional submarine] or ARG warship to attack with less chance of counter-detection.' He also wrote that Graham Libby's effort 'was far beyond the call of normal duty'.

Petty Officer Libby's courageous fight against the perishing cold of the South Atlantic had been echoed further south in the Falklands. Here the enemy was the Argentine air force, and many seamen didn't survive the conflict.

The landings had taken place as planned on 21 May on San Carlos, in a large-scale amphibious operation under the command of Commodore Mike Clapp. During the day, attacks from the air became intense, and, although none of the troop carriers had been hit, five out of the seven escort vessels defending the landings were damaged. The warships had been positioned to draw the air attacks away from the troop ships. HMS *Ardent* in Falkland Sound was hit by seven bombs, sinking her and killing twenty-two of her crew. *Antrim*, veteran of the battle for South Georgia, and *Argonaut* were also badly damaged, but survived.

Thirty-six aircraft attacked the landing force in the first wave, and two were shot down. Another twenty-four came over in a second wave, but by the end of day sixteen Argentine planes had been shot down.

This did not stop the attacks. On 23 May, HMS *Antelope* was hit by two bombs which didn't explode, instead lodging deep inside the ship. Bomb-disposal experts boarded *Antelope*, and over several nail-biting hours set about trying to defuse them. After working into the night, an attempted controlled explosion of the fuse of one of the bombs failed, and it exploded in a massive gout of fire, killing the bomb-disposal expert, Staff Sergeant Jim Prescott, instantly, and breaking the back of the *Antelope*, which burned fiercely throughout the night.

HMS *Antelope* was not the last casualty. On 25 May the Argentine junta threw everything into the fray, in a last desperate attempt to destroy the British beach-head. The Argentine air force flew mission after mission against the ships in San Carlos Bay, more than at any other time in the conflict. *Broadsword* and *Coventry* had been sent to a position outside the north end of Falkland Sound in an attempt to reduce the threat to ships in San Carlos, but they were now deliberately targeted as part of a combined offensive against the carriers *Hermes* and *Invincible*. Six Skyhawks flew along the north of the Falkland Islands, feinting as though they were heading to the beach-head and then changing course to hit *Broadsword* and *Coventry*. Meanwhile two Super Etendards armed with Exocet missiles headed for an attack on the *Hermes* and what was thought to be her sister carrier. The Etendards would refuel in flight and then make an approach from the north, to take the task group unawares.

Two Harriers were in the air flying a combat air patrol at the time, and spotted the approaching Skyhawks, but the captain of *Coventry*, Captain David Hart-Dyke, ordered them to break away, believing he could shoot them down with his Sea Dart missiles. He was wrong. The missiles missed their target, and the Argentine aircraft came on to make a first attack on *Broadsword*. Three bombs missed the ship, but one did find it, failed to explode and travelled with a great deal of force through the ship, departing out of the helicopter flight deck. *Coventry* was less fortunate. *Broadsword*'s Sea Wolf missiles failed to engage any target at first, but when two Skyhawk aircraft, now much closer, started their bombing run against *Coventry*, *Coventry* desperately manoeuvred between the attacking planes and *Broadsword*'s missile launchers, preventing them from engaging the aircraft. The two Skyhawks dropped their bomb loads and three hit *Coventry* along her length. This time they did explode. Nineteen men were killed and *Coventry* heeled over and began to sink.

Meanwhile, the two Super Etendards had made their approach to the *Hermes*, and, launching their missiles, made their rapid getaway. *Hermes*'s and *Invincible*'s escort ships fired chaff rockets in all directions to confuse the guidance radar mounted on the Exocet missiles. The *Atlantic Conveyor*, still with its load of precious Chinook helicopters, had not, however, been fitted with chaff dispensers, and, being the first large ship in the line of supply vessels next to the warships, the Exocet missiles found it and fixed on it as the biggest definable target. One Exocet hit the high-sided container ship, immediately starting fires, and ninety minutes later the order was given to abandon ship. Efforts were made to put the *Atlantic Conveyor* under tow but, three days later, she sank, taking with her enough tents for 10,000 troops, vehicles and ammunition, and the helicopters, whose loss would seriously disrupt the advance on Stanley.

Grave as these casualties were, in the days preceding the 25th, and on the day itself, Argentine aircraft were being relentlessly shot out of the sky. The war of attrition against the Argentine air force had finally been won, mainly by the Sea Harriers flying from the decks of the *Hermes* and *Invincible*. With the British land forces now firmly established on the Falklands, was this the time for the Argentine navy to make another intervention?

Despite further intelligence information that the Argentine navy was preparing to make a sortie from port, *Conqueror* still didn't detect any serious movements by Argentine warships, and the fighting on the islands went on. On 29 May a signal was received that the Argentine task groups 79.2 and 79.4 would be moving down the coast to an area between Puerto Belgrano and Deseado. *Conqueror* was instructed to move north-west to another patrol area to make an interception. Again, they encountered nothing.

Conqueror had been at sea since 4 April and had received a signal from Flag Officer Submarines that they would be required to stay on patrol until Stanley fell – an event that might not happen, according to Northwood, until 14 July. Lieutenant Commander Tim McClement made some calculations and realized that, despite the double-decking at the start of the cruise, food rationing would need to be introduced. In a ship's memorandum the crew were enjoined to:

> Please help to make things easier at this difficult time by NOT WASTING FOOD, EATING SENSIBLY and NOT GIVING THE CHEFS HASSLE. These restrictions have been introduced so that we can continue to enjoy a balanced diet for the remaining time on patrol rather than spending the last weeks on bread and water.

The rations were hardly severe. There would continue to be a choice of two meals at supper, and a full Sunday roast. At breakfast the crew were limited to one egg and a choice of either bacon or one sausage. However, the luxuries – like tinned treacle pudding – that helped to provide some slight comfort during the long boring periods of the patrol had gone.

By this time *Conqueror* was off the coast of Argentina, having received information that the Type 42 destroyer *Hércules* was making its way to port for repairs to its propellers. It was hugging the coastline, staying within the 12-mile limit in accordance with the warning that had been issued to the Argentine junta in May. The rules of engagement prevented *Conqueror* from entering Argentine territorial waters and attacking the destroyer, but Wreford-Brown looked at the chart and made the assessment that *Hércules* might try to save time and shorten her journey by cutting across the bay of the Golfo San Matías, rather than continuing to stick close to the coastline. He decided to enter the Gulf and set a trap. This was a risky manoeuvre for two reasons. Navigator Jonty Powis had to use the only charts he had of the area, which were unfortunately drawn to a very large scale: 'The charts were pretty nebulous, there was very little to tell us where we were, but with a bit of prudent navigation we managed to get safely around.' There was a bar of shallow water in the approaches to the gulf. The sea was rough and the water depth was only 162 feet, leaving barely 90 feet beneath the keel of the 4,000-ton submarine. Any hint that the submarine's presence had been detected would leave Commander Wreford-Brown with absolutely no room for manoeuvre.

Nevertheless, the *Conqueror* eased her way slowly into the bay. Every eye was on the planesmen in the control room. *Conqueror* had penetrated Argentine territorial water by perhaps a mile and was waiting to ambush the *Hércules* should her captain decide that he could make the dash across the open waters of the bay. But the destroyer hugged the coast throughout her transit. Jonty Powis was convinced that he saw the *Hércules* run aground in the bay.

> We were inside Argentine territorial waters – I'm not sure we had permission to be but we were, only by about a mile – and there was this huge great kerfuffle of smoke that I saw through the periscope. I feel sure that I had seen her engine exhaust as she tried to get off the bank or whatever it was she was on.

The navigator's belief was made great fun of in a later 'dit' – a story that appeared in the ship's newspaper, *Black Tin Fish*, distributed to the crew to keep them informed and amused. In a spoof story headlined 'LINER ATTACKED BY WHALE PIRATES', Powis's search for the *Hércules* and the recently introduced food rationing were brought together:

> The liner was overcome by a horde of yellow skeletons dressed in an assortment of jumpers, overalls and shirts. The attackers made straight for the dining saloon where they proceeded to devour every scrap of food in sight. Mr K. Warton of Connecticut said two tall ones rushed by me, the first shouting 'Where's *Hércules*?'
>
> The British Admiralty have declined to comment on rumours that this may be the 'A' class submarine *Conqueror* which sailed on exercises in the Irish Sea on 4 May and has not been heard from since.

*

The *Conqueror*'s crew had little idea of the extent to which the world knew about the existence of their submarine and her exploits. By 8 June she had left the Golfo San Matías and was patrolling off the Argentine port of Deseado. *Conqueror*, along with the other nuclear submarines, had started to become a unique early-warning system for Admiral Woodward's task force. Stationed close to the coast, the submarines using their periscopes and passive electronic detection aerials could monitor the activities of the Argentine air force and transmit a warning of an air attack to the flagship, HMS *Hermes*.

The campaign to recapture the Falklands was in its last week, but the British soldiers on the islands were becoming short of ammunition and were facing a heavily entrenched, larger force of Argentine troops as they approached Stanley. It was a crucial point in the war, when any reinforcements to the Argentine garrison might still prove critical to Britain's chances of success. The presence of the nuclear submarines had been sufficient to impose a total blockade by sea, and only a very limited amount of supplies was reaching the islands by night in flights from the mainland.

The Royal Navy continued to suffer casualties. On the Saturday 12 June HMS *Glamorgan* was hit by an Exocet missile launched from the back of a lorry on the mainland. *Glamorgan* had been firing her gun, assisting 45 Commando in its attack on Two Sisters, two high peaks close to Stanley. At around 05.30 *Glamorgan* had stopped firing and was returning to the task force when the Exocet missile was launched. It hit the stern of the ship, destroying the Wessex helicopter and starting a fire. Thirteen of the ship's crew were killed, but the ship itself was saved and managed to steam away from the Falklands.

Admiral Woodward's task force was now in a very bad way. All but two of the original fleet that had set sail at the beginning of April had either suffered some damage from enemy action, or were affected by serious mechanical problems. On 13 June Woodward wrote in his diary, 'We are now on the cliff edge of our capability, with only three ships lacking a major operational defect . . . Frankly if the Args could only breathe on us we'd fall over.'

Now would be the perfect time for the Argentine destroyers and frigates to make a massed attack with their ship-mounted Exocets. But the Argentine navy remained within the 12-mile limit and the high ground around Stanley was occupied by British forces. Demoralized, and effectively cut off and abandoned, the Argentine commanding officer in the Falklands, General Mario Menendez, surrendered on 14 June.

It had been a bitter and bloody campaign. Given the short duration of the conflict, the casualties had been high, and at times it had been a very close-run thing.

On board the *Conqueror*, the news of the Argentinians' surrender was greeted with jubilation. A day later the signal was received to head north-east, back to Faslane. Operation Corporate was over.

On 16 June the officers and crew of HMS *Conqueror* received a signal from Rear Admiral Woodward:

When the dust has settled on the Falkland Islands campaign it will be seen that the single most significant naval event after the arrival of the task group itself was your sinking of the cruiser *Belgrano*. That action brought the Argentine navy up with a round turn and sent it scurrying to the twelve mile limit, there to stay for the duration while we got on and fought the air war.

That cool and determined attack was typical of your whole patrol. Well done. Bon voyage. Take a well earned break.

Then on 18 June another signal was received from Admiral Fieldhouse, Commander in Chief Fleet: 'The sinking of the *Belgrano* was fundamental to the success of Operation Corporate and took the heart out of the Argentine navy. Well done.'

Conqueror steamed for home, and this time the crew could relax and find the winner of the straggly moustache competition while they made their long journey. A few days later they received a signal that a mail drop from a Nimrod maritime patrol aircraft was being arranged. Lieutenant Commander Tim McClement was sceptical. He had experienced one once before and the sacks of mail and newspapers had plummeted from the aircraft, hit the sea and were never seen again.

But at the appointed rendezvous, just north of the equator, the Nimrod aircraft was circling. The fin of the *Conqueror* broke the surface, the lid was opened, and Tim McClement, the look-out and anyone else who could squeeze up there came to see. The Nimrod passed low and sack after sack – thirty-four in all – dropped into the sea, where they bobbed in the swell. The aircraft waggled its wings and departed.

'Well, don't just stand there,' said Tim. 'Go and get the bastards.' There were letters galore, some with vital family news: Lieutenant Jonty Powis's wife had given birth to a daughter, Megan, on 26 May; a senior rating's wedding date had been booked; there were letters from children, parents, lovers and sweethearts – letters and photographs that reminded the crew that life extended beyond the hull of the black tin fish, that there was a life above the waves.

There were also letters from complete strangers. There were letters from almost everywhere in Britain; from Australia, Canada, New Zealand; some from distant relatives, old school-friends; some from people whom nobody on the crew had ever met or heard of in their lives. Petty Officer Writer Colin Way, the forward planesman, got eighty-four letters. And in the mail pouches they discovered the reason why this strange avalanche of mail had descended on them. There were the newspapers: the *Sun*, with its headline 'GOTCHA'; others – the *Daily Telegraph*, the *Daily Mail* – with pictures of the *Belgrano* surrounded by orange life rafts, all with their centre-page spreads about the torpedo attack, all with their exclusive stories of the attack, and all naming HMS *Conqueror*. It was a complete shock to everyone on board.

Graham Libby thought, 'As a submariner we've done lots and lots of these patrols, and you're used to coming in very quietly, not allowed to say anything, about who you are, where you've been or what you've done. And now it was all over the papers.' Commander David Hall the Chief Engineer was equally perplexed.

> Until then it was always 'one of our submarines', it was never ever named. And it was only then that we realized that people knew the story. It certainly shocked the Captain because he then suddenly realized that he was going to get some press coverage. Then the signals flew thick and fast – what do I say, who's going to help me, where are the PR people and all the rest of it.

Conqueror stayed on the surface for the rest of the day while the crew took the opportunity to swim. Graham Libby remembers that day, the sun beating down on the warm tropical water, and on one side of the casing men swimming and diving, while on the other side were fishermen hoping to catch a shark to barbecue on the fore plane.

A submarine that has torpedoed a ship traditionally flies the

Jolly Roger on her return to port. But no British submarine had sunk a ship since 1945, and no nuclear submarine had ever fired a torpedo in anger before. The publicity about sinking the *Belgrano* complicated the issue further. Was it wise to give yet more publicity to the story? The debate continued for the next two days, and then everyone was persuaded that tradition should be followed. A black flag was run up with white skull and two crossed torpedoes sewn on to it. The symbol of a ship was added, to the right above the skull, to denote the sinking of the *Belgrano*, and a dagger, on the left, to commemorate a secret operation. Finally, to bring it up to date, a symbol for an atom was added under the skull, because *Conqueror* was a nuclear-powered submarine.

There was still some naïveté about the situation that awaited *Conqueror* in Faslane. They were told that there would be thirty-nine representatives of the world's press waiting for them on the quay, and that they should delay their entry into port by two days so that arrangements could be made for a special banquet. But the crew had been at sea for ninety days, living enclosed in the narrow confines of a submarine on active service. Mentally they were completely focused on their fellow crewmembers and the submarine itself. Tim McClement recalled:

They said we'll put a lunch on for you, the wardroom, the senior mess and the junior mess, and we said no, we've been to war together, we'll eat together. And we also said we need a maintenance meeting to plan all the things that we need to do on the submarine, and they said that can wait to Monday and we said no, we can't afford to miss half a day. Later it seemed a stupid thing to have done, but at the time the boat came first. So I suppose we were a bit unbalanced.

HMS *Conqueror* finally surfaced and made its way slowly down the Gare Loch to Faslane. The white ensign was raised at the stern and the Jolly Roger flew at the mast above the fin. Eight crewmembers lined up on the forward casing and as they approached the jetty a tug accompanied them, firehoses creating a fountain in the air.

The press and the men's families were lined up to greet them, and so too were Vice Admiral Herbert, Flag Officer Submarines, and other top brass from Northwood. *Conqueror* was home to a hero's welcome.

A month later, *Conqueror* and her crew put to sea again and disappeared beneath the black waters of the Barents Sea. That patrol, which Captain Chris Wreford-Brown considers the most significant of his career, is still secret.

Epilogue

THE AFTERMATH

The military junta in Argentina collapsed after the defeat in the Falklands and was replaced by an elected government and an elected president, Raúl Alfonsín. Within a few years most of the military dictatorships in South America had also crumbled – a welcome but unintended consequence of the British victory over the Argentine junta.

For many years veterans of the *Belgrano*, and of the whole war in the Falklands, were shunned by the Argentine government, but recently, after persistent campaigning, there has been some belated recognition of the obligation owed to the men who served on the *Belgrano* and to the relatives of those who died, who were only trying to realize the dream of every Argentinian.

The crew of HMS *Conqueror* were feted when they arrived back at Faslane after their lengthy and historic voyage. Various crewmembers received recognition for their service and their contribution towards victory in the Falklands War. The commanding officer, Commander Chris Wreford-Brown, was made a member of the Distinguished Service Order; Weapons Engineering Artificer Charlie Foy and Mechanical Engineering Officer Steve Mitchell were mentioned in dispatches for their struggle to repair the radio mast; and Petty Officer Graham Libby was given the Distinguished Service Medal for his selfless and hazardous attempt to remove the trailing aerial from the *Conqueror*'s propeller.

When these awards were announced, *Conqueror* had left the wall some time ago on her next mission and the news had to be signalled to them below the ocean.

By then the Secretary of State for Defence John Nott had already announced his decision to resign from office, and to retire from politics at the next election, which was held in June 1983 and which saw the Conservative government and Margaret Thatcher re-elected by a vastly increased majority.

I once suggested to Admiral Sir Henry Leach that his forthright request of Margaret Thatcher to form a naval task force had been motivated in part by a desire to prove that the government's policy towards the navy was wrong. He rebuked me, pointing out that it would have been utterly wrong of him to allow those concerns to influence the advice he gave to the Prime Minister in matters where so many lives were at stake. Nevertheless, although after the war John Nott remained unrepentant about his cuts, the decision to sell the aircraft carrier *Invincible* was reversed, HMS *Endurance* was not pensioned off, and the Royal Navy, which had been in danger of becoming, under John Nott, a small localized anti-submarine force, was maintained as a versatile, 'balanced' fleet, preserving its ability to go anywhere on the seven seas.

I think it is true that this was an unintended consequence of Sir Henry Leach's advice. His real motivation was summed up in his words to Margaret Thatcher, and they were concerned with the British state and its position in the world: 'If we don't move very fast and are not entirely successful, in a very few months' time we shall be living in a different country whose word will count for little.' Similar sentiments were expressed later on in the campaign, just before the amphibious forces landed, by Sir Edwin Bramall, the most senior figure in the army. If the landing succeeded, he said, 'In that event Britain's status in the world, the respect shown to her and the strength and credibility of her own deterrent strategy would be that much more enhanced for years to come.' Even at the time, then, the decision to go to war, and victory in that war, was seen as a turning point.

It is impossible to judge whether the successful attempt to recover the Falklands really has brought Britain any greater respect in the world, but it certainly gave Margaret Thatcher more confidence and more determination when she was dealing with other world leaders. It was the Falklands experience, she argued, that enabled her to talk in the way that she did to President George Bush in 1991 when they discussed how to respond to the Iraqi invasion of Kuwait. After the Falklands campaign British forces have never gone to war in isolation from the United States or their NATO allies, but they have taken part in every single foreign military intervention since then, whether it was the first Gulf War, the intervention in Bosnia, Sierra Leone, or the invasion of Iraq. Over thirty years since a British government's defence review called for the withdrawal of all British forces east of Suez, at least one nuclear submarine, now armed with Tomahawk cruise missiles and anti-ship missiles as well as torpedoes, is permanently on patrol in the Indian Ocean.

*

If the Falklands War was as pivotal a point in British foreign and military policy as I believe, then the attack on the *Belgrano* was an equally crucial point in the war itself. The Argentine navy was clearly preparing to mount an attack on the British task force as it approached the Falklands and, having failed, was waiting for the next opportunity. Despite all the mechanical problems that *Conqueror* suffered, the three torpedoes that were fired at the *General Belgrano* completely removed any surface threat to the task group and the amphibious landing force for the rest of the campaign. Within two days of the start of fighting, one of the two major threats to British success had been removed at a single stroke.

Yet rather than being celebrated for its success, the sinking of the *Belgrano* by the *Conqueror* was overshadowed by controversy about whether the *Belgrano* should have been sunk at all.

The controversy really started when the Defence Secretary John Nott made his first announcement about the attack on the *Belgrano* and made several errors of fact. The statement was incorrect about the time that *Conqueror* had first made contact with the *Belgrano*; it was incorrect about the position and the course of the *Belgrano* when she was torpedoed; and it was wrong about the number of torpedoes that had been fired. There were several reasons for these errors, the main one being that the Defence Secretary was relying on what he knew when the decision was made to alter the rules of engagement for *Conqueror*, not what was happening at sea after those changes of rules had been signalled to the submarine. At the time, the Shadow Defence Secretary, Denis Healey, asked Nott whether there had been any loss of political control and whether any efforts had been made to ensure that only minimum force was used.

The opportunity to correct some of these mistakes was missed ten days later when Nott, in another statement, said that the *Belgrano* had been closing on elements of our task force and could have been in striking distance in a matter of five or six hours. Again, no indication was given that the *Belgrano* was steaming away from the task force when she was attacked.

The discrepancies between the statements that the Defence Secretary kept making and what had really happened became more serious when, in December 1982, Tam Dalyell MP accused the Prime Minister of deliberately giving the command to sink the *Belgrano* in order to prevent an agreement with Argentina and to create the conditions for an all-out war. He summed it up in the phrase 'the *Conqueror*'s torpedoes would torpedo the peace negotiations.' From that moment the sinking of the *Belgrano* became the story of a conspiracy to cover up the actions of a ruthless Prime Minister destroying any hopes for peace. The argument was taken up in the press and by Labour party spokesmen, and by Margaret Thatcher's wider political enemies, of whom there were many.

At the time of the general election campaign in May 1983, the Prime Minister was asked in a television debate with the public, 'Why, when the *Belgrano* was outside the exclusion zone and actually sailing away from the Falklands, did you give the orders to sink it?' The question caused another flurry of scandal over the issue and visibly put Margaret Thatcher on the back foot. The story continued with allegations that the cover-up included the loss of the *Conqueror*'s log, and involved, in later years, the murder of Hilda Murrell, an anti-nuclear campaigner, whose death in a bungled burglary was assumed to be because of a family connection to a former member of the naval staff at Northwood.

Initially there were perhaps some reasons for the government and the Ministry of Defence to avoid an accurate description of the events leading up to the sinking of the *Belgrano*. It would have led to the revelation that British intelligence sources were very accurately informed about the movements of Argentine naval units, and were capable of intercepting and decoding the signals that were sent from Puerto Belgrano, the Argentine navy's home port, to ships at sea. It may also have revealed the effectiveness of the sonar equipment fitted to *Conqueror*, although it was not the most modern in the fleet, having been superseded by the Swiftsure class, two of which, *Spartan* and *Splendid*, were on patrol to the north of the Falklands. There may perhaps have been other things to explain that would have proved simply embarrassing, such as why the aircraft carrier *Veinticinco de Mayo* was not as easy to locate as the *Belgrano* proved to be, and why information about the change of course of the *Belgrano*, which had correctly been reported by *Conqueror* to the Flag Officer Submarines, had not been passed on to the War Cabinet.

When the war over the Falklands was won, none of these reasons justified a continuing disinclination by the government to clarify what had happened when the *Belgrano* was sunk, and so an initial mistake by a Cabinet minister, which could have been easily and quickly corrected, was allowed to escalate and assume the proportions of a cover-up.

It has been said by some people that it was perhaps inevitable that the sinking of the *Belgrano*, coming as it did at the beginning of the war and causing so many deaths, was going to arouse strong feelings, not only in Argentina but also in Britain. The truth is that any major incident that caused significant casualties would have come as a shock to public opinion, and it was only a matter of chance that that incident was the attack on the *Belgrano*. The first hostilities had started when Argentina invaded the Falkland Islands and South Georgia, and major casualties were avoided because the opposing British forces on the Falklands and South Georgia were so heavily outnumbered.

There might have been far heavier casualties when the fighting started during Operation Paraquet to retake South Georgia. The Argentine submarine *Santa Fe* could have torpedoed a British ship – they certainly had rules of engagement allowing them to do so; or there could have been far greater casualties when the *Santa Fe* was attacked by British helicopters. Similarly, if the two Super Etendards that took off from Rio Grande air force base on 2 May had not had to return to base because of a mechanical defect with their refuelling equipment, the first major casualties of the war could well have been British. Almost nobody was prepared for war, or understood that war could only be fought with a level of ruthlessness and a loss of human life that would always seem too high.

The rules of engagement for the submarines – and it was the submarines that were the units most capable of taking aggressive action against the Argentine navy – were constantly being changed to take account of the diplomatic situation, but not, as Tam Dalyell alleged, to scupper peace initiatives. Sinking the *Belgrano* cost Britain some diplomatic support. The Spanish government, in conflict with Britain over Gibraltar anyway, said that the attack was 'a serious escalation in the conflict'. The Irish government was opposed to it, as were several South American countries such as Bolivia and Venezuela. Perhaps most important, it caused increased pressure from the US Secretary of

State Alexander Haig to accept some form of ceasefire while negotiations started.

In the light of the shifting international position, the British government accepted new proposals for a ceasefire and a withdrawal of forces from the islands put forward by Secretary of State Haig. These were passed to President Belaunde of Peru, whose initial reaction was sceptical because the proposals insisted that an interim administration carry out its work in consultation with the elected representatives of the population of the islands. This was the crux of the issue, which had not been, and would not be, affected by the loss of the *Belgrano* or the *Sheffield*. Margaret Thatcher would not personally agree to any compromise that left Argentine forces in the islands; she would have never been able to get such a deal through the House of Commons anyway. Neither would the Argentine junta agree to the removal of its forces, and General Galtieri, emboldened by the attack on the *Sheffield*, rejected Haig's latest proposal, opting instead for a military solution. Negotiations continued in the United Nations almost until the start of the amphibious operations, and the rules of engagement concerning the Argentine aircraft carrier *Veinticinco de Mayo* were modified so that an attack on it did not bring these discussions to a premature halt.

If there was any pressure to raise the military stakes, it came primarily from Admiral Woodward, in command of the task group, whose concerns – whether it was to increase his control over the nuclear submarines, remove the threat of the Argentine carrier, or the Argentine submarines – were first to reduce the threat to his own forces and secondly to convince the Argentine junta that a war would end in their defeat and that it might be better to negotiate. This was the reason for his early pressure on the War Cabinet, via Admiral Fieldhouse and the Chiefs of Staff, for rules of engagement that would enable the carrier to be sunk outside the total exclusion zone, and, when this seemed impossible, to urge the destruction of the *Belgrano*. He knew what Captain Héctor Bonzo of the *Belgrano* said to me in Buenos Aires recently: 'There are no roads in the sea.' In other words, you can alter course at will within minutes. But it didn't matter that the Argentine navy's true intentions gradually became known over the years; in the public awareness, *Conqueror*'s actions have been fixed, like a fly in amber, in the snapshot of the immediate arguments.

The effect of this controversy on the crew was mixed. Some were angry about the way they were portrayed. Billy Budding resented being described as a murderer: 'We were only there because of what those politicians had done, or rather failed to do. And then they turn round and blame us for doing our job.'

Commander Hall is both philosophical and sad:

Most of us tended to get angry about certain MPs standing on their hind legs and talking about things they don't know about. But otherwise you're used to politicians not quite getting it right. The only weird thing that happened was a few years later I was out in a fishing boat collecting for the RNLI, going down the yacht anchorage, and of course my friend couldn't keep from saying, 'Have you met my friend? He was on the submarine that sank *Belgrano*.' The reaction was very interesting. Fifty per cent wanted to shake my hand, fifty per cent wanted to punch me.

Petty Officer Libby remained unmoved, and has been largely unaffected. He has now joined his first love, the fire service, and was recently awarded a medal for an act of bravery during a fire.

I have no qualms about what we did. I think we did the right thing. We'd have lost quite a few more lives on our side. We took a pounding after that, but that was only from their air side, because their navy all went home. Had their navy been available, the whole thing might have gone the other way.

However, it didn't. The Falklands War was a success for British arms, and a success for the navy, all of them dependent on the crew of HMS *Conqueror*.

BIBLIOGRAPHY

Arkin, William, and Fieldhouse, Richard, *Nuclear Battlefields*, Ballinger, Cambridge, Massachusetts, 1985.

Bicheno, Hugh, *Razor's Edge*, Weidenfeld & Nicolson, London, 2006.

Bonzo, Héctor, *1093 Tripulantes*, Asociación Amigos del Crucero General Belgrano, Buenos Aires, 2004.

Burns, Jimmy, *The Land That Lost Its Heroes*, Bloomsbury, London, 1987.

Cardoso, Oscar, *Falklands: The Secret Plot*, Buenos Aires, 1987.

Cox, Albert, *Sonar and Underwater Sound*, Lexington Books, Massachusetts, 1978.

Craig, Chris, *Call For Fire*, John Murray, London, 1995.

Destefani, Laurio, *The Malvinas, South Georgias and the South Sandwich Islands*, Edipress SA, Buenos Aires, 1982.

The Falklands Seminar Occasional Paper 46, Strategic and Combat Studies Institute, Wiltshire, 2003.

Freedman, Lawrence, *The Official History of the Falklands Campaign*, 2 vols, Cassell, London, 2004.

Friedman, Norman, *Submarine Design and Development*, Conway Maritime, London, 1984.

'The Gulf War', Frontline, PBS, Transcripts, WGBH Educational Foundation, Cambridge, Massachusetts, 1996.

Hastings, Max, and Jenkins, Simon, *The Battle for the Falklands*, Michael Joseph, London, 1983.

Hill, J. R., *Lewin of Greenwich*, Cassell, London, 2000.

Jane's Fighting Ships 1981–82, Jane's Publishing Company, London, 1982.

Leach, Sir Henry, *Endure No Makeshifts*, Leo Cooper, London, 1993.

Leary, William, *Under Ice*, Texas A&M University Press, College Station, 1999.

Middlebrook, Martin, *The Fight for the Malvinas*, Viking, London, 1989.

——*Task Force*, Penguin, London, 1987.

Morrison, David, and Tumber, Howard, *Journalists at War*, Sage Publications, London, 1988.

Nott, John, *Here Today, Gone Tomorrow*, Politico Publishing, London, 2002.

Nouzeilles, Gabriella, and Montaldo, Graciela (eds), *The Argentina Reader*, Duke University Press, Durham, North Carolina, 2002.

Perkins, Roger, *Operation Paraquet*, Picton Publishing, Bath, 1986.

Ring, Jim, *We Come Unseen*, John Murray, London, 2001.

Rock, David, *Authoritarian Argentina*, University of California Press, Berkeley, 1993.

Schank, John, et al., *The United Kingdom's Nuclear Submarine*

Industrial Base, Vol. 1, Rand Europe, London, 2005.

Sontag, Sherry, and Drew, Christopher, *Blind Man's Bluff*, Public Affairs, New York, 1998.

Thatcher, Rt Hon. Margaret, *The Downing Street Years*, HarperCollins, London, 1993.

Van der Vat, Dan, *Standard of Power*, Pimlico, London, 2001.

Verbitsky, Horacio, *Malvinas*, Editorial Sudamericana, Buenos Aires, 2002.

War in the Falklands, Channel 4, London, 1992.

Watson, Basil, *Commander in Chief*, Royal Navy Submarine Museum, Gosport, 2005.

West, Nigel, *The Secret War for the Falklands*, Little Brown, London, 1997.

White, Rowland, *Vulcan 607*, Bantam Press, London, 2006.

Woodward, Admiral Sandy, *One Hundred Days*, HarperCollins, London, 1992.

Young, Hugo, *One of Us*, Macmillan, London, 1989.

Index

SINK THE BELGRANO

Bernasconi, Lieutenant Commander
Norberto 57, 66, 88, 89, 95, 228, 237–8,
252
Bicain, Captain Horacio 157, 166, 167,
168
black lighting 84
Black Tin Fish (newspaper) 77, 79, 280
Bonzo, Captain Héctor 55, 91, 92–3, 95,
96, 98, 100, 192, 193, 209, 210, 213,
224, 227, 236–7
Bouchard see *Hipólito Bouchard*
Bramall, Sir Edwin 117, 124, 144, 289
Brambleleaf 163
Briatore, Captain 46
Brilliant, HMS 126, 137, 164, 166–7, 201,
202, 269
Britannia 109
British Antarctic Survey 45–6
Broadsword 276, 277
Buchanan, Captain 179
Budding, Bill 155, 156, 166, 295
Burdwood Bank 193, 211
Bush, President George 289
Busser, Rear Admiral Carlos 48, 51, 58,
60–1, 62, 63, 112
Bustos Tacticos 55, 56
Butler, Nick 167
Byron, Commodore John 27

Cabo San Antonio 55, 57, 58, 59, 61–2
Callaghan, Sir James 31, 34, 104
Calmon, Captain Juan 94
Campo Durán 94
Canberra 136, 270
Canberra bombers 203
Canepa, Gerardo 89
Carrington, Lord 1, 35–6, 109, 118
Catena, Arturo 101
Centurion, Juan José 57–8
Chile 100
Clapp, Commodore Mike 132, 198, 275
Cold War 3, 35
Combined Operations Pilotage Parties 21
Comodoro Py 58, 94, 216
Conqueror
ordered to South Atlantic and recalling
of crew from leave 8, 16–17
storing for war and maintenance work
17–18, 19–20

loading of equipment and supplies 22–3
puts to sea and journey south 23–4,
67–8, 77, 78, 79, 140–1
detachment of Special Boat Service on
board 20, 21, 22, 69–74, 171
problem with electrolysis machine 68–9,
72
task of taking SBS troops to South
Georgia and assisting in operations
70, 138
training on board 74–6
communicating with Northwood 83–4
reactor problem 84–6
arrival at South Georgia and
involvement in Battle of 140–2,
145–6, 147, 154
damage to aerial and attempt to repair
148–50
close encounter with *Santa Fe* 155–7
leaves South Georgia to reinforce main
task force 164
returns to South Georgia area to hunt for
Santa Fe 165–6
transfer of SBS to *Antrim* from 171–3
communication problems and damage to
aerial mast 172, 174, 181, 267–8
request to be placed under associated
support 178, 181
fixing of communication problems 182,
194
orders to locate and remain with
Argentine TG79.3 183, 189–90
search for *Belgrano* group and tracking
of 194–6, 206–8, 214, 215, 221,
224–6, 228–9
permission given to attack *Belgrano* and
preparing for attack 223, 229, 230–4
firing on *Belgrano* and sinking of
234–42, 243, 282–3, 284, 290
distancing from attack position and
evasion manoeuvres 240–2
information gained on attack 256–7
orders to protect crippled *Sheffield*
264–5
reactor problem and fixing of 265, 266
communication problems 267–8, 271,
272
other problems faced 271–2
wires wrapped around propeller problem

302

INDEX